Rekindling the ROMANCE

LOVING THE LOVE OF YOUR LIFE

DENNIS & BARBARA RAINEY
WITH BOB DEMOSS

Published by
THOMAS NELSON™
Since 1798

www.thomasnelson.com

To Scott and Theresa

*Your friendship and growth in Christ continue
to be a source of great encouragement to both of us.
We love you and your family.*

—Dennis and Barbara

Published in Nashville, Tennessee, by Thomas Nelson, Inc.

Published in association with the literary agency of Wolgemuth & Associates, Inc.

Nelson books may be purchased in bulk for educational, business, fundraising, or sales promotional use. For information, please email SpecialMarkets@ThomasNelson.com.

Unless otherwise noted, Scripture quotations are from the HOLY BIBLE: NEW INTERNATIONAL VERSION®. Copyright © 1973, 1978, 1984 by International Bible Society. Used by permission of Zondervan Publishing House. All rights reserved.

Scripture quotations noted NKJV are taken from the NEW KING JAMES VERSION. Copyright © 1982 by Thomas Nelson, Inc. Used by permission. All rights reserved.

Scripture quotations noted NASB are from the NEW AMERICAN STANDARD BIBLE®, © Copyright The Lockman Foundation 1960, 1962, 1963, 1968, 1971, 1972, 1973, 1975, 1977. Used by permission. www.Lockman.org.

Cartoons © Copyright Phil Smouse. All rights reserved. Used with permission.

Library of Congress Catalogping-in-Publication Data

Rainey, Dennis, 1948–
    Rekindling the romance : loving the love of your life / Dennis and Barbara Rainey with Bob DeMoss.
        p. cm.
    ISBN-10: 0-7852-8556-3 (tp)
    ISBN-13: 978-0-7852-8556-4 (tp)
    ISBN-10: 0-7852-0001-0 (hc)
    1. Marriage—Religious aspects—Christianity.   2. Intimacy (Psychology)—Religious aspects—Christianity.   I. Rainey, Barbara. II. DeMoss, Robert G. III. Title.

BV835.R3494 2004
248.8'44—dc22
                                                                2004014402

Printed in the United States of America
07 08 09 RRD 9 8 7 6 5

Contents

REKINDLING THE ROMANCE

(for Her)

A Novella

⁂

Trading Places
(Angela's Perspective)

Friday, 3:30 p.m.

The air was actually cool, but I was steaming. The edges of my ears
burned. I felt this sudden urge to jump up and race out of the room.
I shook my head as if to tell the voices inside my mind that I wouldn't
make such a scene. Instead of answering the question, I turned and
stared out the window. The oak tree released several leaves that, like
snowflakes, floated to the ground.

For an instant my mind wandered back to the last time my husband, Bryan, and I went on a picnic. I remembered how we spread a
red and white-checkered tablecloth under a big old tree and nibbled
on grapes, cheese, crackers—and each other. We had a sweeping
view of the Point; that's the spot where the three rivers come together
at the heart of downtown Pittsburgh. Neither of us wore a watch, but
I'd say we must have lingered for hours just talking and admiring the
boats sailing the Allegheny River in the distance.

If you had told me back then that I'd be sitting across the room
from a marriage counselor today, I would have said, "You're a complete nutcase." We had so much in common. I met Bryan at the
University of Pittsburgh. This would have been fourteen years ago.

We were both athletic, although to look at him now, you'd think he majored in pizza. Bryan played soccer until he blew out a knee his senior year. I was the captain of the volleyball team. We were business majors—that is, until we started to major in each other. Bryan and I became an "item" during the last two years of college and got married the summer following our graduation.

I stole a look at my husband and then diverted my eyes. I'll be the first to admit that his thick dark black hair looks as good as the day we first met. He is, after all, an attractive man. To this day, his sea-green eyes sparkle as if he were constantly privy to something funny.

Was it really twelve years ago that we pledged our love to each other? Seems like an eternity has passed between us. What happened? We used to have so much fun together. Not just when we were dating. I'm talking about *after* we were married. For three or four years we did the craziest, most romantic things together.

I guess somewhere along the way we drifted apart. Not all at once. In fact, if you pressed me, I couldn't pinpoint the time when this distance settled on our relationship like a dark cloud. It just did. Maybe we got old. Then again, it's not like we're *that* old. At least, I never pictured myself *feeling* old at thirty-four. But I do. I really do.

Most days I feel old . . . and trapped. That's the truth. Sometimes the walls of my daily routine close in on me so tightly, I feel them squeezing out the few embers of life that remain. I get this claustrophobic sensation, and I almost can't breathe. If honest, I'd say I'm not happy. My life has about as much adventure as a potted houseplant experiences. I've been going through the motions for years. Day after day I struggle with this emptiness, hoping, longing, and praying it will get better. To keep my sanity, I just focus on trying to be a good mom. I know I need to hold it together for the kids.

Now that we have three under the age of eight, I find myself torn between meeting their endless parade of needs and the demands of my part-time job. I can't think of the last time when I didn't hit the pillow at night completely exhausted, like I had just finished a marathon volleyball tournament. There's just not enough time in the day to get everything done.

Of course, this doesn't register with Bryan. He'll jump into bed with that frisky look in his eye. What does he think I am? A machine? In moments like that all I want to do is pull the covers over my tired head and become invisible. Can't he see I'm beat? Doesn't he have a clue what I'm going through? What's with men and their endless need for sex anyway? Why can't he grow up? We made love last week—or was it last month? As usual, he appeared to get more out of it than I did.

Maybe if he tried a little harder at building some anticipation, you know? Bryan used to be Mr. Affection. He'd shower me like a spring rain with his tender words. His life-giving attention opened me up like a bouquet of fresh roses. Nowadays, a peck on the cheek and maybe a pat on my bottom in the kitchen are his idea of romancing me.

Frankly I feel like a lion tamer, cracking the whip to keep him at bay. I hate that about us. I used to have deep feelings for him. There was a time when I even looked forward to our time in bed. But over the last couple of years, I almost always turn him away, or I just go through the motions.

Don't get me wrong. I'm not a whiner by nature. We live in a decent house. Nothing spectacular, mind you. But I've got it fixed up the way I like it. Bryan has a good job. We're all healthy. That counts for something. And I know I should be thankful for these things.

Still, there has to be more.

What I wouldn't give to feel special again. To know that Bryan cares for me as much as he cares for what I call the three S's: Sex, the Steelers, and Sex. If this is it, then marriage is a bad joke. That's all. Which is part of the reason we're seeing John Engle.

John's a soft-spoken marriage counselor with an honest face.

I'd say he's in his midfifties. My best friend from church highly recommended him, and I should add, she said he sometimes used "unconventional methods" to help couples. When I pressed her, that was all she'd say.

So far, there was nothing unusual about John. Sure, someone needs to help him with his choice of sweaters. Other than that, he's a good egg. You can tell he really wants to help. It's just that, well, I find it so hard to believe Bryan and I have come to this.

The truth is, I don't have much hope of recapturing what we once shared. We're *so* different these days. Not to mention I don't know how much longer I can do this. It's really hard for me to go to counseling. You know, to have to spill my guts to a stranger. But what are my options? I really don't care to suffer silently while Bryan and I drift farther apart on different oceans.

In my view, I'm like a rose bush needing to be cared for by a tender gardener who understands my needs. While I may like to bask in the sunshine, I still cherish the cool shade of the day, and I need the occasional rain to quench my thirst. My husband, however, is no gardener. He's more like a meteor, burning a path through my space without taking time to slow down and smell the flowers.

How do you fix that?

When we sat down for our session today, I felt so emotionally distant from him. Like I said, part of me . . . part of us . . . died years ago, and I'm afraid if something doesn't change real fast between us, well—I'd rather not think about that.

I should tell you we've been seeing John for several months. So far it hasn't made an ounce of difference. Okay, I take that back. Bryan has tried to *listen* more when we talk. That's been a refreshing change. If only he could . . . I guess if he could be more like me, maybe then he'd be more understanding about what I really need for this relationship to work. How you can live with someone for so many years and he still doesn't know what's important to you?

"Angela," John said, interrupting my thoughts. "Would you like for me to repeat the question?"

Although his tone was warm, I felt that I was being interrogated by a reporter for the evening news. I brushed a strand of hair from my face to buy another few seconds. "No . . . well, sure."

John smiled and said, "Are you willing to do *whatever* it takes to make this relationship work?" He crossed his legs and readjusted the yellow pad on his lap.

"Yes . . ." I heard myself saying.

"Good," John said with a mischievous wink. "Now, if you folks will give me just a minute." He placed his tablet and pen on the floor next to his chair. He stood and then glided across the room. As he walked, he dug into his right pocket, retrieved a set of keys, and then opened a cabinet adjacent to his desk. He squirreled around inside and retrieved two small brown bottles. He turned and, on the way back, grabbed a single sheet of white paper and two sealed envelopes from his desk.

John placed the items on the coffee table in front of Bryan and me before taking his seat. For reasons I can't explain, my heart began to flutter. What was it about that look on John's face that seemed so curious?

Bryan started to reach for his drink. You'd think after all of these years my husband would have learned a few basic manners. I gave him the elbow . . . you know, the sharp jab couples use that says: "Hold on."

"Not so fast, Bryan," John said, holding up his forefinger. "You might want to know the ground rules before you take a drink of that."

"Huh?" Bryan's forehead creased into a knot as his hand stopped in midair. When the clarification didn't come immediately, Bryan sank back into the sofa.

John studied us for a long moment without saying a word. His trained eyes drifted between Bryan and me before settling on some distant point beyond us. I was tempted to turn around to see what he might have been looking at when he cleared his throat and folded his hands together.

"Here's the way I see it," John said like a coach about to call the winning play in the fourth quarter. "This might surprise you, but your marital difficulty is really not that different from what I find in most couples who come to me for help. You both want to make this work—you said so yourselves a moment ago, right?"

Bryan and I nodded.

"And you both recognize things aren't what they should be," John said. "Now, correct me if I'm wrong, Angela. I hear you saying that you wish Bryan were more romantic, more attentive, more communicative, and more responsive to your needs. You'd also like for him to be more of a spiritual leader. Is that a fair summary?"

"Yes," I said, wondering what this had to do with the two bottles on the table.

"While you, Bryan, wish Angela would agree to sex more often. You'd like for her to be open to greater creativity in the sexual expression and occasionally initiate physical intimacy," John said. His tone remained clinical. "You'd also like for her to put a little more effort into looking attractive when you come home at the end of the day, right?"

Bryan shifted in his seat. "When you put it that way, those things sound so shallow, but, yes. What guy wouldn't?"

John ignored the question. "And it's clear you both feel as if you've reached an impasse. The walls you've built in your marriage over the years appear insurmountable, and you're unsure of how to turn back the hands of time."

John paused again and looked us over. Maybe he hesitated for effect. Maybe he wasn't sure if we were ready for his advice. Whatever his reason, my heart started to skip a beat. Why was I becoming so . . . unnerved? I flattened the end of my skirt, hoping that I didn't appear as unsettled as I was feeling.

When John began to speak, he lowered his voice as if he were concerned about being overheard: "I know a surefire way for you to reignite the passion in your marriage." The mischievous look reappeared on his face. "Are you interested?"

"How's that?" Bryan blurted.

"By walking a mile in each other's shoes for just one week." John's eyes narrowed. *"Literally."*

Bryan and I exchanged a blank look. I could tell neither of us knew what John was driving at.

"I know this might sound far-fetched," John said. He rubbed the palms of his hands together in a slow, patient circle before resting his hands at his sides. "But, please, hear me out. Those bottles in front of you contain a highly sophisticated medication, recently approved by the FDA. It temporarily changes what we call 'your emotional set.' Upon drinking the contents, you, Bryan, will experience life through the emotional set of your wife, and you, Angela, will see and feel life the way your husband experiences it. After one week you'll return here, and I'll serve you the antidote to reverse the transformation."

John leaned back in his chair and fell silent as he observed our reactions. Neither Bryan nor I spoke for a minute while the implication of what we just heard sank in. Was this a joke? Our marriage is a train wreck waiting to happen, and this guy has the nerve to play stupid games.

After what felt like forever, Bryan broke the silence by cracking his knuckles—I hate it when he does that. It's an annoying habit he picked up because one of the Steeler quarterbacks does it. Bryan eyed the bottle and said, "You're serious?"

John nodded; the left side of his mouth curled upward in a playful half-grin. For a split second I couldn't help picturing him like a mad scientist in a lab jacket surrounded by test tubes and bubbling vials of mysterious liquid. With a blink, the room came back into focus.

"So, what do you think?" John said.

"I'm game if she wants to," Bryan said, turning to me for affirmation.

I had a thousand thoughts flooding into my head. *Was what John proposed even possible? Was it legal? Was it ethical? Would it really work? Would I want it to work? And more important, would there really be a way back? The whole thing struck me as rather freaky. That's an understatement, as my racing heart could attest.*

When I didn't respond, John said, "Angela, you and Bryan are excellent candidates for this therapy. I assure you it's perfectly legal and completely safe. In fact, the FDA has approved its usage in supervised settings."

My eyes widened. *Great. Now I'm a human guinea pig. As if I need this on top of everything else.* I felt Bryan's hand give my arm a light squeeze. Our eyes met.

"Babe, you always say you'd like more adventure in our marriage. Well, here's our chance."

I wanted to wipe that cheesy little grin off his face with the bottom of my purse. I know that's not a very Christian thing to admit, but I'm just telling you the way I feel. Even though he's technically correct, how dare he put me on the spot like this? I leaned away and shot him a bewildered look.

"Angela, I can tell you have some reservations," John said, evidently reading my body language. "Naturally I don't want you to do something you aren't comfortable doing. But this medication has no lasting side effects, and it has a ninety-seven percent success rate."

I swallowed hard. I wanted to ask, *Yeah, but what happens to the other 3 percent?* One problem. The back of my throat was as dry as the Sahara Desert, and I couldn't get the words out.

This time Bryan turned halfway around to face me. "Sweetie, how many times have you said to me, 'Try being *me* sometime—then you'd understand'? So what's stopping you?"

I did my best to avoid his gaze for fear that, like a snake charmer, he might seduce me into agreeing. I just *had* to stall for more time to think this through. I used to like Bryan's impulsive side. Not now. This was way outside my comfort zone.

"John, in spite of my husband's enthusiasm to jump off a cliff, this has to be the silliest idea I've heard in my entire life. No offense." I forced a half-smile, although my tone was caustic. "I just don't see how that little bottle of liquid—"

"Medicine—"

"Whatever . . . is going to fix our marriage."

"Actually I understand *exactly* how you feel, Angela," John said. "I had many of the same thoughts and questions you probably have . . . that is, before my wife and I tried this treatment."

My heart jumped. "Excuse me?"

"That's right," John said. "I first read about this approach to therapy earlier this year. However, I refused to recommend it to my clients without having tested it." A playful smile eased across his face. "While my wife and I have a great marriage, we agreed there's always room for improvement. After a week of switching our emotional sets, I have full confidence in the value of this product and the results it produces."

"But how—"

He waved me off. "Don't ask. I can't explain how it works. But it works."

"It's just like that old song 'Love Potion #9,'" Bryan sang with a laugh.

I wanted to slug him.

"Come on, babe. You *know* that was funny."

I stiffened. This was no time for jokes. There were practical matters to address, such as the cost. I ignored my husband and looked at John. "Well, let's say that I were to agree. Isn't it an expensive treatment?"

"It is," he replied. "However, a foundation has provided grant money for the early application of this during the initial rollout. The researchers are doing a study to document the effectiveness when used in the general public. That's why they'll cover it one hundred percent."

Bryan licked his lips. "Come on, sweetie. I'm thirsty over here. Let's go for it."

John suppressed a chuckle as he checked his watch. "Our session is just about over. Now, if there aren't any other questions and if you're ready to see how the other half lives, please sign the waiver," John said, pointing to the paper on the table between us.

Bryan picked it up.

John said, "This is just a formality that indicates you voluntarily agreed to participate in the study." He placed his pen in front of Bryan as he spoke. "Afterward, drink from the bottle in front of you. You should feel the initial effects in thirty minutes or less. Full potency will be reached in a matter of a few hours. You'll also need to take the envelope with your name on it. I'd suggest that you not open it unless you are seriously struggling with the changes during the week."

Bryan scanned the sheet, scribbled his name, and then handed it to me.

I held it at arm's length as if it were radioactive. Was I going to regret this?

On the other hand, was Bryan right? Maybe it would be a good thing for him to see what I go through emotionally every day. It's not like we were switching bodies. Just our emotional wiring or whatever. I should be able to handle that for a week. Besides, John seemed so confident about whatever was in that stuff. I focused on the page and read the lone paragraph. It appeared harmless enough.

I signed my name.

Friday, 4:44 p.m.

There are two ways to get around Pittsburgh during rush hour: slow or stopped. Gridlock is a way of life. It's not that Pittsburghers are bad drivers. It's the hilly topography that, in spots, rivals San

Francisco, complicated by two tunnels, three rivers snaking their way through the heart of town, and the countless bridges.

When we left John's office, I felt this urgency to get in the car and head home. That's the only way we'd beat rush hour. But, no. Bryan insisted on stopping by the appointment desk to schedule our session for next Friday, which we could have done by phone to save time. I told him this, but he ignored me.

In an uncharacteristic move, my clueless husband felt compelled to strike up a conversation with the receptionist. Go figure. They must have talked for ten minutes about *nothing*. Now we're paying for it. We got stuck in traffic on the bridge headed into the Fort Pitt tunnel—just as I predicted. Which is why I'm not speaking to him. I mean, it's a regular Friday afternoon parking lot. We're in the middle lane with cars inching forward at a snail's pace on either side.

I don't know why, but I feel so impatient—which is really weird. That isn't like me. I'm usually the one telling Bryan to chill out and roll with the punches. The only thing I can figure is that maybe the medication is affecting me. It's hard to say for sure. I have serious doubts that the stuff works at all. My bet is that it's a placebo, you know, just water or something harmless John used to trick us into being nicer to each other.

After all, the drink was odorless, colorless, and tasteless. I did think it was unusually cold as I swallowed, considering the fact that the bottle was room temperature. No, the ends of my toes didn't tingle. The room didn't spin or stand on edge. Nothing like that.

Then again, I must confess something has changed. I don't know how to delicately explain the sensation except to say I feel as if I've become acutely alert to every last ounce of testosterone in the universe, you know? It's as if the scales have fallen from my eyes. Everywhere I look, a host of visual stimulants is pushing my buttons—sexual buttons that I never had.

It's not that I haven't seen men before. And yet for reasons beyond my comprehension, I'm seeing them—really *seeing* them. The tiniest detail of maleness catches my attention. I just saw a couple walking down the street, and I couldn't help noticing the way the guy's pants hung off his waist like a curtain shrouding the main event.

And a minute ago, I found myself rubbernecking over a billboard. I've seen it many times before and never given it a second thought. But this time I couldn't resist *staring.* I think a department store was selling jeans. I'm embarrassed to admit that what caught my eye was the guy on the billboard. He was a drop-dead handsome young man—probably not much older than nineteen.

Oddly, I felt compelled to look closer. He leaned against the bumper of a car, bare-chested and as bronze as a Greek god. His flat, tight pecks were complemented by a rocklike set of abs. I had this bizarre, intense desire to run my fingers through his shock of hair.

To be honest, my face flushed as an alien thought popped into my mind: *He's the kind of guy I'd shave my legs for.* Don't ask me where *that* came from. It just did. And for a long moment I actually had this desire to drink in every little detail of his gorgeous face . . . his dreamy eyes . . . his sun-kissed lips. I knew better than to let my mind wander and suddenly felt overwhelmed with guilt.

What was going on with me? Why would I be drawn to a complete stranger like that? Even though things weren't great between Bryan and me, why would my heart actually entertain betraying my wedding vows so quickly? I mean, it's just a dumb picture of a kid almost half my age that's causing my thoughts to spin out of control. I stole another look.

As I was wrestling with these conflicting emotions, a brown UPS truck inched forward and pulled alongside us in the next lane, blocking my view. Thankful for the diversion, I rechecked my makeup in the visor mirror to regain my composure. Satisfied, I looked out my side window to avoid eye contact with Bryan. It's my husband's fault, after all, that we're stuck on the bridge.

That's when I noticed the driver's door was pulled back, revealing the inside cab. The driver wore brown shorts and a matching brown shirt. I gave him the once-over. I'd say he was about thirty. What I could see of his face was definitely tanned. A moment later, I caught myself admiring his calves. I mean, they looked so lean and muscular. Probably rock-hard to the touch.

My eyes drifted up to his waist. Nice. The guy was trim, unlike Bryan. I wish Bryan would lay off the chips and soda, you know? He could stand to lose a good fifteen pounds—right around the middle. I couldn't help studying the guy's angular jaw line, wavy blond hair, and dark sunglasses. As I savored the details, I concluded he'd make a great model . . . and was probably awesome in bed.

It's funny how the mind works, you know? Out of the blue a slogan for UPS popped into my mind: "This Is What Brown Can Do for You." I started to consider a few tempting possibilities and was lost in these private thoughts when the driver glanced over at me. He flashed me a smile as his truck inched forward. My heart jumped.

What's with that? I turned and stared straight ahead. This was different. *Really different.* Why in the world was I . . . well, picturing us in bed together? Trust me when I say that I'm not one to have sexual thoughts, at least not usually, certainly not like that, and especially not with a stranger. Yet here I was captivated by his looks and craving his body.

"Babe?" Bryan said, lowering the radio.

"Yeah?"

"Is something wrong?"

My face flushed. "No . . . why do you ask?"

"You gasped."

"I did?"

"Yeah. Just a second ago."

"Uh . . ." I hesitated, scrambling for a good explanation. I felt like a kid caught with her hand in the cookie jar. "I thought you were going to bump the car in front of us." It's not like I could ever admit, *Honey, I was lusting over the UPS driver.*

Bryan studied my face. "We weren't moving."

I felt the blood rush to my face. "Oh. Gee. Well, maybe that stuff John gave us was playing tricks on my mind," I said with a weak smile. At least that much was plausible.

Bryan grunted, unconvinced.

I went to steal another peek and was disappointed to find the truck had started down the exit ramp before the tunnel. Don't ask me to explain it, but I craned my neck for a final look. It's like I didn't want to take my eyes off him. These new impulses pulled me along almost against my will, as if I were caught in a salacious riptide.

"What are you staring at?" Bryan said.

"Nothing." I snapped my head around.

"Admit it, Angela. You were gawking at that guy in the truck."

"Me? *Right*," I said, trying to save face. I hooked my hair behind my left ear, guilty as charged.

"You could have fooled me," Bryan said. He tapped a finger on the steering wheel. We pulled into the tunnel as traffic picked up. Still tapping his ring finger against the wheel, he asked, "Am I not good enough for you?"

I detected a sadness in his voice. Now I was *really* puzzled. From the day we met, Bryan always impressed me as Captain Confidence. He never seemed to worry what others thought about him. He was like a rock, unshakeable. For him to ask a question like that revealed a side of insecurity I had never seen before.

"Well?" he said, persisting. His voice almost cracked.

I was stumped. I didn't know how to answer that one. If I said, *No, I wish you'd lose some weight and look more like Mr. UPS*, I'd be digging my own grave. On the other hand, if I said, *Yes, dear, you're the best; I can't imagine being with someone else*, I had this distinct feeling he'd see right through me. I bit the inside of my bottom lip and held my tongue.

If there's one thing I've learned when you're about to lose an argument, change the subject.

"Oh, I've been meaning to tell you, Bryan" I said, hoping to sound natural. "This morning I noticed in the paper that the Steelers are playing a preseason game tomorrow afternoon. Why don't you and I take the kids?"

He hesitated. "No thanks, I'm not interested."

"*Now* who's not being honest?" I said.

"See—you just admitted it. You *were* checking him out."

"I . . . huh?"

"When you said, '*Now* who's not being honest,' that implies you weren't honest with me a minute ago. 'Fess up, Angela, you're busted." Bryan leaned his left arm out the window.

"I will do no such thing—this is so ridiculous." I shifted in my seat. "What are you? The thought police?"

"No, just call me the janitor."

"Huh?"

"If you were drooling any harder back there," he said, "I'd need a mop to clean up."

୧୭ ୧୭ ୧୭

When we got home, Bryan offered to make dinner and watch the kids while I ran my errands. I'd like to say that was the end of this barrage of sexual thoughts, but the rest of the evening wasn't any better. At the mall . . . at the grocer . . . at the mini-mart . . . everywhere I went, I found myself fighting to keep my mind from daydreaming about other men.

At one point I even whispered a short prayer for strength to keep my eyes from wandering. By the time Bryan and I got in bed, I was beat. Not in the usual physical sense. After all, Bryan surprised me by making dinner *and* he cleaned up afterward *and* he chased the kids into the tub *and* he read them a story before bed.

I have no idea what came over him.

No, I wasn't physically tired. I was emotionally exhausted from fighting the endless war in my mind. The steady stream of ungodly thoughts was sparked by the slightest stimulation: a magazine cover, a billboard, a guy standing in front of me in line. You name it. I never felt so *surrounded* by temptation in all of my life. I actually had to wonder if fighting this onslaught was possible, you know?

Even as Bryan was putting the kids down to sleep, for example, I clicked on the TV to unwind. Once again I found myself captivated by a flood of fresh male eye candy—if you know what I mean. By the time 11:00 p.m. rolled around, I was just glad to shut off the world and fall into bed with the man I pledged to be faithful to. And, boy, was I ready for him now.

Bryan, who lay on his side of our queen-sized bed, was breathing softly. I inched closer under the covers and started to snuggle against his chest.

"What are you doing?" he asked. His body tensed.

"I . . . you know, it's been a while since we made love, and I thought we could—"

He rolled on his side away from me. "I'm not in the mood."

Believe me when I say *that* was a first. I pressed myself against his back and traced a line with my finger along his shoulder. "Why? What's wrong, hon?"

He sat upright, clicked on the lamp, and folded his arms together. "You don't know, do you?"

He had me there. "Enlighten me," I said, squinting as my eyes adjusted to the light.

"This afternoon. When I was talking to the receptionist," he said, sounding as if his concern should be crystal clear. "Does that ring any bells?"

I racked my brain but—

"I didn't think so," he said, indignant. "You jumped all over me when I was just trying to be nice to her." He searched my eyes. "You don't remember how rude you were, do you?"

I blinked. He had a point. I *was* abrupt. But that was this afternoon. This was tonight. The two are separated by at least eight or nine hours . . . and he's still fuming? I had all but forgotten about that little lapse in judgment. Why was he bringing it up at a time like this?

"Can't you just hold me?" I said, dripping with desire.

"Can't you apologize?" he countered. His sea-green eyes resembled two frozen patches of ice.

This was unreal. "Fine. I'm sorry."

"Are you?" He didn't budge. "You don't *sound* sorry."

"Well, I *am* sorry."

"You must think I'm a fool . . . I know perfectly well when I'm being snowed," he said. "Besides, what planet are you living on, Angela? For the last five hours I've been juggling the kids, dinner, dishes, clean-up. Can't you see it's late? I'm tired. Now you want me to just flip a switch and suddenly be your teddy bear. It's not gonna happen. So deal with it."

I could see this was going nowhere fast; I turned on my side, frustrated. And angry. How I longed to feel his touch. Which is odd, considering the problems we've been having. Somehow none of those issues mattered in this moment. I can't explain the deep ache inside, but I hungered to be intimate . . . to taste his lips . . . to drink our fill of love. What right did he have to push me away when I needed him to quench this fire that only he should be satisfying?

Without saying another word, he snapped off the light.

I was dumbfounded. This was so unfair. I yanked the sheet over my head and turned my back on him. I wanted to put as much distance between us as possible. If someone could arrange to have the Grand Canyon delivered and placed between us, that would suit me just fine.

Of all the nerve.

In a secret corner of my mind, the stranger in the UPS truck reappeared. He flashed a smile, and with a wave, he winked at me.

Saturday, 8:27 a.m.

The aroma of fresh coffee gently nudged me from my sleep. I could hear the kids with Bryan at the breakfast table down the hall. He probably made pancakes. That's the one thing I can count on—Saturdays he makes them green pancakes with sprinkles. My eyes, opened half-mast, glanced at the clock. I had overslept. Usually, I was up before the family. But this morning I stuffed a pillow over my head, hoping for just five more minutes of unconsciousness.

As if last evening's barrage of temptations wasn't insane enough, my dreams weren't much better. The truth is, I'm not sure how much sleep I got. I actually woke up once in the dead of night horrified that I had allowed myself to be ravished by the kid on the billboard. I can't tell you the last time I had a dream like that.

Right then in the darkness I had started to confess my ugly, lust-filled thoughts to God. And yet I felt the whole thing was unfair. How could I be responsible for my dreams? I didn't ask for them, did I? Surely this round-the-clock ambush of sexual thoughts was a distortion of my husband's emotional set brought on by that mystery drink. Come to think of it, maybe I was experiencing a bad chemical reaction or something. I mean, how could anybody live with these temptations day after day?

I know I couldn't.

Even now, I hoped Bryan would come back to bed so we could, well, you get the picture. Funny, I was so angry with him last night, and now I wished his legs were entwined with mine. Boy, I don't recall the last time I woke up in the morning with sex on my mind.

This is so . . . *weird.*

With sleep out of the question, I swung my legs over the edge of the bed, pulled on my robe, and shuffled to the bathroom. On the counter next to my sink was a pile of magazines. I moved them to the edge so I could brush my teeth, but managed to knock the magazines onto the floor. Bending down to pick them up, I saw that one of them had flopped open to a fragrance ad.

It wasn't the perfume that caught my attention. My eyes, like heat-seeking missiles, zeroed in on the male model. Frankly he wore nothing but a watch, although his midsection was masked by a strategically placed plant. I caught myself, averted my eyes, and thanked God for small victories. Right then and there I was determined to switch our emotional sets back sooner than later. I couldn't imagine going a whole week like this. No way.

It was then that I remembered the note John Engle had handed each of us. He told us to read it only if we were seriously struggling with the changes. *That would be now*, I thought. I opened the vanity drawer, found it, and then tore into it like a kid opening a present on Christmas morning. Maybe this held the key, something to help me unlock a strategy for coping.

Inside he had typed three words: *Now you know.*

That's it? Now I know *what*? Know that I'm ready to tear my eyes out? Or that this mental war is beyond my power to beat? Or that I hate my husband for pushing me away when I needed him last night? I clenched my hands into tight fistfuls of rage, crumpling the paper into a useless wad. Was this a joke?

I collapsed on the vanity stool and reflected on his words: *Now you know.*

What kind of twisted puzzle was this? I bet John was laughing somewhere across town knowing full well that I've completely lost my mind. I was tempted to call him and read him the riot act. I looked around for the cordless phone when a new thought emerged. The idea materialized slowly at first. As it came into focus, I wasn't sure I wanted to comprehend its full meaning.

Now you know.

I flattened the crumpled note on my lap with the palms of my hands. Yes, I think I just got the message in the bottle. Like a parting in the clouds, the significance of John's words came into view.

I had walked a mile in Bryan's shoes. I had experienced a small portion of what my poor husband has had to deal with every day of his life. For reasons I don't fully understand, God had wired him to be moved visually—way beyond what I could have imagined. No question, Bryan possesses a heightened sensitivity to visual stimulation. And in this fallen world, that means he experiences a daily battle over purity. I confess I hadn't the slightest clue how difficult that actually was—that is, until now.

I also can imagine how hard it must be for my husband to keep his thought life pure. No wonder he gets bothered by those bikini-clad billboards and commercials. And when the swimsuit issue of his favorite sports magazine arrives, he asks me to throw it away. He's been taking a stand all along. Those little things have been his way of saying he loves me. I just never valued it.

What's more, it dawned on me that in the midst of Bryan's struggle to stay on course, he needs me to be there for him. To give him the strength to remain faithful. To give him the reason to stay home. I was about to get up and share these thoughts with him when he appeared at the bathroom door.

"Hey, babe," he said, bringing me a cup of coffee.

Our eyes met. "Morning, hon," I said with a smile.

"We need to talk," he said, placing the mug on the counter.

I nodded. "I know. There's so much—"

"Shh." He brought a finger to his lips. "Me first."

This was new. Bryan rarely initiated a conversation. I wasn't about to stop him, even though I was burning to unload my new insight.

"I've been thinking, honey," he said, his eyes warm and inviting. "Whatever was in that stuff yesterday has done some crazy things to me—"

"To me too," I was quick to add, but then stopped myself from saying more. The last thing I wanted to do was stifle him when he was expressing himself.

His eyes widened. "Talk about freaky stuff."

"I'll say." I was dying to ask him if he was as ready to switch back as I was, but I held my tongue.

"It hasn't even been twenty-four hours, and I've already come to appreciate—"

"Our differences?"

He squinted at me. "Angela, if you'll just let me get the words out . . ."

"Oops. Sorry." I know how he hates it when I finish his sentences. "Not another word, Scout's honor," I said, holding up two fingers to seal my pledge.

"What I'm trying to say is that I've come to appreciate you . . . and what you do for the family."

I sipped my coffee.

"I can see how I've been missing out too," he said, leaning against the doorjamb. "I mean, spending time with the kids last night and this morning has actually been a blast. They're so cool. I feel closer to them now than I have in a long time."

I was genuinely surprised. This wasn't like Bryan.

"The truth is," he said, circling around behind me. He started to gently massage my shoulders. "I've been selfish. I've let the things *I* want to do get in the way of being a part of our family. I've been so focused on sex that I stopped romancing you the way you desire to be romanced. So, I've been thinking . . ."

"Go on," I said. For some strange reason, my heart was starting to rattle.

"Well, this little experiment has been so good for me—for us— I thought we should call and ask John if we could just leave things the way they are."

I scrunched my forehead. "You what?"

"You know, I'd like to forget about switching back our emotional sets, or whatever he called them, when the week is up," Bryan said, beaming. "Bet you thought you'd never hear me say that, did you, sweetheart?"

For a long second I couldn't breathe. I studied his face for the slightest indication that this was a prank. His gaze didn't change, prompting my heart to play tag with the bottom of my throat. I turned halfway around and faced him. "Please, tell me you *are* joking."

Bryan's eyes twinkled . . .

. . . to be continued

ngela and Bryan's story is fictional. Yours is not. Are you wishing for a "magic" pill for you and your husband? Life would be so much easier, it seems, if such a medication existed. In an instant we could experience and gain insight into how the other half lives. Too bad, but this is not an option.

So, where and how do you start to rekindle the romance you once enjoyed with this man of yours? Is he still a Prince Charming? Or has time transformed him with the help of a little extra weight, a little balding on top, and a few bad habits into just an ordinary married man? Are you frustrated in your attempts to nudge him off of the sofa and back onto his White Horse—the one he rode when he first swept you off of your feet?

I believe far too many of us try to "reform" or "fix" our husbands. That is the wrong approach. By God's grace only *you* can change *you*, and only *he* can change *himself*.

That is why we have two parts to this book. One half is for you and the other half is for your husband.

You'll need a few supplies: a willingness to try, a teachable heart to grow, and a hope in God that He alone can work miraculous transformations.

Learning to romance a spouse is not necessarily a simple task. Romance is wonderful, but it takes work.

Marriage is often complicated. For our part, we women are frequently confused in our role. Some wives become martyrs in their marriages, completely denying their feelings and needs and ideas. Others become masters, insisting their feelings, needs, and ways of doing things rule. Still others become mothers, fussing over the husband's life and activities and interests like he's a child.

None of these—martyr, master, or mother—is what God had in mind for married women. His goal is far higher and greater. He wants us to experience all He intended for marriage: passion, comfort, peace, companionship, fun, laughter, great hope, and much more for the future.

My hope and prayer for you is that you'll find a measure of encouragement, a dose of hope, a fresh motivation toward creativity, a greater faith in Christ, and a renewed vision for the future. Without passion, tenderness, and physical oneness, marriage fizzles into a joyless endurance contest. Without romance, marriage is destined to lose intimacy and wither in isolation and loneliness. And that's a sad place to live.

You might be thinking, "Yes, that's exactly where I'm living. I feel like there's no hope for us." One of my favorite verses in the Bible is Luke 1:37 (NKJV): "With God nothing will be impossible." Your husband is not impossible; your marriage is not impossible; your present circumstances are not impossible. Nothing you will face is too hard for God. Always remember, with God nothing is impossible.

Have fun reading and growing together.

Part One

THE
SEASONS
OF ROMANCE

When I fall in love with you, it will be forever.
—STEVIE WONDER

Chapter 1

New Love Is Easy

nce upon a time . . .

There's nothing like a fairy tale to arouse delight in the soul of a little girl. As her mom turns the colorful storybook pages, her heart dances with anticipation. She knows the handsome prince must ride his tall white horse through the storm to rescue a fair maiden—before it's too late. She can barely contain herself when, just in the nick of time, the prince reaches down from his horse and sweeps the maiden off her feet.

Safely behind him in the saddle, the maiden holds her arms around his waist. As the story draws to a close, the child's heart soars. The valiant prince and the young maiden ride off into the sunset . . . to a faraway castle deep inside never-never land . . . where the grass is always green.

. . . and they lived happily ever after.

Like a well-worn Raggedy Ann doll, a little girl will carry that ideal picture of romance around in her head for the rest of her life. She's too young to understand why she resonates with such tales of chivalry. But she does. Deeply. And whether she knows it or not, the seeds of her dream lover are being cultivated in her fertile imagination. As the longing takes root, she might not say the words aloud, but she dares to believe that . . .

One day my prince will come too.

And then he does.

From the first touch of his hand, her childhood fantasy begins to take flight. He's so perfect. He's absolutely charming. He thinks she's beautiful. He brings her flowers, writes a little poetry, and laughs at her jokes. He even thinks her freckles are adorable. They talk for hours. These early days of love have her sailing above the clouds.

She's found her one and only true love. Her soul mate.

After much fanfare—and breathlessly discussing every little detail of Mr. Wonderful with three girlfriends—she and her prince decide to marry. They find the "perfect" one-bedroom apartment and begin their life as Mr. and Mrs. Prince Charming. Standing in her own kitchen, she realizes she's all grown up. She's arrived.

And she couldn't be happier.

But a fairy tale is not real life.

One day, when she least expects it, she awakens from her dream and, with a look at the disheveled prince beside her, wonders if she's made the biggest mistake of her life. Like Snow White's mirror, the truth of his shortcomings and failures are revealed. The more she dwells on these deficiencies, the more she feels as if she's bought a ticket on the *Titanic*.

Why didn't she see it before? Now what?

THE SEASONS OF ROMANCE

Maybe you're in the same boat as this young bride. Whether you've been married a few months or many years, it's possible you're tempted to jump ship. Or maybe you've just decided to settle for being seasick. Let me encourage you not to give up hope. Here's why. Cinderella and all of the other *fairy-tale love stories end at the wrong place*—at the beginning! The grand finale is the wedding. No fairy tale dares to go beyond the honeymoon to show us the rest of the story.

After more than thirty years of marriage, I know more now than I could ever have imagined on that day when Dennis and I said, "I do." One thing has become crystal clear: romance is seasonal. Dennis and I have discovered that every marriage progresses through three seasons of romance—and most couples revisit them as the years go by. These seasons are:

- New love
- Disappointed love
- Cherishing committed love

The first season of romance, *new love,* begins during dating and continues through engagement, the wedding, often into sweet days as newlyweds, and perhaps even into the first few years of marriage. This season is characterized by an intense focus on each other, a strong mutual attraction, eager anticipation and enthusiasm for building a life together, and a great freedom (hopefully after marriage) for expressing physical intimacy.

Couples in *new love* are eager to sacrifice time and money to fuel this new experience. It feels so good. Their fears are minimized by the emotion of love, and they will talk for hours about their lives and dreams and hopes. New love is easy, delightful, and intense. It is intoxicating. It is living a dream.

Romantic Interlude

Did you have your wedding ceremony or the reception taped?
If so, dig out the old tapes and watch them together
with your husband. Just for fun, bake a cake with
white frosting to share as you stroll down memory lane.

In his book *The Mystery of Marriage,* noted author Mike Mason writes, "Being engaged is like entering a new stage of childhood, right down to the feeling of strange new chemicals being released into the body. It is, in fact, like having a new body, like being a brand new creature just emerged from a cocoon . . . The world is so bright, and this crazy new body is so incredibly sensitive to everything."

His picture of a new creature shedding her cocoon came to

mind as I was passing through the Dallas airport. There, not long ago, I ran into a business acquaintance, a young woman who was on her way to visit her fiancé. I had not seen her for a year and was unaware she had become engaged. In our brief conversation I was amazed at the visual transformation in her. No, she hadn't had plastic surgery or changed her hair color. But she was glowing. She had come dramatically alive in a way she hadn't appeared a year earlier. She was clearly in love—she was radiant.

Such is the transforming power of *new love*.

ICING ON THE WEDDING CAKE

Our media-saturated culture encourages and celebrates *new love* by placing an inappropriate emphasis on the early days of courtship and romance. Just look at the ratings for the wildly popular "reality" dating shows such as *The Bachelor, The Bachelorette*, and their many imitators. Millions of Americans tune in every week to follow the romantic adventures of complete strangers.

Hands down, the best example of turning romance into a spectator sport had to be the wedding of Trista Rehn and Ryan Sutter. On ABC's *The Bachelorette,* Trista chose Ryan as her knight in shining armor out of twenty-five competing suitors. Nine months later, Trista and Ryan exchanged wedding vows in front of family, friends . . . and more than seventeen million viewers via an ABC television crew.

In true Hollywood fashion, no expense was spared.

From head to toe Trista looked like Cinderella when she walked down the aisle—wearing a diamond necklace worth $1 million and a strapless designer gown that cost $70,000. And it was only one of three dresses she chose for the occasion: one for the wedding, one for the reception, and the third as she and Ryan departed the grand event to live happily ever after.

Although she didn't wear glass slippers, her shoes were a real work of art. Costing $50,000, they were covered with 282 diamonds—which, according to several estimates, were the most expensive wedding shoes ever created.

Not that anyone could see them.

As it turned out, Trista's gown hid the platinum and diamond-studded heels. On hindsight, she could have worn any cheap pair of shoes from a local discount store. But money was no object. It was, after all, what many have called "The Wedding of the Decade." Which explains why the bill was $73,000 for a celebrity makeup artist, $83,000 plus postage for custom-made fan-shaped wedding announcements, and $250,000 for the flowers, including 30,000 pink-and-ivory roses flown in from Ecuador and Holland.

But wait, there's more.

The wedding banquet featured food from 14 countries and included 200 pounds of shrimp, lobster, and crab—not to mention the swordfish, filet, and ravioli main dishes accompanied by 600 bottles of wine and 4,300 cups of coffee. A $15,000 seven-tier cake offered the perfect finish to a perfect evening where guests toasted the now famous newlywed couple with 180 bottles of champagne.

And all before the clock struck twelve.

Never mind that, as American weddings go, their $4 million bill for this modern-day fairy tale is slightly out of line. The national average is less than $20,000. But who's counting? This is true love we're talking about.

ABC scored millions of viewers because the network tapped into every woman's little girl dream to be a real Cinderella. The problem is, we think creating the perfect circumstances will make the dream a reality. But if the truth be known, that dream is the source of profound disappointment and disillusionment in millions of marriages today.

Here's the "real reality" of this extravagant reality TV show. After the caterers had packed their bags, the camera crews had unplugged their cables, and the masses of Cinderella wannabes had changed channels, Trista and Ryan's chances of experiencing a lifelong, romantic marriage are *no better* than those of the couple who decide to stand before a justice of the peace and pay the $20 for their license.

In fact, I believe their chances may actually be less than those of an average couple because their expectations—as well as those of their friends, families, and seventeen million viewers—are higher than normal. When everything has been orchestrated to perfection, how will they cope with the inevitable imperfections they are soon to discover?

The same is true for most couples. Creating the perfect wedding has been elevated to an art form. Preparing for a marriage has been demoted to insignificance. The blind assumption is that the fire of this unique love can and will conquer all.

But the harsh realities of difficult marriages, separations, and divorce statistics tell the real story. Just as Prince Charles and Princess Diana discovered, fairy-tale weddings do not guarantee *happily ever after*.

In the end, great damage has been done by such high-profile weddings of the rich and clueless. Their actions perpetuate the notion that couples can stay together only as long as the romance burns hot; furthermore, their example lends weight to the belief that breaking up is both inevitable and okay when the romance cools down.

Romantic Interlude

What was one of the most romantic things you and your husband did together during your season of new love? What's keeping you from enjoying something like it again?

When our focus is on the glitter of the wedding event, we forget that romance is *more than what you do to catch your Prince Charming*. Granted, a romantic attraction gets a couple launched during the first season of romance. But then reality comes along and exposes the fairy tale for what it truly is: an illusion. As the saying goes, if love is blind, marriage is a real eye-opener.

A couple wrestles with the fact that marriage isn't what they thought it would be—or should be. Real romance, they discover, is not like the fairy tales or the passionate stuff on TV. As Henry Ward Beecher, a clergyman, noted, "Young love is a flame; very pretty, often very hot and fierce, but still only light and flickering. The love of the older and disciplined heart is as coals, deep burning, unquenchable."

How do we move from new love to a heart that burns with an unquenchable romantic fire? We start by learning in the next chapter how to handle the second season of romance, *disappointed love*.

New love is easy.

Happily ever after is hard work.

You don't bring me flowers
You don't sing me love songs
You hardly talk to me anymore
When you come thru the door.

—BARBRA STREISAND AND NEIL DIAMOND
(WRITTEN BY NEIL DIAMOND, ALAN BERGMAN, AND MARILYN BERGMAN)

Chapter 2

Disappointed Love Is Normal

One of the greatest challenges faced by virtually every newly married couple is moving from *event romance*—the picnics, dinner at an exclusive restaurant, and other creative "mini-productions" couples enjoy while dating, to *everyday romance*—those less "glamorous" expressions of love and affirmation that a couple maintains amidst the busyness of everyday married life. Newlyweds of all ages must learn to move beyond the first burst of new love that carried them through courtship and engagement, and turn it into the kind of love that sustains a marriage for life.

Like the jarring, repetitive beep of an alarm clock, the shocking jolt of disappointment eventually affects all couples. This wakeup call may start on the first day of the honeymoon, after a few months, or even a year into the marriage. The disillusionment can be a sudden, dramatic eye-opening moment or a gradual, growing realization that *marriage isn't what I had imagined.*

The second season of romance, *disappointed love,* awakens every newly married couple from their fairy-tale dream. And it will visit their marriage again and again in the years to come. Disappointed love, however, can be a healthy experience and a very necessary ingredient in the making of a great marriage.

"AN OLD-FASHIONED LOVE STORY"

Dennis and I met at the University of Arkansas, where we were involved with Campus Crusade for Christ. We spent many hours together helping create and plan revolutionary ways to reach our campus for Christ. Dennis's leadership, integrity, passion, and conviction impressed me, but he was just a friend, more like a brother to me.

After college graduation, we joined the staff of Campus Crusade full-time, but we moved to different states, Dennis to Texas and I to South Carolina. We agreed to keep in touch with letters—old-fashioned snail mail.

And then came the summer of 1972 when my friend became much more than a friend. We were assigned to work in Dallas for two months on a special project. Dennis offered to take me to lunch so we could catch up on the past year. The next day, being unfamiliar with the city, he offered to give me a ride to work. And the next and the next and by the end of that first week, we'd spent every day riding to and from the office together, going out to lunch together, and spending time in the evenings together. I felt safe in his presence, accepted for who I was, and confident in his passion for Christ.

Our courtship was nothing like Ryan and Trista's. We didn't spend time in a hot tub. There were no exotic dream dates and no cameras to record our every move. And I'm very thankful for that. Instead, over six weeks, our friendship changed quickly. Although we didn't kiss once, we realized that our relationship was now much more than an ordinary friendship.

Two weeks later, serving as attendants at the wedding of mutual friends, we considered marriage for ourselves. Getting married was a simple decision for us. It made sense. For three years we had known each other as good friends. We had watched each other's Christian walk match the talk, and we felt confident that God was in our relationship after we prayed for direction. In a very unromantic, no fanfare way, Dennis proposed over the phone at two in the morning!

I spent the first week of engagement back in South Carolina trying to adjust to this new reality in my life. It had happened so fast. I honestly hadn't seen the possibility of engagement coming until the last minute. There had been no time to anticipate this sudden change in my life. I was unprepared for what lay ahead.

Our engagement was only six weeks long, and those weeks were a flurry of activity—setting up a wedding, packing to move, having three wedding showers, meeting family, and going through premarital counseling. In a blink it was over. We were married. In three short months my best friend became my husband.

For us the *new love* season lasted for the first couple of years of marriage, primarily because our courtship and engagement were so short that in many ways we began to fall in love only after the engagement and the wedding. Disappointments came, but they came slowly at first and, thankfully, in small doses.

Romantic Interlude

What disappointments are you struggling with
in your marriage? Who are you most disappointed with—
your husband, yourself, or God? Why are you disappointed?
Have you believed fairy-tale thinking?

"IT'S MY PARTY, AND I'LL CRY IF I WANT TO"

For other couples, like our son, Samuel, and daughter-in-law, Stephanie, *disappointed love* can begin the day after the wedding. They now refer to their first week of marriage as the "honeymoon from hell," and the first six months of marriage as a disaster. They followed their parents' pattern for speed and began dating in

January, were engaged in March, and married in May. Their wedding day rivaled any fairy tale with their long-anticipated first kiss at the altar, the *Star Wars* theme recessional music, and a horse-drawn white carriage ride around historic Franklin, Tennessee, in absolutely perfect weather.

Watching our son get married was one of the greatest delights of my life. I reveled in God's provision of Stephanie for Samuel, how He so clearly orchestrated every detail. It was magical and memorable. But their perfect wedding day was only His inaugural gift for the main event, the marriage.

As I said, *disappointed love* visited them immediately. Their differences were glaring and sharp. "New husband" miscues like missing their honeymoon flight, their sightseeing tour, not to mention their individual expectations about married life got them off on the wrong foot. Then they moved to more serious issues, not the least of which were their assumptions about the roles each of them would play in the marriage, and normal newlywed fears of not being accepted or of being abandoned. These mistakes and misunderstandings, even though most were unintentional, caused unexpected grief and hurt. For Samuel and Stephanie their initial ride was turbulent. But because they knew God had called them together, they weathered the initial storms of disappointed love and have grown more deeply in love with each other.

Just as Samuel and Stephanie learned through their difficult experiences, Dennis and I discovered early on in our marriage that married life wasn't exactly what we thought falling in love would be—or should be. It wasn't like Cinderella. Experiencing disappointed love meant going from falling in love to deciding together to go forward in pursuit of a better love. It wasn't easy.

It became hard work. Really hard work.

Dennis and I discovered what we knew to be true: I'm selfish, he's selfish, and we're *so incredibly different*. Why didn't we see that before?

STAND BY ME

The reality of disappointment is a surprise for most couples. No one expects it really. Why? Because most engaged couples, in the flush of new love, think that their relationship will be different. They feel a sense of destiny. They believe their love will stay strong and fresh in spite of all the odds.

Love is demanding, however. Once we have tasted the experience of being loved, accepted, cared for, appreciated, and served, we want more. We got married not for less love, but for more love.

So, what do we do with disappointment? Most of us just try harder and harder in those early years. We try all kinds of new approaches to salvage the dream in hopes that we'll recapture the magic.

And where is God in all of this? He's waiting . . . waiting to give us understanding, compassion, and His love for each other. He wants us to see that we can't iron out the wrinkles on our own. The kind of love we are looking for isn't a love either of us can self-produce.

Far too many couples bail out of the marriage at this point. Why? The light, airy feelings are gone—or are greatly diminished. The wedding gown is in a box, the music has stopped, and as Barbra Streisand sings, "You don't bring me flowers anymore." They never fully accept that new love is just that . . . new. It's only the beginning. They decide that they'll pursue "happily ever after" in another relationship.

Other couples, upon reaching the disappointed love season, don't quit, but instead, they give up hope. Perhaps the pain of facing their struggles is too great, and the fear of what it might take to move beyond the disappointment of reality paralyzes them from moving forward. Not willing to consider divorce, and finding it impossible to believe their relationship could ever get better, they stalemate, move into denial, and go through the motions in their relationship.

As the experience of disappointed love becomes a daily lifestyle, couples fight with their words, retreat to separate corners, and walk on eggshells in their relationship. They experience what someone once described: "When I got married, I was looking for the ideal. But it soon became an ordeal. Now I want a new deal." This is when love, romance, and marriage require a new level of courage.

The season of disappointed love is inevitable and necessary, but it doesn't need to be fatal. The apostle Paul reminded us, "In all things God works for the good of those who love him" (Rom. 8:28). Yes, even in the midst of intense disappointment, God wants you and your husband to discover the most important ingredient for a lasting, rich, and dynamic romance.

Philippians 1:6 tells us that "he who began a good work in you will carry it on to completion until the day of Christ Jesus." This passage refers to salvation and maturity in our walk with Christ, and I think it is important to realize that as we continue to mature in Christ, God will bring maturity to the marriage relationship as well. God is also in the business of redeeming and completing marriage. He wants us to know real love. He wants us to move on to the kind of rich, deep, mature love that heals and inspires and nurtures and sustains. He and He alone is the source of that kind of love.

We can't know that kind of love until we are willing to let new love go and honestly confront our disappointments. We have to release our fairy-tale thinking.

How? The secret is found in one word. *Commitment.*

THROUGH THICK AND THIN

Commitment is choosing to take your husband's hand and *walk through* the reality God has allowed in your life, believing that on the other side, you will find a deeper love and a healthier relationship than you had before. Sometimes moving past disappointed love will mean restating your wedding vows, literally, as one couple did at the *Rekindling the Romance* arena event that FamilyLife hosted in Orlando. Facing a time of extreme trial, John and Amy wrote,

> After going through a painful separation and getting back together, renewing our wedding vows had a profound effect. We both were crying so much that we barely got through it. We had not been wearing our rings for about a year and thought there was no hope. Restating our vows helped to put us on the right track. Funny how our vows meant so much more to us now than they did 19 years ago.

At other times commitment is an inner resolve to keep going, a realigning of your thinking to conform to what you know to be true in spite of your feelings. It's similar to reciting the Pledge of Allegiance. In America we often repeat the words of the Pledge in classrooms, at sporting events, during national holiday celebrations. The Pledge is a reminder of what we hold dear in this nation. We don't think of these recitations as being burdensome just because we recite them every so often. Renewing the commitment in marriage to the one person we have promised to love, honor, and cherish should be no more difficult.

Romantic Interlude

Have you and your husband ever renewed your wedding vows?
If not, or if it has been a while, consider refreshing your pledge
by restating your vows over a candlelit dinner.

In marriage, God wants to take us on a lifelong journey to become what we were meant to be, to experience Him more and more, to understand a hint of the relationship and unity God

Himself knows within the Trinity. This intimacy is a mystery, but it makes marriage a heavenly journey and not merely a biological coupling.

God allows disappointment to bring us face-to-face with what we really believe and value, sometimes on a daily basis so we have to depend on Him for the grace to continue to love as He intends. But the promise is this: on the other side of disappointed love is the hope of a greater taste of heaven. The apostle Paul put it this way, "we also rejoice in our sufferings, because we know that suffering produces perseverance; perseverance, character; and character, hope. And hope does not disappoint us, because God has poured out his love into our hearts by the Holy Spirit, whom he has given us" (Romans 5:3–5). Just as we look forward to the peace and joy and comfort and love of heaven, so in marriage we can know the flavor of that experience. It's God's intention for us if we will choose to courageously follow Him with our commitment.

Your covenant of commitment to God and each other is the heart of what remains once reality has edited the illusion of *what you thought* marriage would be. Think back to your wedding. You stood before God at the altar and promised to *never* leave and *never* forsake your husband, in sickness and in health, for better or for worse. Now, staring "worse" in the face, you have a choice.

Will you honor that commitment?

PRESSING ON

When you reach this crossroads of decision, you can reject your vows, you can believe there is no hope, or you can trust God that He is able to help you rekindle the smoldering ashes and transform them into something vibrant. As our dear friends Jim and Debi Godsey said to us when Dennis and I were in the middle of a very difficult time in our lives: "What an awesome opportunity to see God work." They were right.

When you choose to take the high road and trust God to

rekindle your romance His way, you set your marriage on a course to experience the third and most exciting season of romance, *cherishing committed love*. As you read on, you'll find this season is well worth the work. I know. It's what we have experienced and our married children are still discovering.

Love seems the swiftest, but it is the slowest of all growths.
No man or woman really knows what perfect love is until
they have been married a quarter of a century.

—MARK TWAIN

Chapter 3

Cherishing Committed Love

*N*ew love is admittedly shallow, but it's great fun. Disappointed love is clearly inevitable and is not fun at all. The season of *cherishing committed love* is worth the work and the perseverance.

Commitment doesn't sound romantic on the surface. But it is absolutely essential for success in every marriage. Genuine romance is impossible without it.

Commitment begins at the wedding with our vows and pledges to each other and to God. But when we face disappointment, we have to decide again to live by those vows. We must choose commitment. Contrary to what some might think, however, choosing commitment is not a one-time decision. As I've come to see, this act of the will is often a daily resolution to stand by our vows. Why?

Because you will repeatedly experience disappointment with each other and with the state of your marriage. Trials will come, responsibilities will grow, children will continually challenge, and temptations of escape will float by again and again. What is your source of hope in the midst of all that lies ahead? There is only one way to make marriage and romance last: *A renewable commitment to each other that has no escape clauses and hopes only in God and not in each other.*

Commitment creates a wall of protection around your marriage. Commitment creates a safe place for two people to be real with each other without fear of rejection. Commitment not only protects your marriage from outside intruders, but also creates the security that allows you to discover love and romance in fresh ways and deeper levels of intimacy and joy.

Dennis and I found our intimacy was free to grow every time each of us realized the other person was really committed for life. And it's not a resigned, "I guess I'm stuck" kind of commitment. Instead it's a renewable resource in marriage, like trees in a forest. Trees take years to grow to maturity. As they mature, they provide rest, shade, and nourishment for humans and animals alike. With sufficient soil depth and water, a tree's roots grow deep and provide stability for the inevitable storms.

Commitment in marriage is like the growing root system of an oak tree. Yes, there are roots in every new little tree, just as there is often a heartfelt commitment in new marriages, but it takes time for roots to grow deep. Likewise, it takes time for commitment to grow deep and strong. Far too many couples uproot their love in the early stages of growth and, as a result, never have the privilege of experiencing the majesty of a mature forest of long-term love.

Keep in mind that while commitment provides the context of stability every marriage needs for intimacy to grow, as you'll see in chapter eight, a marriage also needs passion. You might say that *commitment is the tree* and *passion is the luscious fruit adorning the tree.* Both are necessary.

ON THE ROCKS

I'll never forget when disappointed love crashed on our marriage with a vengeance during our sixth year of marriage. It left us tattered and worn. Not surprisingly, disappointed love surfaced during our first season of real suffering. And yet over time, this rude awakening provided the ideal soil conditions for growing a deeper root system.

By the way, we saw none of this coming. Suffering always slips up on us with the element of surprise. With it comes an enemy who lurks in the shadows of our struggles, whispering that we shouldn't trust God in the midst of trials and difficulties of life. This enemy hopes to lure us into unbelief about God and our spouses and our marriages.

In the summer of 1976, we moved to Little Rock with two young children to help start FamilyLife. Soon afterward, we found, much to our surprise, that we had been cheated out of some money on the sale of our house. Undaunted, we moved into our "vintage World War II–era cottage," only to discover that while vintage was charming, it was also dusty and moldy and a serious assault on my allergies. Cleaning provided minor relief. My battle with allergies was an almost daily dilemma for the eight years we lived in that house.

Then shortly after our move, Dennis's father died suddenly, necessitating a three-week stay in Missouri with his mother in the tiny two-bedroom home of his childhood. Making matters worse, in October and November a funding shortage meant a cut in our paychecks. Christmas came and went, and we dared to hope that the new year would be better than the last six months had been.

But it was not to be.

In January Dennis's brother had an apparent heart attack, and Dennis returned to run the family propane business while his brother recovered. In one of the worst winters in decades, Dennis spent two weeks in subfreezing temperatures delivering propane to homes on hilly, snow-covered back roads and unhooking propane tank cars from trains in the middle of the night. He was exhausted and alone, wondering if God had abandoned him.

Then in early June of 1977 came the trial that nearly ended our marriage—literally. About 9:00 a.m., I suddenly felt faint. I almost passed out and realized my heart was beating at an uncontrollable rate. Within an hour I was rushed to the hospital in an ambulance, terrified at what was happening. I wondered if I was dying. Dennis worried, too, as he battled his fears of being a widower with two children under three years of age.

For several hours my heart continued racing at more than three hundred beats a minute. We believe God intervened in answer to a dear widow's prayers as my heart instantly returned to a normal beating pattern at four o'clock that afternoon. Though I was released from the hospital in a couple of days, we lived the following weeks in fear that the racing would happen again at any minute. It was a condition that could not be controlled by medication or prevented by any action.

In July I discovered I was pregnant. As you might expect, I wondered whether the pregnancy would threaten my health. Would the baby be normal? There were no answers. Only questions. Only more waiting.

We were exhausted and on the verge of burning out. We were young and inexperienced, and we had *no preparation* for handling all of this suffering. Neither of us really knew what the other was feeling. To look beyond my fears and needs to my husband's needs was beyond difficult. I was empty emotionally. There was nothing to give. I was numb.

Romance? The thrill of our new love was a distant memory. We didn't sign up for this. There was never trouble of this magnitude in my Cinderella storybook.

And what about God? Could I trust Him? While the Bible clearly teaches in Job 1 that God permits suffering, my confidence in Him was shaken when hardship happened to us. Yet I knew that I could ultimately trust God in spite of what my circumstances looked like.

Was my husband meeting all my needs emotionally, spiritually, and physically? No. He couldn't. Dennis was only human. We had made our commitment to each other for better or worse, and divorce wasn't an option, so we pushed forward one day at a time. It was all we could do.

Recognizing our need for a break, some good friends invited us in August of 1977 to join them on an all-expense-paid trip to

Mazatlan, Mexico. Thrilled by the opportunity to put the chaos behind us for four days, we packed our bags and headed south.

When we arrived, the warm ocean breeze and the steady sound of breaking waves spoke of serenity and peace, and gave us hope. The taxi left us at our beach-front hotel that night. We slept in the next morning and wandered around town the next day with our friends.

That night the four of us enjoyed a wonderful dinner on the restaurant patio. Afterward, we even tried to do a little dancing— which I'm sure was an interesting sight for the locals. When we returned to the room, a gentle breeze was blowing. The edge of the moon was peeking around a thunderstorm on the horizon. As we lingered on the tiny balcony watching the last fading colors of the distant sunset, we were serenaded by the music from a nearby cabaña.

While the setting was close to perfect, the two people were not. And we were about to find out how different our needs were.

When we walked back into our room, the first thing Dennis did was to light some candles. He was making assumptions that seemed logical to him. We were finally away from the stress of the last year. We'd had time to relax and unwind a bit with a nice dinner and some dancing. There were no children to interrupt, the room was warm and quiet, and there were no schedules the next morning. We had time to connect and have a meaningful time of making love. He needed to feel close to me. He was ready to move on with life.

I also had some assumptions. Even though we'd had a relaxing day, we hadn't had much time alone for the two of us to just talk. Since that day in June when my heart had raced wildly, I had become fearful, timid, confused, and introspective. I hardly knew what I was feeling or how to express it.

So, on this perfect night in this perfect location what I needed was not what my husband needed. I didn't need sex. I wasn't opposed to making love eventually, but first I needed him to help me sort through what I was feeling and reassure me that everything would be okay in my life.

How did we resolve our differing needs?

We had a fight!

Not right away, of course. Dennis tried to talk to me. He tried to love me. I wanted to talk but didn't know what to say. I knew he wanted to make love and he needed me, so I tried to deny myself and serve him, but I just couldn't respond in that moment. Of course, given a less stressful set of life circumstances, making love would have been a wonderful ending to a romantic day.

Our situation went from bad to worse. I felt guilty, and he felt frustrated. I hated myself for being so complicated. He was stressed over his inability to love me enough to make me forget my fears.

Finally the tension became too much, and Dennis grabbed a bottle of hand lotion on the side of the bed and threw it across the room. Instead of hitting the wall, the bottle broke a small pane of glass in the window. It also shattered our wills.

The room became very still. We again heard the waves continuing their relentless crashing on the beach. Palm tree branches rustled each other gently in the breeze just outside the now broken window. I began to cry. I loved my husband and didn't want to hurt him. For a few more moments Dennis was silent.

Then Dennis rolled over to face me in bed and said something that I never expected to hear. Something that became a milestone in our marriage. Something that was unexpectedly liberating. He tenderly cupped my face in his hands and said from his heart, "Barbara, I want you to know that I love you, and I am committed to you. I will love you for the rest of your life, even if we never, ever make love again."

Then he kissed me on the forehead and gathered me into a warm embrace with no strings attached, and we eventually fell asleep in each other's arms. No gift of any price could have meant more.

Romantic Interlude
What could you or your husband say or do
that would bolster the level of confidence you share
in the commitment to your marriage?
Why not talk about this over coffee tonight?

Interestingly the next afternoon as we were on an offshore fishing trip, I discovered a growing desire to be with him sexually. I couldn't wait to be alone with him again. It was something I hadn't felt in many, many months. Suddenly my needs and fears didn't matter so much anymore. Why? I was motivated to be in the presence of that kind of sacrificial love. I saw what kind of love my husband had for me. His heartfelt assurance was what I needed. I, in turn, wanted to express love to him, which was what he needed.

After six years of marriage, his declaration of unconditional, sacrificial love let me know he loved me for who I was, not just for what I could do for him. It's not that I really thought he was interested only in sex. But when he spoke those words, he took the pressure of performance off of me. It was as if we'd gone back to the altar of our wedding and renewed our vows. It was a holy moment. God was there, and it was a new beginning. We discovered the profound peace of committed love, and we cherished it.

That evening in Mazatlan was a make-it-or-break-it moment in our marriage. Either of us could have chosen to walk away because the disappointment and pain were too great. We alone knew how difficult life had been for us.

We learned that *sacrifice is the language of romance,* and selfishness is the language of isolation and rejection. Commitment inspires one to sacrifice, and sacrifice makes commitment a rare jewel to be cherished.

ALWAYS AND FOREVER

Although you may wish your husband would say to you something like Dennis said to me, such an expression shouldn't be forced. My husband's words of sacrificial, committed love were born out of desperation and death to self. In his declaration that night, and my romantic response the next day, we experienced the truth of Philippians 2:3–4 (NKJV): "Let nothing be done through selfish ambition or conceit, but in lowliness of mind let each esteem others better than himself. Let each of you look out not only for his own interests, but also for the interests of others."

While looking out for the interests of another person doesn't come naturally, when a couple commits to self-sacrifice and cherishing their commitment, they discover a whole new side to romance. Is this hard work? Absolutely. Is it worth the effort? You bet. After years of hard work, there is no question in my mind about the payoff: *our love for each other and the romance we share are richer today than at any time in our marriage.*

This can be true for you.

After all, marriage is not just about a grand beginning. It's about committing to a strong finish. It's weathering the storms of disappointment and the turbulence of life, never losing the ability to sing with Solomon, "How delightful is your love . . . How much more pleasing is your love than wine" (Song 4:10).

That, my friend, is a real storybook finish.

Part Two

MEN AND WOMEN EXPRESS ROMANCE DIFFERENTLY

Deep in his heart, every man longs for
a battle to fight, an adventure to live,
and a beauty to rescue.
—JOHN ELDREDGE

Chapter 4

Why Sex Is So Important to Your Husband

ave you read your husband's part of the story about Bryan and Angela? My guess is, you have. You wanted to see if the prescription worked correctly on his mind and body. You probably thought, *I'm not sure if Angela's experience is accurate, but Bryan's better be!*

Speaking of those differences, Dennis and I received a cute e-mail about the romantic differences between men and women. It began by asking, "How do you romance a woman?"

Answer: "Wine her, dine her, call her, cuddle with her, surprise her, compliment her hair, shop with her, listen to her talk, buy flowers, hold her hand, write love letters, and be willing to go to the end of the earth and back again for her."

That sounds about right, doesn't it?

Who wouldn't want that kind of treatment?

Ahhh . . . men.

The e-mail continued, "How do you romance a man?"

Answer: "Arrive naked. Bring food."

A woman's picture of romance tends to revolve around her emotional needs and her thirst for a relationship with her husband. It's a package deal, like going on a cruise. Your cruise ticket doesn't just allow you to enjoy sailing on a ship through beautiful waters to exotic locations; it includes three meals a day plus all-you-can-eat midnight buffets, access to swimming pools, games, exercise facilities, entertainment, excursions to ports of call, and a host of other amenities and experiences.

While a man has emotional needs, too, as Dr. Willard Harley asserts in *His Needs, Her Needs*, a man's view of romance is much more focused on a single experience: sexual affirmation. In that regard, God wired men and women very differently. As you probably have experienced, these radical differences in approach to romance set the stage for repeated clashes in marriage—the husband pursues romance based on his sexual passion, and the wife goes after relationship. This romantic two-step is what Dennis and I experienced on our trip to Mazatlan, Mexico, as I shared in the last chapter.

Unlike Angela, you and I as women have no idea what it is really like to be a man. For example, as Dennis and I worked on this book, we invited several close members of our staff to preview portions of it. One woman read Bryan and Angela's story and couldn't believe that her husband actually struggled with sexual thoughts. After all, she had been married thirty-seven years, and *they never had a conversation on the topic*. She assumed lust wasn't a battle he had to fight. What did she do?

She went home and talked about it.

Guess what? He read the story and said, "Yup, that's about it."

Likewise, men are often clueless about being a woman. In the above example, this man couldn't fathom that his wife, as a woman, lacked the same struggle with lust. He had made the assumption that both were engaged in a constant battle for the purity of the mind.

We have to be educated and nurture a desire to learn. Colossians tells us to "put on a heart of compassion" (3:12 NASB). If I love my husband, then I'll want to know him, to understand him, to have empathy for him so I can love him more. It's what we wanted in marriage: to know and be known by another in the safety of unconditional love.

Genesis chapters one and two teach that man and woman are made in the image of God. As I understand how God made my husband, I can better complete him as a man. We are "fearfully and wonderfully made," the Bible declares (Ps. 139:14 NKJV). My husband's maleness is as essential as my femaleness in the working out of God's design in our marriage.

I SAY TOMATOE; YOU SAY TOMATO

About a dozen years into our marriage, I discovered a book that dramatically altered my understanding and perception of how God made my husband and his need for sex. Just as Angela experienced a change in perspective through cutting-edge medication, I gained fresh insight into my man and how he thinks thanks to *Men and Marriage* by George Gilder.

Gilder is a sociologist and economist who writes that women have a taming influence over men through the institution of marriage. Without women—and in my view, without Jesus Christ—men would become uncontrolled barbarians, living on impulse, wandering in life, fighting, competing, and chasing after power. But a man will willingly surrender all his barbarian ways for the love of a woman. Women inherently possess this power over men. I'll have more to say on this in the next chapter.

Another insight I gained was *how vastly different we are* as men and women. I shouldn't be so surprised, but as a woman I view the world through my female senses. I continue to forget that Dennis doesn't think like I do—and I can't think like he does!

When God created woman, He gave her multiple avenues for expressing the essence of her sexuality—her *femaleness*. Because I am a woman, I can participate in sexual intercourse with my husband. I can conceive a child and experience the miraculous process of creating a life in my body over nine months. My husband can only watch and wonder, but he'll never know what giving life is like.

After my child is born, I can physically nurse her for months and even years if I so choose. There is no way a man can feed a baby with a bottle and begin to experience the same deep fulfillment and satisfaction women feel when they successfully nurse their child.

The experiences of childbearing and nursing are affirmations of female sexuality. Women were made to nurture life. It is an expression of our inherent femaleness, even if we never have a biological child. We are nurturers by God's design.

By contrast, a man's sexuality, his manhood, is primarily expressed through sexual intercourse. Of course this isn't the only way he demonstrates his sexuality, but his sexual performance with his wife is an inseparable part of who he is. This area of his masculinity is subjected by the design of the Creator to a brief performance *with a woman—his wife.*

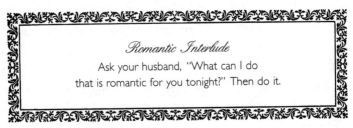

Romantic Interlude
Ask your husband, "What can I do
that is romantic for you tonight?" Then do it.

My point is this: when it comes to affirming your sexuality as a woman, you can participate in intercourse with your husband without having to become aroused. Your husband, however, cannot. His sexual affirmation requires him to be able to perform to complete the act of intercourse. Gilder writes, "His erection is a mysterious endowment that he can never fully understand or control. If it goes away, he often will not know exactly why, and there will be little he or his partner can do to retrieve it" (p. 10).

A wife must understand that temptation can get a foothold when her husband's sexual needs (including the need to feel *desired* by his wife as we'll discuss later) remain unmet. There are many voices in a man's world tempting him to fulfill his needs through illicit and perverted recreational outlets. Counterfeit pleasures beckon from every street corner—and every modem.

Take, for instance, the pornography industry which exploits the visual wiring of males of all ages. Again Gilder writes, "Unless men have an enduring relationship with a woman—a relationship that affords him sexual confidence—men will accept almost any convenient sexual offer. The existence of a semi-illegal, multi-billion dollar pornography market, almost entirely male-oriented, bespeaks of the difference in sexual character between men and women" (p. 11).

Is it any wonder that *all* of the warnings about sexual temptation in Proverbs are directed at men? While women are not immune from the pressures of sexual temptation, I find it remarkable that there are a host of examples of men falling into this sin throughout the Scriptures (Judah sleeping with his daughter-in-law thinking she was a prostitute, David and Bathsheba, Samson and Delilah, or Amnon raping Tamar—not to mention the examples of women trying to seduce men (such as Potiphar's wife luring Joseph to her sofa), but there are no examples of women being seduced by men.

As I'll discuss further in the next chapter, we as women have a unique and powerful opportunity in marriage to understand and find creative ways to affirm our husbands in an area that is clearly central to their manhood.

THE VISUAL WIRING OF WOMEN

But what about women? Is there a corollary?

I believe there is. Just as the pornography industry is built around a man's visual attraction to women, so the fashion industry is built on the visual wiring of women. God designed a woman to want to be attractive and to look good for men, specifically for the man she marries. God designed a man to be attracted to women, specifically the one woman he chooses to marry. We are built and wired to attract and need each other.

Recently Dennis and his co-host on *FamilyLife Today*, Bob Lepine, recorded an interview with three women on the subject of beauty. Dennis came home that evening talking about his amazement at how much these mature, godly women thought about how they looked. He suggested to me that perhaps women think about how they look as often as men think about sex.

That idea intrigued me, and I began paying attention to my thoughts. I've been surprised how often I have fleeting thoughts about my appearance.

I've posed Dennis's observation to other women and asked for their response. At first they'd say something like, "I probably think about how I look three or four times a day." When pressed about those fleeting thoughts about appearance that pop in their minds when walking by a mirror or a store window, when entering a room full of people, when looking in the rearview mirror, or when standing or sitting in view of others, they'd admit that they thought about their appearance more than they realized.

Unlike me, my husband would never start thinking about what to wear and how he'll look for an event more than thirty minutes before he has to leave. Unless, of course, a hunting trip is approaching, and then he'll start gathering gear a week ahead. He wants to be properly equipped for the wild of the hunt. It has nothing to do with how he looks.

Just as young men experience their sexual peak in their teens and twenties, so young women are fixated on their beauty, appearance, and attractiveness in this same time frame. A young man's sex drive does diminish some with age as does a woman's intense need to be attractive to potential suitors. Yet neither loses that unique God-given wiring during this life.

CHANTILLY LACE

What did I do with my newfound insight into a man's sex drive after reading Gilder's book? I started by asking Dennis if my understanding was accurate. We had a long conversation about it, and as I listened to him, I sensed for a moment what it must be like to be a man. I felt compassion for him and was motivated to love him more fully and better meet his needs. I resolved to remember this knowledge and improve by becoming a better wife.

We were on a trip in another city conducting a *Weekend to Remember* conference when this heart-to-heart conversation took place. Because we were away without kids, it was fairly easy for me to move to a new level beyond the ordinary in our lovemaking that night. I still remember some of that evening because I gave myself to him in greater abandon. I wanted him to know how much I loved him and appreciated him as a man. I wanted to meet his deepest needs for affirmation.

Was I suddenly transformed? I had hoped so. In my heart I certainly felt that way . . . for a while . . . a short while. The rest of our marriage would have been so much easier if my perspective had been transformed the same way that the medication had changed Angela in our novella. But it didn't. I couldn't maintain that way of thinking. I lost what sensitivity I had for his perspective and returned to thinking and feeling like a woman. But did I forget?

No, I've never lost sight of how important this is to my husband. Many times in the midst of everyday life with kids and carpools, lessons and lectures, meetings and messes, I've had to remind myself of my husband's needs. Knowing what affirms my husband requires that I plan for him and keep my relationship with him my number one priority. Romance and love take work.

Romantic Interlude

When was the last time you wore something to bed
at night that *he* would call "interesting"? If it's been a while,
why not surprise him tonight by wearing a new nightgown?

LIKE OIL AND VINEGAR

Looking back, it's interesting to reflect on how much Dennis and I have grown in our understanding of each other. One misconception we believed in the first few years of our marriage was that even though we seemed to have differing sexual needs, with time and love we could eventually be more alike.

We honestly brought into marriage the notion that my lesser interest in sex was because of cultural conditioning of women to be more inhibited and reserved. Dennis believed that he could free me to discover greater sexual desire like his with his abundant unconditional love. While there has clearly been a growth in greater freedom and enjoyment in my life in this area over the years, I have not been transformed into a female version of my husband. And that is good. I am a woman by God's design.

Over time, the reality of our inability to change the way we were made by God diminished our wildly idealistic notions of sexual equality. Our repeated experience of disappointed love in the sexual area forced us to renew our commitment to each other many times. As a result, we grew into a greater level of acceptance and love. Our commitment kept us moving toward understanding and sacrifice in our marriage, which are the basis of romance. In turn, we enjoy a deeper, richer intimacy.

Now we understand and appreciate our differences, and we marvel at God's grand design. In a way, the blending of our romantic differences is similar to making a good salad dressing. Oil and vinegar are about as dissimilar as condiments get. The only thing they have in common is that they are liquids. Oil is smooth; vinegar is sharp. Oil is thick; vinegar is thin. Left alone in the same bottle, the two will always migrate to opposite ends and remain there forever—unless shaken.

Interestingly even after the bottle has been shaken, the two retain their unique identities. And yet they complement each other in a perfect unity; together, they serve as a zesty finish to an otherwise bland mix of lettuces. And so it is in marriage. No matter how many times a husband and a wife come together, they always remain unique. He will always think like a man; she, like a woman. While their innate design will not change, they can better understand each other and move to love each other with compassion, knowing that, in so doing, they give each other life.

I'M ALL OUT OF LOVE

At this point you might be saying, "The exact opposite is true in our marriage. He's passive when it comes to sex, and I'm the one initiating. Is there something wrong with us? Doesn't he need the same affirmation sexually that you say other men need?"

First, being more interested in physical oneness than your husband is not wrong. A wife can feel a greater need for sex because she is longing to feel wanted by him, connected to him, and attractive to him. And, yes, there are some women who have a stronger interest in sex because they enjoy sex. This is good and healthy. However, rarely do marriage partners experience totally balanced sexual interest in each other. Our differing desires and needs, when it comes to romance and sex, are a part of a life-long opportunity in marriage to love and be loved for who we are.

Second, there may be any number of causes for a man's lack of interest in sexual relations with his wife: childhood sexual abuse, guilt or shame over past sexual sin, significant rejection in his life that makes the risk of any potential rejection by you frightening, workaholism, exhaustion, health issues, prescription medications, fear of his potential inability to perform sexually, pornography, and masturbation. Dennis writes more about this point in Chapter 10 for the men.

Two other factors shouldn't be overlooked. Our family physician told Dennis that male patients have confided in him that their wives have gained so much weight, they find it difficult to be attracted to them sexually. (More on this in Chapter 8.) The doctor also said that unresolved conflict and resentment can render a man impotent (I'll discuss this in Chapter 11). Viagra may have its place, but no pill can cleanse the heart or stimulate romance in the heart of an angry man.

If the sexual roles are reversed in your marriage and you are reading this book as a couple, I trust that your husband finds hope and help in the men's half of the book. As the Song of Solomon demonstrates, God intends for your marriage to be a relationship where two hearts are inseparable, knit together as one, a place where physical intimacy meets both spouses' needs for love, acceptance, and affirmation. Solomon put it this way: "Even much water cannot put out the flame of love" (Song 8:7 NCV). That is our prayer for you.

GRATEFUL FOR GOD'S DESIGN

For many years, reconciling our seemingly opposite sexual needs and design felt impossible to me. Perhaps yours do, too, regardless of who is more interested and who isn't. At times our situation even felt like a mistake. I've had women ask me, "Could God possibly design such a gigantic flaw?" Could He really not know the implications for His children? Hardly. God's design isn't a mistake. God is in control. He fashioned us together as husband and wife the way we are wired, with our unique backgrounds, for a specific purpose.

And He has done the same for you.

I turned a corner in our relationship when I chose to begin thanking God for His design of my husband and me. As a result, I started to see how important it was for my husband to need me, and I began to appreciate his greater sexual drive. Our coming together sexually was a key part of what has kept our relationship a marriage—not merely friendship, a roommate living arrangement. Sexual intimacy with my husband gives both of us the comfort of being known and accepted on a deep level that is unlike any other human relationship. Safety and security are the result when we experience being "naked and not ashamed" as did Adam and Eve in Genesis chapter two.

Have you ever thanked God for the way He created you and your husband? God doesn't make mistakes, and thanking Him for His design is the first step in finding peace in your situation. And doing that will give God the opportunity to change your thinking.

Thanking God is a decision I choose to make. From there, I choose to love my husband even if I don't have strong feelings. Love, ultimately, is a commitment to seek the best of the one loved. I can choose to exercise my power as a passionate, nurturing, fully alive woman, or I can withhold and withdraw.

You face the same decision to love your man today.

Your husband will never be the man God created him to be if you don't validate his maleness and understand and satisfy his need for sexual intimacy. You are God's primary instrument of love and affirmation if he is to became God's man. You have the power to make him or break him because *men are not born, they are made.*

"Draw me after you and let us run together!"

SONG OF SOLOMON 1:4 NASB

Chapter 5

The Power of a Woman

*E*veryone loves a good story. A well-written tale captures the imagination and transports us to another time and place where we are invited to wander through new experiences that are different from our own.

Fairy tales were intended for children. These timeless legends entertained but also communicated profound truths about life on a level that a child could understand. The story of Cinderella, for example, is full of life lessons. Cinderella models being patient in difficult circumstances, serving with kindness and charity those who are self-centered or spiteful, persevering to overcome seemingly impossible odds, and making the most of what you've been given. Somehow those ideals get lost in the telling, and little girls remember only Cinderella's magical transformation, Prince Charming, and "happily ever after."

Another well-known fairytale illustrates the power of a woman. A young man who is pampered in his youth becomes increasingly arrogant and demanding as he grows older. Eventually he is transformed by a spell into a literal beast as a punishment because it is a reflection of his true nature. His only hope for release is to be truly loved by a maiden, a seemingly impossible achievement. In his anger he demands to be loved, but his beastly behavior only drives people farther away until eventually he is totally alone, isolated from the world of humans.

You know this story as Beauty and the Beast.

There are many variations on this story in different cultures, but all have the same ending. A woman sees something of value in the Beast and begins to love him, changing him from a beast back into a man—and not just the man he was before, but a new, changed man. How could she have loved him as fearsome as he was? It's a mystery, but it illustrates the power of a woman's love.

Both tales mirror another story I know—the story of the Bible from Genesis to Revelation, which reveals humans as rebellious, proud, and unlovely. But God loves us in spite of our sinful nature. It's the amazingly wonderful story of redemption. God's love is also a mystery with great power in our lives.

God tells us in the Bible that marriage is a picture of Christ's redeeming, transforming relationship with the church, His bride. Marriage is intended to be redemptive for both men and women. God has given us women the privilege and the ability to bring life to our husbands with our love. Women have enormous power with men, and we can use it for good or for evil.

A WOMAN'S POWER OVER MAN

Consider three examples from the Scripture. Take the power of Delilah with Samson. Samson, the strongest man in the world, could take on an army of warriors, but he surrendered to the powerful charms of one woman. In *Killing Giants, Pulling Thorns,* Chuck Swindoll describes Samson as a "He man, with a she weakness."

Take King David, who faced and felled a nine-foot Goliath, yet fell under the spell of Bathsheba. David was so obsessed, he was drawn away from his God into immorality, lies, and ultimately murder. Consider Solomon. He ruled over the golden years of Israel, but was captivated by the power of women. Actually make that seven hundred wives and three hundred concubines.

A woman's power over men has not lessened since those biblical days. Today, the advertising industry exploits this power in order to sell everything from cars to toothpaste. Magazines, billboards, posters, and store windows use attractive women, seductive women, and blatant sexual images to catch a man's glance and capture his attention. Every day men walk away from wives, children, friends, parents, siblings—risking career and reputation. For what?

Another woman.

Even more tragically, in the Middle East, young men and teenage boys willingly become human bombs, causing endless grief to thousands, for what? The promise of seventy-two beautiful virgins in paradise.

Female attraction can be deadly.

But death was not our Designer's intention. Feminine power was intended to give life. Eve, as a woman, was designed to complete her man, to nurture life in him and to create new life in children.

Just as Beauty's feminine loveliness transformed Beast into a prince, your femininity caught your husband's attention. The way you looked at him, the way you dressed and fixed your hair for him, and perhaps even the way you kissed him—all were expressions of your power as a woman.

You "caught" him and awakened in him a new dimension of life.

But now that the prize has been won, have you pulled the plug on your power source? It's very easy to do. We see a woman's power used in endless negative ways outside of marriage, but we have little vision for the life-giving power of a wife with her husband inside of marriage. Women seldom talk about how to use this unique power they have with their husbands after they are married. Wives have few models to follow. We rarely hear about and never see another wife using her power. A married woman's sexual power is a private, hidden strength, as it should be.

Many wives do not understand how profound this power is. God has blessed you with a feminine ability that you can use for great good in your husband's life. God has plans for your man. And he wants to use you to help grow him into a godly man. Your power can meet his aloneness and companionship needs, bless his sexual identity, protect him from temptation, and keep him for life.

MEETING HIS RELATIONSHIP NEED

Something is missing in every man. And it's by divine design. As I mentioned a moment ago, after God created Adam, He said, "It is not good for the man to be alone" (Gen. 2:18). It's an astounding truth that the perfect God of the universe created a perfect human being and then declared, "it is not good." God intentionally created the first man with an aloneness need. Man was incomplete. God orchestrated the perfect drumroll for His grand finale of creation: a woman, the "helper suitable for him." God fashioned the woman to complete her man and make whole that part of him that God purposely created incomplete; his aloneness need could only be met by Eve.

Your husband has this same "aloneness" need.

God brought you into his life to be his "helper"—to meet his companionship need. In Christian marriage, this oneness is a unity of mind, body, and soul, and is celebrated through the sexual union.

Of course, now after the fall of mankind, no one is totally complete without the indwelling presence of Jesus Christ. Further, perfect completeness cannot occur this side of heaven. But in marriage we can touch the holiness of God; we can recapture a taste of what was lost in the Garden of Eden when a husband and a wife express love, transparency, trust, and sacrifice in the mystery of marital intercourse.

BLESS HIS SEXUALITY

Every wife has a deep, life-altering responsibility to her husband to be a *helper*, and help him feel like the man God created him to be. If I love my husband, I won't view his sexual needs disapprovingly.

A number of years ago after Dennis spoke about marriage at a seminary, a young wife came up to him with a question. She said, "I was driving home with my husband the other night after church and decided to ask him a question. I asked, 'What could I do to make you feel more like a man of God?' There was silence in the darkness of the car as we were driving home. Then my husband said, 'When I come home from work at the church at the end of the day, meet me at the front door with no clothes on.'" With a bit of a blush, she asked Dennis, "Do you think I ought to do that?"

Basically, this newly married wife was asking my husband what sex has to do with godliness. She was expecting her husband to ask for her prayers or help with sermons, but not a strip show!

Dennis encouraged this young woman to please her husband sexually because he knew that in doing so, she would be profoundly validating his God-ordained manhood. Since all men are created with an aloneness need, they journey from boyhood into adulthood needing to know that their maleness is good and positive. Apart from parental validation, humanly speaking, this is a question that only his wife should answer, a blessing only she should give.

To bless another person means to set them apart or make holy.

Your attitude toward your husband's sexuality and sex drive is important because you *alone* have the power to bless him sexually and affirm his male identity. Your responsiveness is a major component of how he feels about himself. Your husband needs to feel that when he initiates intimacy with you, you "welcome" him and want to "receive" him. By doing so, you affirm him—indeed, you affirm his leadership and initiative, the very essence of manhood.

It's not easy being a man in marriage. Don't get me wrong. There are risks for us women, too, but at the core, when a man initiates sex, he must perform. He's on the line, and he risks rejection and failure every time. As a wife, you have the opportunity to place your stamp of approval on his manhood, or you can refuse him and turn him away.

Repeatedly rejecting your husband's sexual initiative creates a profound wound and a part of him dies. This wound is so deep that far too many men, wrongly, go elsewhere to be received and validated sexually. When a wife consistently makes excuses for avoiding physical intimacy, repeatedly expresses disinterest in something so vital to her husband, she is emasculating her husband. To emasculate means to weaken, to soften, to maim, to castrate, to effeminize. It's a word rarely spoken in our culture, but it happens regularly in marriages.

Listen to how a man can be wounded by the repeated rejections of his wife. Steve, a listener to *FamilyLife Today*, writes,

> We have been married 15 years and have sex less than once a week. I regularly masturbate to relieve stress, tension, to compensate for a lack of sexual satisfaction, and feelings of rejection by my wife.

Sometimes it takes a lot of effort and self-control for a husband to work through the process of warming up his wife, reassuring her that the sounds she hears outside of their bedroom are really nothing to be concerned with, and helping her focus on receiving pleasure. Our sexual interest and arousal are fragile things that can be quickly broken by an unintentional mistake or misunderstanding or by the faintest noises from down the hall.

Be aware of his efforts on your behalf. Ask God to help you feel compassion for him. No, I'm not talking about feeling sorry for him, but seeking to understand his needs and his struggles. Your husband wants a genuine romantic love relationship with you that is mutual. He takes little pleasure in just doing the deed and getting it over with. He wants to connect with you on a deep, emotional level. Through physical intimacy he makes that connection and receives that affirmation.

One note of caution: there may be parts of your husband's

sexuality that are not holy and should not be blessed by you. You should not bless and affirm any of his interests in satisfying his sexual need apart from you or in ways that are degrading to you. By the way, *Intimate Issues* by Linda Dillow and Lorraine Pintus is a great resource as you seek to affirm your husband's sexuality and learn to enjoy your feminine power with him while at the same time defining appropriate boundaries.

Can you bless and appreciate and approve of your husband's male sexuality the way God made him? Are you willing to consider finding a way to bless him sexually that would make him smile with confidence? Rather than disapprove, can you instead see his interest in you sexually as God directed? Can you imagine your feminine power being used to encourage him in becoming a godly man?

Questions Your Husband May Be Asking When He Initiates Physical Intimacy

1. Do you want me? Will you welcome me? There is no other person I can go to who will affirm this side of me.
2. Will you trust me with your body?
3. Do you really want to please me? Do you have any idea how important this is to me? Am I important enough in your life to focus on what I need sexually as a man?
4. How did I do? Did I do just okay, or did I really bring great pleasure to you? I gain my greatest satisfaction from knowing that you have received and enjoyed pleasure.

The sexual fulfillment of your husband is directly related to how you communicate your sexual love to him. Do you communicate you need him? Do you usually "wait" for him, or do you initiate? Do you respond, or do you resist? Your attitude and actions are essential.

PROTECT YOUR HUSBAND
FROM TEMPTATION

As Angela discovered in our opening novella, her husband lived with an almost constant mental pull toward women, whether fully alive or mere photographs. If a man willingly yields to the temptation to lust for or engage in relations with another woman, whether she is just a photograph or a real woman, he is following his internal need to affirm his manhood. He's following his longing to be wanted and needed by a woman. He's just doing it in the wrong way.

Protecting him from temptation means making sure his sexual needs are met by you and you alone. I have a good friend who said it this way: If you don't want to do his laundry, your husband can take his clothes to the cleaners. If you decide you don't want to cook anymore for him, he can go out to any number of great restaurants to eat.

Or maybe you have great friends and you enjoy them so much that your husband doesn't have you as a friend anymore. He can decide to spend more time with his buddies at work or his hunting pals or his golfing partner. If your husband really needs to talk about his problems and the struggles in his life and you aren't available, he can go to a counselor. But if your husband isn't getting his sexual needs met at home with you, and he goes somewhere else, God calls that a sin.

Don't misunderstand what I'm saying. If your husband sins in this way, he's responsible before God. But at the same time, understand that you play a powerful role in empowering him to turn away from temptation. This is not a guilt trip. It's just the truth. God created us as men and women with profoundly inherent differences. If you love him, you'll want to protect him from the limitless temptations that the enemy of his soul floats by him day after day.

Andy Stanley, a pastor in Atlanta, illustrates how temptation enters a marriage. Imagine a wife asking her husband to carry her responsibility in the marriage for a while. Perhaps she's having a baby or going back to school or doing a big project at work. Andy demonstrates this by handing a volunteer a heavy rock to hold. He explains that we may have the best intentions in the world and that we may actually love the person to whom we gave the rock of responsibility, but after some time, the rock becomes too heavy and it cannot be held any longer. As Andy continues to illustrate his point, the volunteer holding the rock discovers that physical exhaustion overtakes his mental willingness to be helpful; he has to put the rock down.

That is true of far too many men.

They want to be strong for their wives, they want to stay pure, they want to be a faithful husband; but the longer they are deprived sexually, the more their physical need will conflict with their faithfulness. Many men yield to temptation because their wives have put their responsibility on hold. This in no way excuses a man who chooses to meet his sexual needs in illegitimate ways. But it does explain why the temptation becomes so overwhelming.

When a wife resists meeting her husband's needs and never thinks of pleasing him sexually, she leaves him vulnerable to some other woman willing to delight him with her body. You are most powerful as a wife when you become a student of what your husband likes and use that knowledge and your feminine skill to affirm him and protect him from temptation and sin.

Romantic Interlude

Buy a spicy tube of lipstick, and just before
you give him a smooch, put it on thick. When you kiss,
watch his surprised eyes light up. Then demonstrate desire.
With a whisper, say, "And that's just the appetizer."

KEEP HIM FOR LIFE

When we stated our vows at the wedding altar, most of us repeated the words "to have and to hold" till death do us part. We signed up for life. But have you ever thought about what it means to "have" and "hold" your husband?

To *have* implies a possession. It means he belongs to you and no one else. He is your responsibility, and you are his. Are you fulfilling your sexual responsibility? For frequency? Creativity? Have you turned him down more often than you have invited his love? Do you put his needs *before* or *after* those of your children or your work?

To *hold* means to keep or bond, much like a magnet. A magnet has the power within to pull another polar opposite to itself. My husband and I are virtual opposites in nearly every way. It's what attracted us to each other in the first place. But I must continue to be a magnet in his life if I am to keep him. Too many women would love to have him if I let him leave home for work or travel constantly in a state of sexual deprivation. First Corinthians 7:5 (NKJV) tells us, "Do not deprive one another except with consent for a time, that you may give yourselves to . . . prayer; and come together again so that Satan does not tempt you because of your lack of self-control."

Dennis tells me that I am a magnet to him when I communicate that I am "available." I've seen the magnetic forces at work when I've planned a special evening together or a weekend getaway. He's talked about some of those getaways for years. And he tells me that I'm a magnet when I focus on romance practically and make him feel like a man.

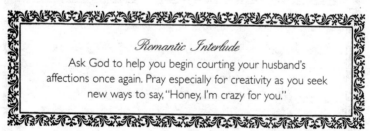

Romantic Interlude

Ask God to help you begin courting your husband's affections once again. Pray especially for creativity as you seek new ways to say, "Honey, I'm crazy for you."

This may come as no surprise to you, but most men want—*really* want—their wives to passionately desire them. And when you express sexual longing for him—whether verbally or nonverbally—your husband is unlikely to refuse your magnetic power. Let me illustrate.

For a number of weeks I planned a special, romantic two-night getaway to a bed-and-breakfast in another town. As Dennis knows, I am not one to plan romantic retreats regularly. I'm also not a big risk taker. And with our large family, executing the details of this getaway took some sacrifice of time, energy, and emotion. Still, I followed through with my plan for an unforgettable "feast" for my husband.

I planned and shopped and organized all the right elements for our time together. Then I called him while he was away on a speaking engagement and told him that I would be picking him up at the airport—but we would *not* be going home! I also dropped more than a few subtle hints about what kind of adventure he could expect.

Power? Absolutely.

Attraction? Ask him.

My husband is a man's man, but when I picked him up at the airport, he was as excited as a child on Christmas Eve.

That weekend was memorable for both of us. We had a wonderful time. It was especially so for my husband. He talked about it for months and still mentions it from time to time after all these years.

The more a wife affirms her husband's God-given manhood, the more she helps build him into the man God wants him to be. This power of a wife to affirm him, bless him, protect him, and keep him is blessed by God. It is a very good, nurturing, life-giving gift. Knowing this, I've often wondered why we women don't want or choose to use our God-given powers to affirm and nurture our husbands more often.

EARTH ANGEL

I must tell you a story about a friend, Crystal, who understood her feminine power with her husband and was willing to take a risk by using it. I know this young wife well. Crystal does not have a bold, outspoken, uninhibited personality. She is truly a southern belle: sweet, proper, gracious, and kind. Listen to her love for her husband.

When Crystal knocked on the hotel room door, she was completely out of her comfort zone. Inside, her husband, Travis, and ten buddies were having a much anticipated "boys' night out" to celebrate his birthday. She knew the guys planned to watch movies (*manly* movies—bursting with explosions, car chases, and martial arts action), eat barbeque and beans, and drink sodas through the night.

She also knew she didn't belong there. The invitation had been clear: no girlfriends or wives allowed. As a thirty-something busy mother of four, she had never—and I mean *never*—dared to do something so radical. She almost changed her mind several times.

When the door opened, she stepped inside the lions' den, clutching a small overnight bag to her side. A war movie projected on the wall provided the only light in the room. Although it took several seconds for her eyes to adjust, she couldn't miss the high voltage of testosterone coursing through the rather stuffy air.

Like a timid cat, she scanned the crowd for Travis, then walked up, whispered something into his ear, and disappeared into the adjacent bedroom and closed the door. Although the movie played on, all eyes were on the birthday boy who sat in stunned amazement by his wife's unexpected appearance. Two minutes later, Travis stood and announced that the party was over—for his friends.

He, however, like King Kong, went to claim his precious beauty in the next room. And in that moment Crystal's reputation rose to legendary proportions for the friends as they left the hotel room.

Crystal's bold, purposeful, and sacrificial act of love reached deep inside her husband's heart with a wise, generous deposit. Her investment paid wonderful dividends in their marriage. What man wouldn't go the extra mile for his bride after she so publicly honored him?

By using her feminine powers in such a powerful way, Crystal ignited a fire in the soul of her mate that blazed for weeks. This is, after all, a biblical principle. Jesus said, "Give, and it will be given to you. A good measure, pressed down, shaken together and running over, will be poured into your lap. For with the measure you use, it will be measured to you" (Luke 6:38).

This principle, as Crystal and Travis learned, applies to much more than being generous with money. Jesus wants us to be generous with our love and care for one another.

This power you and I have as wives is blessed by God. It is a very good, life-giving ability. The question remains: What will you do about this power you possess? Are you going to put it to death, bury it, deny it, or will you choose to exercise your sexual power to create a soul-satisfying confidence in your man?

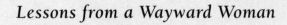

Lessons from a Wayward Woman

There's virtually nothing in your world that validates your unique assignment to affirm your man sexually. Most of your day is focused on your other "duties" that scream for your attention—none of which remind you that you are, or should be, the single most powerful sexual woman in your husband's life.

I, Dennis, am about to make a potentially controversial statement. But, please, for the sake of your marriage and your husband, hear me out. Solomon wrote in the Proverbs about the "wayward woman" who used her charms to seduce men. You might not have considered that the same sexual power that this adulterous woman used for evil can be used by you for the good of your marriage.

I am *not* suggesting that you need to be like her in her life choices—a fool; an evil, cheating, deceiving liar. But I am encouraging you to be all that God created you to be romantically and passionately with your husband. With that in mind, let's go to the Scriptures so that you may learn from this passage how to be a powerful wife to your husband.

- *Her words were like honey, smoother than oil* (5:3). Say things to your husband that you know will quicken his pulse with anticipation and excitement.
- *She operated at twilight, in the evening, and in the middle of the night* (7:9, 18). Sometimes start your romantic encounters early and finish late. Make it last a while.
- *She used her beauty, especially her eyes, to capture his attention* (6:25). It's easy to glare at your husband, but do you know how to invite him with your eyes? Does your husband like you in a certain dress? How about

your nightgown? Do you go to bed in what's comfortable or what he'd like? (You can always change into your flannels later.)

- *She seized him and kissed him* (7:13). One evening when he arrives home from work, or when the kids are in bed, engage him in a passionate, earth-stopping kiss. Not a peck on the cheek, but one that says, "Let's go!" And then *go!*
- *She had a bedroom that was prepared for him* (7:16–17). Set the mood for making love. The use of candles, lotions, powders, and scents creates an irresistible environment.
- *She talked of a night of pleasure, followed by more nights of the same* (7:18–20). She promised him that this wasn't a one time event. Don't be afraid to make similar promises and watch how it motivates him to please you.

While romance is *not* the center of a marriage, it *is* an indispensable component. You have been assigned a very special responsibility to love, to please, and to protect your mate from the tempting lure of the wayward woman. A wife cannot ignore the competition of the adulterous woman.

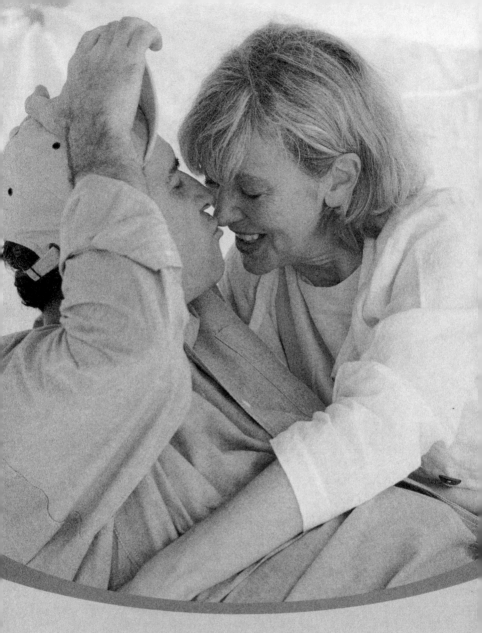

*Like an apple tree among the trees of the forest
is my lover among the young men. I delight to
sit in his shade, and his fruit is sweet to my taste.*

SONG OF SOLOMON 2:3

Chapter 6

Why Wives Don't Use Their Feminine Power

oes the story of Crystal's bold, courageous display of love for her husband feel way too risky for you? Either you can't imagine doing what she did, or you might be uncertain of your husband's response. In either case, it's an idea that can seem a bit frightening or perhaps a tad extravagant.

It's understandable *why* a woman would feel out of her comfort zone in attempting something like this.

Marriage is a delicate dance. He initiates; I follow. He learns how to invite me, and I learn to respond. He may not do it all correctly, but he will never get better if I criticize him every time he steps on my toes or misses a beat. My job is to encourage him by responding to what is good and minimizing what isn't.

The old saying "It takes two to tango" explains why many husbands are standing on the dance floor alone, waiting on wives who can't or won't be engaged in the romantic dance. I believe there are four distinct reasons why wives withhold their sexual power to attract, affirm, and nurture life in their husbands: (1) the fear, risk and sacrifice are too great, (2) they believe lies and fairy-tale notions, (3) they are hindered by past sexual abuse, or (4) they are selfish and unwilling.

1. The Hindrance of Fear, Risk and Sacrifice

Using your feminine power for your husband's good to create a significant and memorable romantic experience, to initiate a small, meaningful love encounter, or even to respond to his initiation of sexual love often requires *overcoming fears*, *risk* and *sacrifice* at some level.

A wife may face a host of emotions and fears when she initiates lovemaking or even when she just needs to respond to her husband's initiation: the fear of transparency, nakedness, and the vulnerability of being known; the fear of rejection or ridicule; the fear of feeling ashamed, used, or "cheap"; the fear of feeling underappreciated, undervalued, taken for granted for the gift of her body, soul, and spirit; the fear of being hurt physically or emotionally; the fear of being interrupted by children; or other emotions that aren't healed from past hurts, pain, and failures.

Facing these fears and moving past them is in and of itself a sacrifice. It requires you to release the fear that tells you to hold back, be cautious, trust your feelings instead of trusting your husband. It's also choosing to be with your husband even when you don't have romantic feelings initially and that it can be a risk, because there is no guarantee your sacrifice and choice to risk loving will be adequately rewarded.

Love is *not* just a feeling, but a commitment to be purposefully passionate. Making love with your husband does not necessitate sexual feelings first. Instead, as I've learned, a commitment to love him and serve him often precedes sexual feelings.

Moving beyond these emotions and fears is the first sacrifice to be made in using your sexual power for good with your husband. But there are others.

I don't want to overlook the myriad practical sacrifices a wife makes. Often you must choose to give up *time,* when you finally make it to bed, to read, relax, do your nails, or best of all . . . sleep. Sometimes you must make a *personal comfort sacrifice*—delaying the things you feel you want or need to make room to do something he desires. Other times you must set aside your *personal interests,* such as projects, hobbies, house decorating, or opportunities for personal advancement, for a season so he can be more important in your life.

In short, the greatest cost is a denial of self, a setting aside of self-interests for the purpose of demonstrating love for another. In a small way such self-sacrifice is a picture of Jesus' love for us when He emptied Himself so that He might show His great love for us. Marriage mirrors God's relationship with His people.

2. The Hindrance of Believing Lies, Fantasies, and Fairy Tales

There's a second reason why women experience a feminine power outage in marriage: They believe the wrong things. Fairy-tale wishes, celebrity fantasies, magazine psychologists, book authorities, videos, "sextique" parties, and talk show hosts offer a plethora of beliefs and information for adding sizzle to your relationship.

Some of it is good; much of it is not. A lot of it is simply not the truth. When it comes to romance, what are the lies women believe?

Lie #1: I deserve Prince Charming and a happily ever after life.

Lie #2: Love is a feeling. No feelings equal no love.

Lie #3: Romance should be easy, like it is in the movies.

Lie #4: It's his fault that I feel this way. If only he'd talk more, if only he'd lose weight, or if only he was more romantic.

There are more lies, many more.

Which of these lies do *you* believe? And how do they influence your thinking about your husband's need for your affirmation and blessing of his sexuality?

You see, these lies short-circuit a woman's power because they rob her of motivation. How can she be motivated to action when she believes that her husband's sexual needs can just wait? Why would she spend the time and energy to creatively meet his needs when she believes his needs are not as important as her children's needs, or that it's all his fault?

The answer is found in knowing and embracing the truth. Jesus said, "You will know the truth, and the truth will set you free" (John 8:32). Knowing the truth gives you the choice of affirming the truth and acting on the truth to meet your husband's needs.

May I encourage you to believe the truth about him as a man? Don't believe a half lie that results in your focusing on his weaknesses.

3. The Hindrance of Past Abuse

Many women who feel blocked or hindered from enjoying a healthy sex life with their husbands may need to confront their own pasts. Children who are abused verbally, physically, emotionally, or sexually face repercussions for the remainder of their lives. The increase in sexual abuse over the last few decades has been especially shocking. The sexual permissiveness of the past generation and the pervasiveness of sexual images in the media have unleashed a wave of inappropriate sexual contact and activity outside marriage that has damaged countless children, adolescents, and adults.

For clarity on this important subject, let me give you a definition of sexual abuse by our good friend Dan Allender from his book *The Wounded Heart:*

> Sexual abuse is any contact or interaction (physical, visual, verbal, or psychological) between a child or adolescent and an adult (or a significantly older child/adolescent) when the child/adolescent is being used for the sexual stimulation of the adult (perpetrator) or any other person. (p. 48)

Based on the above definition, Dan estimates that up to 65 percent of women have been sexually abused at some time in their lives. Whether it was actual physical contact, verbally seductive comments, or a psychologically inappropriate parent-child relationship, all sexual abuse leaves damage at some level.

The guilt and shame that are left in a person's heart and soul in the wake of sexual abuse make enjoying a healthy sexual relationship in marriage difficult in proportion to the degree of abuse. Those who have been abused feel confused emotionally. They feel ambivalent, which means they experience conflicting emotions at the same time: love and hate, pleasure and shame.

Dan writes, "I have never worked with an abused man or woman who did not hate or mistrust the hunger for intimacy. In most victims, the essence of the battle is a hatred of their hunger for love and a strong distaste for any passion that might lead to a vulnerable expression of desire" (p. 59).

If you have been abused in your past at any level, no matter how minor it may seem to you, and you haven't talked about it with your husband, let me challenge you to risk letting him know this about you. My guess is, he intuitively knows something isn't "right" anyway. Your marriage will never grow to the place of mature, cherishing love without this difficult disclosure.

God is a God of redemption. And it is His greatest delight to take a willing broken human being and redeem that life, making it whole and beautiful again. We see a picture of this act of redemption in Joel 2:25 where the Lord offers this promise: "I will repay you for the years the locusts have eaten." This would include the years where the locusts of abuse devoured your innocence and left you with shame.

God wants to redeem your life, not just sexually, but in every way and make your marriage a reflection of His love. He wants it for you, for your husband, for your children, and for others who know you to see what wonderful things God can do.

In his book, *The Mystery of Marriage*, author Mike Mason says, "One of the most fundamental and important tasks that has been entrusted to marriage is the work of reclaiming the body for the Lord, of making pure and clean and holy again that which has been trampled in the mud of shame." Marriage is to be a place of healing, redemption, and restoration. Every person is broken and in need of repair by the Great Physician. You are not alone.

But it requires trust and risk and hard work. You will need the help of an experienced pastor or counselor who knows how to help you seek healing. Facing the past takes courage. Indeed, nothing is harder than the work of facing past sexual abuse. And yet nothing is more important to the health of your marriage.

One last thought. If there is even a suspicion in your thinking that sexual abuse occurred in your past, I strongly suggest you read Dan Allender's *The Wounded Heart* and then discuss with your husband the significant portions.

Don't ignore the possibility that sexual abuse might have happened to your husband, for it's true with about 25 percent of all men. Be sensitive to him in this. It won't be easy for him or for you to work through the shame and guilt of the past. And there won't be a quick fix. But God is able. He is the Great Physician and Healer. Be patient and remember He delights in redemption.

4. The Hindrance of Selfishness

In the last half of the twentieth century we saw a female-focused revolution. The feminist movement successfully shifted the thinking of corporations, advertisers, writers, and everyone else in American culture to think about women's needs first. While there was some need for change in many areas, the pendulum swung way past the center point of balance. The result is a generation of women who have become more self-focused than ever.

As wives we have the challenge of renewing our minds to think biblically—not culturally—about our marriages. The world's philosophy would tell your husband to "get over it" (his need for affirmation and sexual love) and help you with your load. And while he ought to help you with children and household duties, he doesn't need to "get over" his God-designed sexual need.

I realize what I'm about to say might be a tough message for you to hear. But please hear me out. I'm convinced that, for the most part, women in America have become pampered to the point of being spoiled rotten. We have heard hundreds of thousands of messages over the past forty years that say in various ways: "Stand up for your rights," "Don't let him run over you," "You can have it all," "Women deserve a break," and on and on.

Almost all advertising, most book promotions, radio and TV programming, and nearly all retail businesses are aimed at women. Our affluence is feverishly feeding women's selfish nature with the result that women are more self-focused than at any point in our nation's history.

Listen to one husband's perspective on his wife's lack of interest:

> I read with interest your article "You're Stressed, Exhausted, and Not in the Mood," by Dennis & Barbara Rainey and find Dennis's statement "Remember, men, that our wives long for real intimacy with us" to be rather amusing, and difficult to accept. The reason I say this is our marriage has been celibate for 18 of the 23 years we've been married, certainly not by my choosing! Over these years, I've tried all of the things you suggest in this article, and many other things, and just cannot get my wife to realize how important this issue is for me. As a consequence, we are having, and have had, significant difficulties in our marriage.

It appears this wife has chosen to put her needs and wants above her husband's. I wonder if this is what she promised when she married him twenty-three years ago.

The antidote for selfishness is serving. And sacrifice is the language of romance. Therefore, it's impossible to have the marriage you once dreamed of without self-denial.

Remember Philippians 2:4 (NKJV): "Let each of you look out not only for his own interests, but also for the interests of others." Take an appreciative look at your husband. Take a good, hard look at what he does for you and your kids, and then thank him for it. First Thessalonians 5:18 (NKJV) reminds us: "In everything give thanks; for this is the will of God in Christ Jesus for you."

IN THE MOOD

No husband is perfect or ever will be. No marriage will be perfect. Find all the things he does right and serve him with a healthy dose of praise. He will *never* do it all right, so don't wait until he does.

Then give him affirmation as a man. Make him feel welcome when he comes home from work. Greet him with genuine love and affection and a kiss or two. Be patient and wait for the best time to talk to him about your day. You don't always have to be first.

Finally remember his need for sexual fulfillment. It's not incidental; it's essential. Choose to be interested in him sexually. Plan a time to initiate a special romantic time for the two of you, as Crystal did for Travis. But know what your husband would like. Some men might not respond the same way Travis did. They would want something subtler and less public. A little attention and affection of the kind your man would like go a long way.

God's divine design endowed you with a magnetic feminine power that He intends you to use to draw your husband from wherever he's been back to his marriage, back to the celebration that was intended only for you as a couple.

I believe that the death of romance and love isn't found in the hands of those who hate each other. Oftentimes it's the silent rejection of indifference and the chilling coldness of apathy when two people allow their passion and their romance to just go away—because they were too stubborn to deny themselves and take the first step to place another log on the fire.

Are you waiting for him to take the first step?

Part Three

How to Begin a Romantic Makeover

You're still the one I want to talk to in bed
Still the one that turns my head
We're still having fun, and you're still the one
— "Still the One" by Orleans
(By John Joseph Hall and Johanna D. Hall)

Chapter 7

First Love . . .
Putting Your Husband First

*E*ach of our three married children is really into photography, especially now that all of them have babies. Two of my daughters have small part-time photography businesses and have acquired lots of photographic gear. In every photo session, whether it's a scheduled event like a wedding or a family portrait, or just quick snapshots of the babies at home, one thing is essential for great photos: focus.

Focus is more than making sure the image is not blurred. Focus is about what you choose to see and what you choose to ignore or hide. It's how you decide what is important in the photo you are about to take. Do you want to focus on the background and the landscape, or the people nearest to you? Is it more important to focus on a person's face or the whole body? It's up to you.

The same is true if you want to rekindle romance with your husband. What are you focusing on? His flaws? His weaknesses? Or are you choosing to focus on the qualities that made you fall in love with him in the first place? Are you focused on caring for him, his need for respect, and his need for sexual affirmation?

The choice of focus is yours.

I recall early in our marriage that I was disappointed in Dennis because he was not the spiritual leader that I had envisioned he'd be. I wanted to do the right thing, so I began to pray about all the things I wanted God to change in this area. The result? I became preoccupied with what he was *not* doing instead of appreciating who he was and what he was doing right. I had to take a step back, adjust the lens of my heart, and refocus.

The first step in your romantic makeover is to take your focus off his flaws and weaknesses and failures. Quit looking at them. It's not your job to change his life. Only God can change people. You need to *repent* from your focus on his imperfections.

The second step is to *remember* what you love about him and focus on these things. A very practical way to do this is to ask God to open your eyes to see what is admirable and good and attractive. Then write them in a note or a letter to express that admiration. It's capturing what you love on paper like a photographer does on film.

One weekend our two photographers, Stephanie and Ashley, were together taking photos of Ashley's little boys with Stephanie's professional camera. My favorite is one of little James, who was about eighteen months old at the time, in his birthday suit. Stephanie and Ashley set up a black backdrop to hide the distraction of the living room furniture. The dark backdrop also highlighted the purity of his new little body with its clear, soft skin. The pose they captured showed James innocently and playfully on his hands and knees, looking to the side with a precious grin on his face. It will be a treasured photo for years to come.

As photographers Stephanie and Ashley had a choice. They could have placed little James in the backyard in the mud and then irritated him to make him mad so they could capture his little sin nature on film forever. Instead they chose to focus on his best qualities. And because he was naked, they carefully chose an angle that hid his male parts from view, knowing that it would be distracting in the final photo and that James would likely be embarrassed someday.

Like little James, we are naked and exposed before each other in marriage. No one knows your husband's sin and shame and failures as you do. But marriage was designed by God to be a place of comfort and safety, not condemnation and critique. Yes, you and I are flawed too. Husbands and wives can cause and experience great suffering in marriage, but it is still the best place for two imperfect people to find acceptance and the courage to change and grow.

Frankly it is unkind for us wives to so focus on our husbands' faults and shortcomings that we can see nothing else. It's also arrogant to think we are so much better than they are. As wives we have a tendency to see the negative in our husbands.

The apostle Paul wrote, "Whatever things are true, whatever things are noble, whatever things are just, whatever things are pure, whatever things are lovely, whatever things are of good report, if there is any virtue and if there is anything praiseworthy—meditate on these things" (Phil. 4:8 NKJV). While no man is perfect, and some men have serious issues that must be addressed, I bet there is much that is good and virtuous in that man of yours. Remember those qualities, repent from your critical focus, and *return* to seeing the good in him, as you once did. Then choose to love him as you did at first by spending time with him as your best friend and lover.

PUTTING YOUR HUSBAND FIRST

Another way to recapture your first love for your husband—to do the things you once did—is to make him your highest priority. As a wife, I am aware of my inadequecies and failures. Sometimes I lose perspective and feel that I haven't done many things right. But one thing I have worked at consistently over our thirty-two years of marriage is to keep my husband my number one priority. I haven't even done that perfectly, but when I spent too much time on the children or projects and that became apparent, I made the necessary adjustments.

Have you made the decision that, no matter what, your husband is number one? (Obviously your ultimate number one relationship is with Jesus Christ.) You married him for life. You are not guaranteed how long that life together will be. Putting him first says, in effect, "I choose to make the most of whatever time we will share on this earth."

Romantic Interlude

What are some delaying tactics that you use to put off your husband's sexual advances? What do you think he feels when he sees that you have energy for everything and everyone but his need for physical intimacy? Think of one thing you can do today to make your husband a priority; then do it.

At one level, keeping him your priority means making sure his needs for romance and physical oneness are met. At another level, it means going beyond just meeting a physical need to choosing to give him the gift of pleasing him in whatever way you can. More on this in the next chapter.

Do you have a heart for him and his needs? Do you show appreciation for his efforts to remain pure in his thinking and faithful to you in your marriage? Do you value how God designed him and his manhood with any kind of admiration and gratitude?

It's been said that less than 20 percent of all married couples have conversations about sex. Is that true of you? Do you and your husband talk about what you like and don't like? Do you know what would please your husband? You can't rekindle your romance if you don't know what his needs are and what would communicate love to him.

For centuries, married Christian women assumed they had a duty to their husbands. They took at face value 1 Corinthians 7:3–4 (NASB):

> The husband must fulfill his duty to his wife, and likewise also the wife to her husband. The wife does not have authority over her own body, but the husband does; and

likewise also the husband does not have authority over his own body, but the wife does.

This passage is a radical call for wives—we should be more concerned with the physical and sexual needs of our husbands than we are about our own needs. God actually says that our husbands have authority over our bodies—and then makes the principle even more profound with the statement that wives have the same authority over husbands.

Today, women have taken back the ownership of their bodies in contradiction to the clear teaching of the Bible. *The Bible is not instructing you to become your husband's slave;* the idea is that you are to use your body to please him . . . while he uses his body to please you.

As I've traveled and worked with thousands of women at our various FamilyLife *Weekend to Remember* marriage seminars, I'm painfully aware that far too many of the wives that I have met have lost this sense of duty and responsibility in marriage. As a culture, we've rebelled against male domination (which is not biblical) and have traded places with men, becoming domineering and expecting our men to serve us. We must instead become biblical and seek to be wives of God's design. Choosing to focus on your husband and his needs—choosing to serve him sacrificially—will breathe life and romance into your marriage.

MAKING TIME FOR HIM

As I've said, your husband longs to feel wanted and needed sexually by you. He wants to know that you want to share love with him. He'd like to know that having sex with him isn't just another item on your "to do" list—somewhere down at the bottom, just after changing diapers, cleaning toilet bowls, and sweeping the floor. Where is the satisfaction for him if he gets the impression that he's a burden to you?

There are some simple, practical things I've done over the years that reflect the commitment I made in the early days of our marriage to keep Dennis my priority. One is an unspoken agreement not to go to bed at night without the other. Usually we go to bed between ten and eleven o'clock, so I know when it's nearing ten that it's time to finish what I'm doing. We haven't done this legalistically, and there have been seasons—those years when the kids were teens, for example—when it has been more of a challenge.

But going to bed together at the same time at night has been healthy for our marriage for several reasons. It gives us time to talk if we want to. We always pray together at night, and being together in the same place makes that a possibility. We always hug and tell each other, "I love you," no matter how we feel. And going to bed together definitely makes it easier for me to meet my husband's sexual needs and share a time of intimacy together.

Another practical application of this for me was that I worked to keep my schedule and the kids' schedules reasonably balanced so that all our evenings weren't booked late into the night. I also tried to take naps on days that I knew I would need extra energy, even in the years I home schooled our children. I knew, in a general sense, how many days it had been since we'd made love, and I tried to save some energy for my husband.

Sometimes Dennis would request that we go to bed early, so we could have extra time together to talk and have a more meaningful sexual experience, and I would work to honor that request.

It wasn't always easy, but I needed to remember that Dennis was my "first love." Guess what? It was good for the kids to know that as well!

JESUS COMMENTS ON NEW LOVE

There is another love story of a bride and her Groom in the first three chapters of Revelation: the Groom, Jesus, delivered brutally honest report cards to seven churches (His bride) of the day. He told them where they were succeeding and where they were failing.

In chapter 2, Jesus gave the believers in Ephesus good marks for their work, their labor, and their perseverance with patience for His name. But after commending them, He rebuked them by saying, "I have this against you, that you have left your first love" (v. 4 NKJV). Those followers of Christ had wandered away from the enthusiasm and joy of those early days of their new faith. They were "all work and no relationship"—they served God well, but they neglected their relationship with Him.

They lost their focus.

To me, that sounds like the change in most marriages. Because Christianity and marriage are intimate personal relationships, the comparison is appropriate. Couples experience new love with great enthusiasm and joy like new believers. And they, too, get busy with the responsibilities of life and drift away from their first love.

While we can't return to the same experience of new love and no responsibility, we can rekindle the embers of the romantic love we used to enjoy into a warm flame of mature love that will sustain our marriages for a lifetime. How? The solution Jesus delivered to the Ephesians was to "remember from where you have fallen; repent and do [or "return to" NASV] the works you did at first" (Rev. 2:5 ESV).

The application for your marriage is the same: *remember, repent,* and *return.* You must *remember* what you loved about your husband, then you must *repent* from negative attitudes, and finally you must *return* to fanning the flames of the relationship as you did so willingly at first.

Where are you right now?

Are you in need of going to the God of the universe and asking Him to help you refocus? Perhaps as you pray, you could ask Him to enlarge your heart for your husband. Ask the Lord to help you recall the "things you did at first" to please him. And then ask Him to give you the ability to really please your husband; what's more, pray that these steps toward your first love would become mutual.

Take each other for better or worse
but never for granted.
—ARLENE DAHL

Chapter 8

Ingredients for Romance

erhaps you are one of the 51 million women in North America who read romance novels. More than 50 percent of all paperback novels sold in America are romance books. Harlequin Books, the largest publisher of romance novels, has printed more than 3 billion books since 1992.

Or think about the movies we women love, our favorite "chick flicks," like *An Affair to Remember, Roman Holiday, You've Got Mail, Pride and Prejudice, Sleepless in Seattle, While You Were Sleeping, First Knight* among others. Hollywood knows we thrive on romance.

I've never read a Harlequin romance novel primarily due to the often racy elements, but I have seen most of these movies and have read other novels with romance woven into the story. Most novels and movies contain a romantic theme. It goes like this: a handsome, intelligent, adventurous, single man on a mission unexpectedly meets a beautiful, equally intelligent single woman under improbable circumstances, often in an exotic foreign location or in a lavish historical setting. Though their personalities may clash at first, and though they may even be on opposing "teams," eventually they fall madly "in love." And while this love is often impulsive and *always new*—never mature—in most cases the story ends with the unspoken assumption that they will live happily ever after.

Has there ever been a romance novel or an all-star chick flick featuring a faithful husband and wife with two, four, six, or eight children, living a normal life (whatever that is!) going to work and school and church, and enjoying passionate romance on a regular basis? Not any that I know of.

How many couples really live like people in the movies and novels? Who can maintain that level of intensity? Or adventure, intrigue, and surprise? Does that sound like your marriage relationship? I'm guessing it doesn't.

Everyone must come down from the high of new love and make the transition to everyday romance. But as we saw in the previous chapter, it's also important to work at renewing some elements of that "first love." That's why a good book or movie with a romantic theme, as shallow as they may be, can also be instructive; they can cause us to reflect on and remember the flavor of new love. They show us how couples in love act with each other, and they remind us of the effort that many of us once put into our marriage relationship.

IMAGINATION AND CREATIVITY

Couples in the new love season of romance are often so focused on pleasing each other that they devise ingenious means of capturing each other's attention and create endless ways to say, "I love you." Their courtship is marked with creative notes and gifts, interesting dates, surprise parties, and much more. But at some point complacency sets in to a relationship, and creativity often goes out the window—or is refocused toward the children.

The ability to imagine and create sets humans apart from the animal world. It's a connection to God Himself—using your mind to think of something that is different or unique or distinct and then expressing that idea in some kind of action.

In an article titled "God Is Not Boring," John Piper suggests that using our God-given imagination is a Christian duty. He writes, "Jesus said, 'Whatever you wish that others would do to you, do also to them' (Matt. 7:12). We must *imagine* ourselves in their place and *imagine* what we would like done to us. Compassionate, sympathetic, helpful love hangs much on the imagination of the lover."

The application for romance in marriage is this: As we seek to understand our husbands, feel some of what they feel, and think of what they think, we can imagine what would spark their romantic interest.

Here are some ideas and thoughts to spark your imagination so you can become creative in your unique way with your husband. Remember, creativity can come in lots of sizes: small, medium, large, and supersized. While special events are great, a little surprise can also go a long way.

Small actions of creativity can include phone calls, e-mails, and little notes that express your gratitude and praise for who he is and what he does. Whisper in his ear, telling him you enjoyed your most recent lovemaking; that will make him proud to be your man. Thank him verbally for his manly qualities that you love—his strength, his work, his leadership, his faithfulness, his way of serving you and your children.

Then, there are those medium-level creative touches that contribute more directly to a romantic rendezvous. Buy candles and romantic music for your bedroom. Replace your worn-out panties and bras with something new and more interesting. Demonstrate greater affection by giving him a back rub or more passionate kisses or some other affectionate means of extra attention. A new night-gown is always appreciated by my husband because he knows it's not important to me what I wear to bed as long as I'm warm. The truth is, I'd wear the same thing for years until it wore out if it weren't for my husband!

Ultimately, the best creativity is your imaginative new ways to give yourself to your husband sexually. Depending on your background and your husband's level of interest in trying new things, this could require a great amount of risk for you (as we discussed in Chapter 6). The only guidelines for your creativity are that it be pleasing to your husband, not offensive to either of you, and within the boundaries of Scripture. Plan a special love feast for his birthday; find different places to enjoy love; dream up different things to wear . . . or not wear.

You'll find additional large-size creative ideas to fuel your imagination (and give you practical suggestions) at the end of the women's chapters called "Fire the Desire." Dennis and I have also helped put together a couple of resources that offer a number of creative ideas for romance and intimacy: *Simply Romantic Secrets* and *Simply Romantic Nights*. FamilyLife has received many glowing responses from couples who have used the ideas in these resources to bring spice, fun, and adventure to their romance. To order, call 1-800-FL-TODAY (1-800-358-6329) 24 hours a day, or visit www.FamilyLife.com.

A gift is most meaningful when it comes from the heart, requires some sacrifice of cost or time, and goes beyond the ordinary or the expected. One year, for example, I worked to plan and put together a gift for Dennis based on the song "The Twelve Days of Christmas." I won't go into the details, but each night I had a special, intimate, "super-sized" gift of love for him.

The Twelve Nights of Christmas

The best Christmas gift I (Dennis) ever received was the gift that truly kept on giving. About ten years ago, on December 12, I arrived in bed to find Barbara with a slight grin on her face. She told me to close my eyes. She explained she had a little gift for me. This was unusual because our tradition was to exchange gifts alone on Christmas Eve. When she surprised me with an early gift, I thought this *must* be good. And good it was.

Barbara had privately schemed and created her own rendition of the festive song "The Twelve Days of Christmas."

There were no partridges in a pear tree . . . no French hens . . . or golden rings. She rewrote the song completely.

I opened my present titled "The Twelve Nights of Christmas." Barbara had given a series of gifts to me that spoke *my* love language as a guy, namely, physical intimacy. This remains the most memorable Christmas gift she's ever given me. Why? Twelve nights demand no less than twelve reasons:

1. She gave me gifts that she had spent a lot of time on.
2. She gave gifts that she *knew* I'd love.
3. She gave without reservation.
4. She gave repeatedly.
5. She gave generously.
6. She gave creatively.
7. She gave to me and then participated.
8. She gave by creating great anticipation. Many of those nights I'd be in bed by 6:45 . . . not really!
9. She gave joyfully—not begrudgingly.
10. She gave abundantly . . . hey, by the time you get to the twelfth night, you have some momentum. The grand finale was unforgettable.
11. She gave the gift of focus—she focused on us and me, which was difficult because of six children, three of whom were teens at the time.
12. She gave me the most important gift of all—she gave me herself.

ANTICIPATION

If you want to learn about the power of anticipation, try this: if you know you are interested in making love to your husband one night, give him a hint that morning of what you're thinking. Watch his eyes light up. Chances are, he'll be unusually focused and attentive that day or in the evening when he comes home.

If your first step in creativity is to purchase new candles for your bedroom, whisper to your husband when he comes home that you got a little gift for him. Then after the kids are in bed, go into your room, and light the candles so the scent begins to fill the room and drift beyond.

When you go to bed, welcome him with a warm hug, and tell him you love him. Your lovemaking doesn't even have to be more than the ordinary (although it might be) because you've made the overall experience one of anticipation for him. Knowing that you thought of him and your romance together and took steps to express creativity communicates love.

He will be grateful.

ADVENTURE

Dating your husband was probably a wonderful adventure. You were continually discovering new things about each other—your likes and dislikes, tastes and habits, interests and hobbies—all of which made your interaction a delight. The problem with marriage is that communication can become predictable and boring. The discovery is over. Routine sets in. While some comfort and stability come from knowing what to expect about each other, it can be terribly uninteresting. Boredom is the enemy of romance—it can tempt a spouse to find excitement and adventure elsewhere.

Oswald Chambers, the great British author, pointed out that we all need adventure: "Human nature if it is healthy demands excitement; and if it does not obtain its thrilling excitement in the right way, it will seek it in the wrong way. *God never makes bloodless stoics. He makes passionate saints*" (emphasis mine). The question is, Will you celebrate how God made you and your husband by becoming a more imaginative lover?

The Top Five Romantic Needs of Your Man

When it comes to romance, your husband has a few predictable needs. While this list would not be true for every man, it's likely true for yours. Show him this list and ask him if the needs are true. If they are, ask him to prioritize them in order of importance.

1. He needs his wife to respect and celebrate who he is as a man and how God made him sexually. A wife who is critical of her husband can create an impotent man.
2. He needs his wife to make his romantic needs (frequency and creativity) a priority in their relationship.
3. He needs his wife to desire and make him feel wanted sexually. He needs his wife to be unashamed of her passion for him.
4. He needs his wife to be adventuresome, fun, and imaginative sexually. He needs his wife not to be afraid or passive about using her sexual power as a woman in his life.
5. He needs his wife to let him know that "he did it!" That he is a great lover. That he brings his wife great pleasure!

For some, it might be an adventure just to go out on dates again with your husband. If you have young children, find a babysitter and get away for an evening . . . just the two of you. Or maybe you date each other regularly, but you're stuck in a rut—all you ever do is go out for dinner, return home, and then watch a movie. It's time to try something new—go to a play or a concert; plan a picnic at a local park; borrow a friend's fancy car for your date; do whatever it takes to add a sense of adventure.

Another way to add adventure to your marriage is to plan trips to another location. Solomon's wife said, "Come, my lover, let us go to the countryside, let us spend the night in the villages . . . There I will give you my love" (Song 7:11–12). Her agenda was clear. She wanted to spend time together and make love. She initiated getting away with her husband. Forget about ruling the nation—I bet Solomon had his bags packed, the chariot loaded, and the babysitter arranged in record time.

I've told Dennis for years that part of my difficulty in connecting with him in the evenings is that I live in my "office." At the end of each workday he can leave his office and all his work behind, but I can never leave mine. My work at home is always around me, and it's never finished. The old saying "A woman's work is never done" has certainly been true for me. Because I'm task-oriented instead of relationship-oriented, leaving work undone to go to bed early with my husband can take a lot of willpower.

However, I discovered that leaving town with him made it much easier to invest in our marriage and focus on our sexual relationship. How long has it been since you got away together even for one or two nights?

For us the best places have always been remote, like a state park we've been to several times that has nice log cabins. We sleep in, take walks, talk, and read. We focus on each other without the distractions of phones, computers, children, malls, and work that needs to be done at home or the office. When we take time to get out of our familiar neighborhood and go to new environments and surroundings, we give ourselves the opportunity to discover different experiences together. Just like we did when we were dating.

When you plan these getaways, use your creativity to plan extra special times of lovemaking. Make memories that are known only by the two of you. A man loves a wife who is adventurous, who is fun, who welcomes variety.

A SHARED MISSION

Though a shared mission is not usually thought of as an essential ingredient in romance, it is one that will add depth and meaning to your relationship. In many romantic movies, the leading characters are engaged in a quest to solve a mystery, discover a lost artifact, or struggle against a common enemy. What is your mission as a married couple? Are you living for a common goal? Or have you become two independent people with individual goals?

One of the best ways to foster unity in a marriage is to work on reaching the same objectives. Raising children is the first mission of every couple, but in addition to that lifetime task, find something outside your family that you can live for or work for.

We naturally gravitate toward self-focus in marriages and families and forget the hurting world out there that would benefit from even a small portion of our time and energy. Dream with your husband about the difference you could make as a couple and with your children. It will give you another avenue for admiration, and you might discover things about him you never knew. And that could be very romantic.

BEAUTY

God made women to be beautiful in two ways: internally and externally. No matter our age, wives need to cultivate both. Internal beauty is born in the heart. It is the most important kind of beauty, and as we learn from 1 Peter 1:22–25, it is imperishable in contrast to the external body that will perish one day. What we cultivate there will last forever.

The essence of this internal beauty is found throughout Scripture. God tells us to have a heart of gratitude, compassion, and hope; an attitude of humility, service, and joy; a mind transformed, focused, and at peace. And then God tells us in 1 Corinthians 13 what love looks like. If you love your husband with patience, kindness, goodness, and humility, refusing to let envy, pride, evil, or revenge live in your heart, you will be beautiful to him.

While God expects men to love this way as well, a woman possesses softness, gentleness, and grace that a man does not. These qualities make her more beautiful. This blossom of beauty matures very slowly and never fades.

How well we know the fading glory of the external. External beauty barely reaches full bloom before our bodies blossom with babies and then begin to deteriorate and droop like a flower past its prime. This inevitable decline should not, however, be an excuse for giving up the care of our appearance.

Every human being is attracted to things of beauty. We long for beauty because God is the source of all beauty and our hearts were made for Him. Your husband was attracted to you because of your unique beauty. He still desires to be delighted by that beauty. But he can't enjoy beauty that has been hidden by neglect.

Your body was made to please him, not just sexually, but visually too. Carrying around too much extra weight, always wearing sweat suits day after day, and ignoring your face and hair are not pretty sights. Your body is the temple of the Holy Spirit if you are a believer in Jesus Christ. You have a responsibility to take great care of that temple, not to let it fall into disrepair.

It's too easy to become complacent and lazy in marriage. When that happens, romance fades, and the lure of another becomes a greater temptation. Instead, a woman ought to be attentive to looking attractive for her husband. I know it's difficult when you have a houseful of little ones. I've been there. There were days when I never put on makeup. Even then, I always tried to make a quick pass at my appearance before my husband walked in the door.

I also know losing weight after having a baby is not easy for every woman, and weight loss gets harder with each pregnancy and with age. But it can be done. You don't have to look like you did at eighteen or when you married. If you want to romance your husband, find out what you need to do to be more attractive. And then keep that goal for the rest of your marriage.

Yes, he's commanded to love you unconditionally, but don't make it hard on him. If I may be so bold, I believe refusing to take care of your appearance is both selfish and dishonoring to God.

Romantic Interlude

Go on a five-minute walk today. Drink in the fresh air. Stretch your legs. Even modest exercise can do wonders for your self-esteem and overall fitness. Invite your husband to take a walk with you after dinner.

External beauty is important to cultivate for your husband, just as internal beauty is. Women can be very attractive and beautiful even in their seventies, eighties, and nineties. Even with the inevitable decay of aging and disease, the great hope of marriage is that our husbands will still find the lovely in our female forms when lovely hearts inhabit them. Heed Proverbs 31:30: "Charm is deceitful, and beauty is passing, but a woman who fears the Lord, she shall be praised" (NKJ).

VARIABLES AFFECT BAKING A CAKE

One last thought as you sift through these elements for creating your own romantic marriage. In some ways, renewing romance is like baking a cake. Many common ingredients, such as flour and sugar and eggs, go into every cake recipe, but there are also many variables that affect the baking. Oven temperature, altitude, humidity, and the inevitable mistakes of inaccurate measuring, incorrect ingredients, or inadequate equipment have an effect on the final product.

Each partner brings to the marriage a host of romantic variables. Each of us brings a way of thinking from the past. Each of us has experienced disappointment and failure and rejection in life unrelated to romance and sex that influence the ability to take further risks. Many marriages deal with repeated health issues for one or both spouses.

Your individual personalities will also be factors. Some are very expressive verbally and physically. Others enjoy new experiences, are somewhat impulsive, and think fun is more important than frugality. Still others are extremely practical and evaluate the actual monetary cost and the emotional cost of each decision. More cautious, not impulsive, and less expressive would better describe them. Be careful not to ignore or minimize these variables in rekindling your own romance.

In the end, renewing romance in your marriage means taking the time to work on your relationship by gathering the right ingredients and being willing to "love your neighbor as yourself"—and your nearest neighbor in this case just happens to be your husband.

Then be ready for the variables that you can't always control to make it more difficult. Always be willing to fight for your relationship and to try again if the cake falls in the baking. I promise it's worth it in the end. How can I be so sure? Not long ago I was talking with my dear friend, Vonette Bright. Vonette is the wife of the late Dr. Bill Bright, founder of Campus Crusade for Christ. As we talked about romance in marriage, with a twinkle in her eye, she said, "If there's a better way to bake a cake, I'd want to know about it!" No wonder she and Bill had been married more than *fifty years*—she never stopped working to perfect their recipe of romance.

Part Four

WHAT TO DO ABOUT . . .

*Love is patient, love is kind . . . It always protects,
always trusts, always hopes, always perseveres.*
1 CORINTHIANS 13:4, 7

Chapter 9

"Little" Interruptions to Romance

I always dreamed of having a family. It was one of my hopes for the future when Dennis and I were engaged and newly married. And of course, my dreams were only about good, peaceful, happy times with children who loved and obeyed their parents. I was unprepared for the perpetual demands parenting would require of me. From 2:00 a.m. feedings, potty training, ear infections, nightmares, and coloring on the walls to braces, birthday parties, and driving lessons for teens, mothering is a full-time, 24/7 job with few vacations and a delayed payment plan.

How do you balance being a mother with your first calling as wife? How does motherhood mix with romance? Not easily, at least if you are like me.

I have a vivid memory of standing in my kitchen sometime after child number three was born, feeling conflicted internally over my role as wife and mother. It seemed incongruent to be a mother and a sexually interesting wife at the same time. I had no model for that. I had questions but no answers.

Children are just one of several common threats to romance. FamilyLife conducted a survey of more than ten thousand couples, asking them to name the culprits that robbed their marriages of romance. The most commonly mentioned factors were children, stress, fatigue, busyness, misplaced priorities, anger, and unresolved conflict.

In the Bible we find an appropriate name for these romance robbers. The bride of King Solomon described him in endearing, poetic terms and then said, "Catch the foxes for us, the little foxes that are ruining the vineyards, while our vineyards are in blossom" (Song 2:15 NASB).

In those days, a wise gardener would protect his vineyard from foxes. The nocturnal bandits would sneak in during the dead of the night and eat the most tender parts of the vine, rendering them fruitless and useless.

The vineyard is like your marriage. The foxes are the things that sneak up on you and snatch the fruit of passion before it can bloom. These sly creatures are relentless. Drop your guard, and they'll reduce the vineyard of your marriage to a barren, lifeless place where romance shrivels on the vine.

"CHILDREN ENDED OUR ROMANCE!"

Without question the biggest deterrent to romance for moms is children. The sweet, precious, innocent, little ones, given to us by God, are also self-centered, untrained, unending "need machines" who aren't naturally going to think once about helping our marriages. In fact, they can suck the life out of our marriages. For us as wives and mothers, our children will be the greatest distraction and hindrance to growing a healthy, romantic marriage.

Our mailbag at FamilyLife is filled with letters from mothers dismayed at how difficult it is to feel romantic or sexual. One woman wrote, "During this season of life, I have three children, four years and younger, plus a full-time job. I cannot even think of doing anything romantic."

Or maybe you feel like the mother of a "rambunctious two-year-old," who said, "It's ironic: Romance gave us our children, and children ended our romance!" It's sadly true for too many women.

Oftentimes, motherhood can be a tempting excuse for giving

up sex. Caught up in her responsibilities day in and day out, a mother can experience a slow shift in loyalty from husband to children. She begins thinking she has more important things to do than getting involved in the frivolity of playfulness with her husband. She thinks the needs of her children, because they are so helpless and formative, are more important than the needs of her husband. After all, she reasons, he is an adult.

One reason this is so common is that we as women are able to express and experience our femaleness (as we talked about in Chapter 4) by nurturing our children. We feel fully alive as women when we care for our children—except for the times when we are fully exhausted. Women feel a deep, innate sense of well-being and fulfillment when we give birth, nurse, and nurture babies and children. It is an indescribable privilege that brings profound satisfaction. It's what we were made to do.

But it's only part of being a woman.

Raising children, as wonderful a calling as it is, is not *all* we were designed to do. Children were given to us for only a short time. They are not possessions but a stewardship. Our job is to train them in godliness and then to let them go. You will always have a job as wife, but motherhood is only temporary.

One of the most important parts of your job as mother is to be a model to your children. If your children see a mother who has resigned from her duty as wife, they will grow up confused about marriage; that is especially true for your daughters. Your children desperately need to see Dad and Mom as husband and wife who love each other, care for each other, and are loyal to each other above all others.

God didn't create women with the ability, the capacity, or even the compulsion to nurture just for the sake of our children. He also meant for us to nurture life in our husbands. Maintaining that balance with your children will probably be your biggest challenge in the parenting years.

TOO MANY HATS?

How do you balance being a mom who deals with spit up, poopy pull-ups, modeling clay ground in the carpet, and frogs and lizards escaping in the house with being an attractive, romantic, interesting wife? The first step is to *teach your children that they are third on your list of priorities.* They cannot be more important to you than their father, and certainly they cannot be more important than God.

Clearly they will take more time on a daily basis, and meeting their needs may be your number one priority when your husband is not home. But when he is home, they can be taught to wait unless it's an emergency. Your marriage will not grow and there will be no chance for romance if your kids are allowed to constantly interrupt, make demands, and dictate your lives. They will be much more secure if they learn that they have a place in the family, but that they are not the center of this little family's universe.

Parents—not the children—must be in charge. Again, you are modeling what a Christian marriage looks like for them, and that includes being romantic together. They are watching you more than you may realize.

A wise older woman said to me years ago, "Honey, one child will take all your time, two children will take all your time, and so will three. It doesn't matter how many children you have, they will take all your time." She was right. They will *if* you let them. It's up to you if they get all your time or you save some for your husband.

Second, *realize that your children have great value, but so does your "work."* Yes, you want your children to know they are more important than a perfectly ordered house, more important than possessions, and more important than jobs, financial success, and status. But you also must teach them that parents have to work, and part of your work is to make time to be an attractive, interesting wife.

When you pay attention to your husband, children begin to see that their needs and wants do not have to be met immediately. They learn patience when they have to wait on Mom and Dad to finish their tasks or their conversation. They learn responsibility and greater independence when you and your husband leave them (well-supervised, of course) to go on a date or a weekend away to "work" on your relationship.

It's healthy for them and for you.

SEASONS OF STRESS

As you raise your children, two distinct childhood seasons will typically threaten your romance more than any other. One is the preschool years (zero to four years), and the other is the teenage years (thirteen to eighteen years). Each arrives with a completely different set of challenges. And sometimes these seasons overlap— at one point we had a toddler, and a budding teenager at the same time, with all ages in between! But you can still find solutions for building your relationship and cultivating romance if you are willing to make the hard choices and be creative.

The Preschool Season

When we had two and then three little ones, Dennis and I got time alone the usual way—we hired a babysitter and went out for dinner. We also managed to arrange a few out-of-town weekends in those years for extended focus on our relationship.

And then there was time at home. At our house bedtime was 8:00 p.m. sharp. We are strong believers in scheduling little ones for their security and for the parents' sanity! We'd put the children to bed after reading a story or two or three, giving them kisses and hugs, and saying prayers. We were tired, but the routine was fairly simple, and it gave us time to unwind together in the evenings.

It was especially helpful for me as a mom to have time to transition to my role as wife, and to have some time for adult conversation. I've always needed more time to switch roles than my husband does.

As our family continued to grow, going out for an evening became increasingly difficult. Finding a sitter mature enough to stay with our growing brood, not to mention the cost and the hassle of having to return the sitter afterward, required more involvement than we had energy to deal with. We applied our creativity to the problem and came up with a new option: we preserved the spark of romance by opening Café Rainey.

While I gave the kids their baths, read stories, brushed teeth, and said prayers, Dennis prepared the food and then brought it to the bedroom, along with china and silverware. It was a great deal for me. I didn't have to cook, which he enjoys doing occasionally, I didn't have to call a babysitter or deal with the frustration of arriving home at 10:00 p.m. to a mess she failed to clean up, and there was no expense other than the cost of the food.

We have a small table that we moved to our bedroom and placed at the end of our bed, and there we would have a late, but delightful meal. We'd talk in complete sentences (without a jillion interruptions), interact, and laugh. If the evening progressed into physical intimacy, that was fine. By setting aside the time in our marriage to get alone, we allowed a chance for relationship and romance to occur.

Those special dates at home—which we pulled off only six to ten times a year—were lifesavers for our marriage for about five years. We still went out occasionally, still tried to get away for a weekend or two a year, but having these times at home gave us another creative option for keeping our marriage healthy and alive.

One thing is always true with children: the seasons *do* change. Nothing stays the same. As soon as you get one stage sort of under control, you're in a new season. It seemed like almost overnight that our oldest two began the metamorphosis into these new people called teens, which presented us a new challenge to keeping our marriage and romance alive. Regardless of the season of childhood, the key is to realize your children will ultimately come, grow and then leave the home, but your husband is there to stay. Don't neglect to invest in the two of you.

The Teen Season

Unlike little children, teens talk on the phone, stay up late, and graze for food in the refrigerator at all hours of the night. At one point in our marriage, *four* teens could be found at any random moment wandering through our house well past their parent's preferred bedtime. While our first choice was to know our teens were in bed before we retired for the night, it wasn't always possible. So, Dennis and I were forced to face this question: How would we maintain our romance when one of these teenage foxes might just barge in without warning? The truth is, one of our teens had a habit of doing just that—in spite of our efforts to declare our bedroom a kid-free zone after the door was closed at night. She'd burst through our bedroom door . . . after hours . . . long after the lights had gone out.

Trust me, we had many conversations with this fox in an attempt to preserve our space. Still, it happened again and again. One night, she plowed into our room and stopped by the edge of the bed. The room was pitch black. I remember how Dennis sat straight up and paused for effect. He said, "Honey, one of these days you're going to bust through that door, and you're going to get a sex education that you will never forget!"

In the darkness after a moment of silence, she said, "Gross!"

She never came into our bedroom again without knocking.

Apart from the privacy issue, parents of teens have far less time for nurturing their marriage relationship than parents of younger children who can be put to bed early enough to allow mom and dad some time in the evening. We quickly realized that the only way we could get uninterrupted time with each other was to leave home! So we began a weekly date every Sunday night, a tradition we maintained religiously until our last one left for college.

We also discovered that the challenges of parenting teens far surpassed the challenges of parenting preschoolers, and with that additional work came greater stress on our marriage. The decisions on whether to spank or not for a particular offense, whether to let them eat dessert or not, whether to let them watch an extra kid video or not paled in comparison to the decisions we faced regarding driving a car, going to a party at a friend's home, and attending school dances.

> *Romantic Interlude*
> What boundaries have you set to protect
> your bedroom from late-night interruptions from the kids?
> Do you sleep with your bedroom door open? If so, close it
> and declare your room a "kid-free zone" after 9:00 p.m.

These decisions required much more discussion between us as parents and left us with less time and energy as a couple. Younger children can be controlled, and you know they are safe under your own roof. Teens face life-altering choices often on a daily basis, and parents have much less control over their safety. All this can impact your romance, which is why I'm a firm believer in committing to a weekly date night with your husband. Those precious few hours provide time for you reconnect in the midst of the storm of activities and stress.

Our Sunday night dates were literally the salvation of our relationship for many reasons. They gave us uninterrupted time that was nearly impossible to get any other way. We spent our date nights coordinating our calendars so both of us were on the same page with parenting issues that swirl around teens, the kids' activities and events, and with our own responsibilities and obligations.

We often talked about the needs of a particular child and tried to create solutions to the problems. Sometimes we agreed *not* to talk about a particular child at all so we could focus on our relationship (and romance) for a while. Some teens, when they are rebelling, will try to take control of a family through their negative behavior, thereby becoming the center of attention. Moms and Dads need time away to think and establish a united battle plan.

The importance of establishing and maintaining a regular date night is absolutely imperative. You need it to keep your marriage relationship healthy and alive. Your kids need it so they can continue to see Mom and Dad keeping their priorities straight. They need you to be in control of your lives and theirs, even though they will fight you for that control sometimes with everything they have.

You cannot have romance without a relationship, and you cannot have a relationship without time together.

A LIGHT AT THE END OF THE TUNNEL

Without question children are the greatest interruption to the romance relationship you began with your husband when you married. But they are just that—an interruption. Eventually they will leave home, and it will be just the two of you again. There will be time again for spontaneous decisions that foster relationship and romance. There will be freedom to travel together, go out to eat together, go for walks together, have picnics together.

As you enter and journey through the teen years, begin to talk and dream and plan for your life together after children. The teen years may be the most difficult of all and, as a result, may strain your marriage to what *feels like* the breaking point. But if you work to keep your relationship and your romance of utmost importance and you look to the future together, hope will grow.

On the other hand, if you let your relationship falter and you let the hope of romance die, you will arrive at the end of the parenting years as total strangers. Even as we devoted our lives to strengthening marriages and families around the world, and worked hard at keeping our relationship strong and vibrant, we still found ourselves in the early days of empty-nesting realizing that as we raised our six, we'd missed each other in some areas.

I can't imagine the profound sense of loss that many couples experience when the children leave and they find themselves totally isolated, with little attraction to each other and no romance. What an unnecessary tragedy.

Keeping children from robbing your marriage of its romance will be an ongoing challenge. Finding that balance between my role as wife and mother was the subject of many conversations with my husband during our full-time parenting years because I was so often off balance. It was not easy to manage both roles well at the same time.

"Gee Honey, I know the laundry is piling up,
but can't we just get naked now and worry about that later?"

Often Dennis felt he was getting the leftovers of my time and energy, and he was right. There was only so much of me to go around. We laughed one day while writing this book when I told him that because I had six children to take care of and him to serve too, he got one-seventh of my attention. He said it was often less than that!

Growing romance in marriage during the seasons of life is hard work. A good question to ask is, Where does my loyalty lie? Am I loyal to my husband first or my children? Answering this question will be a litmus test of your romantic allegiance.

You may be thinking, "Yes, I understand I need to be loyal to my husband . . . but you don't understand my real problem . . . Raising kids is exhausting! I'm just too tired for romance." How well I remember that feeling. If that sounds like your situation, read on.

*Do not deprive each other except by mutual consent
and for a time . . . Then come together again so that Satan
will not tempt you because of your lack of self-control.*

1 CORINTHIANS 7:5

Chapter 10

Multiple Distractions to Romance

o you ever wonder how we can feel so fatigued today, despite all our modern conveniences that are supposed to save us time and make life more comfortable? How can we be so busy, so stressed, so fractured? For many, the pace of life presents the biggest deterrent to marital romance.

Couples just don't have any energy for romance. For Sandra, a listener to *FamilyLife Today*, the hurried life has drained the romance from her marriage. She writes,

> My husband and I continue to have problems in one main area of our marriage. You guessed it: sex. We have three preschoolers, and I am mentally and physically exhausted at bedtime. My husband thinks we are having problems in our marriage because we only have intercourse once a week or so. I try to explain about stress, exhaustion, etc., but all he sees is that I don't desire him.

The natural results of parenting children are fatigue and stress. Moms experience normal everyday fatigue from just executing the duties of the household. Kids naturally fight and compete, complain and whine, spill milk and "forget" to do chores. They present challenges day after day for years and years. It's a draining job. Exhausted mothers don't make great lovers. Felicia, who took our online survey, confessed, "Getting sleep is almost always more important than sex to me."

In addition, mothers typically experience additional stress from worrying. Questions constantly swirl through our heads over the choices we make. Are we raising our kids well? Are they prepared to make choices on their own? Will they ever make it to adulthood alive?

Children bring a certain amount of healthy stress to any marriage. It's part of God's design for teaching us as adults to die to self and depend on Him. Moms and dads need Jesus, too, and they find they need to pray as never before. God knows what He's doing.

Dennis often said he'd be a wealthy man if he had a dollar for every time he heard me say, "I am *so* tired." And he's right. I said it a lot because I felt depleted and bone weary during most of our parenting years.

At the end of the day, all I wanted to do was fall into bed. Being intimate with my husband was not my greatest "felt" need. Frankly I craved sleep, not robust romance. The temptation was to believe that my needs were more important, that my husband's needs and the needs of our marriage could wait.

The other temptation was to believe that tomorrow would be different or somehow better. I remember thinking, *I won't be this tired tomorrow night. It's just because of all that happened today. I'm so tired that I'll sleep great tonight and will feel refreshed tomorrow.*

Tomorrow I'll feel more like focusing on Dennis and our marriage. I didn't want to neglect our romance. But my feelings overwhelmed me and threatened to rule my choices.

Because I had already decided in the early years of our marriage to keep Dennis as my number one priority, I refused to let this tenacious thief of fatigue win in our relationship. Many nights, Dennis graciously gave me a kiss and a hug, prayed with me, and said good night.

On other nights, recognizing that my husband was carrying a lot of stress from work, or I just knew we needed to reconnect in our marriage, I chose to deny the fatigue, set aside the stress, and give myself to him that we might enjoy each other. As the Nike slogan states, wives need to "just do it."

Fatigue and stress in parenting are normal. While you can't eliminate them, you *can* learn to manage fatigue and stress by evaluating your level of busyness and your lifestyle choices. Simplifying life is the best way to reduce fatigue and stress.

BACK TO THE FUTURE

I remember driving home alone in my car years ago (that in itself was always a minor miracle, since we had so many children) and contemplating this question: How did I get to this place in life where I (and everyone I knew) feel out of breath from the daily race? I found myself imagining life would have been simpler in the days depicted on *Little House on the Prairie*. It was a pleasant escape for a few minutes.

Romantic Interlude
If busyness has your schedule in a blender,
slow down and simplify your life. Need a few ideas?
In *Simplicity*, author Kim Thomas offers a collection of ideas to
declutter our lives, our spirits, our schedules, and our homes.

If I was living on a farm one hundred years ago, I thought, I would not worry about the continually multiplying details that cluttered my life—such as getting my hair cut and highlighted regularly, which is where I'd just been for two hours. What time that alone would save! We'd be living miles from our nearest neighbors, so I wouldn't have a whole town full of people to compare my house with.

There would be few, if any, magazines telling me how to dress myself, how to dress my children, how to accessorize my house, and how to manicure my yard and gardens. Running errands would be a simple event, for there was only one store in Walnut Grove, and it had everything you needed. No running to dozens of places all over the city to get your errands done and then never finishing.

It sounded like heaven.

Then I got stuck in traffic at a busy intersection, and my moment of bliss on the prairie was gone. As the commercial used to say, "We've come a long way, baby." I'm not so sure I like it. There is a one-word explanation for why we've become so busy.

Prosperity.

Our lives are cluttered with lessons, parties, activities, trips, classes, events, rallies, meetings, and campaigns. We spend countless hours working so that we can spend countless hours spending money on countless things we don't really need—clothes we don't wear, leisure accessories we don't use, books we don't read, and food we can't or won't eat.

Prosperity is a blessing from God. His Word makes that clear. But His Word also makes it clear that prosperity can kill us, for in our abundance the very real danger is that we forget God, the true source of it all. In Deuteronomy, God told His people through Moses that if they obeyed Him, He would bless them and give them great abundance. But God always followed His promise with a warning, saying, "Beware that you do not forget the LORD" who brought you out of slavery into a land of plenty (Deut. 8:11–14 NKJV).

Thomas Carlyle said, "For every one hundred people who can handle adversity, I can only show you one who can handle prosperity." Adversity reduces our choices and many times crystallizes our priorities. Prosperity, however, increases our options, choices, and activity. Stress soon follows!

Romance cannot compete with and win the battle of busyness that prosperity has brought unless, as a couple, you and your husband decide that romance and relationship are more important than the success of the world.

"I CANNOT DO IT ALL"

Charles E. Hummel wrote a wonderful little booklet called *The Tyranny of the Urgent*. His simple message was this: *don't let the tyranny of the urgent rob your life of what's really important*. The most important relationship in a family, the marriage relationship, is the easiest to ignore in the urgent demands of sick kids, diapers, ball games, job deadlines, and a host of other daily life demands.

The tyranny of the urgent occurs when you plan a date with your husband, but your boss informs you there's a project that *must* be done that evening, so you cancel your date. It occurs when a friend, a neighbor, or your sister calls at the last minute needing you to drop everything to watch a sick child so she can attend an important event because the sitter fell through. In turn, you give up the important time you were going to spend studying your Bible.

The reasons for the *urgent* winning over the *important* always sound pressing. And on some occasions you have no choice. But there are just as many times when you could have said, "No, I'm sorry, but I can't," to rescuing your friend or to letting your boss control your life.

Here's another example: it's nearly impossible to live in any city in America, raise a family, and not feel the pressure to have your child in the best schools, learning the best lessons, playing on the best teams. Most parents feel a sense of desperation for their children to succeed in many areas of life, giving them multiple opportunities to excel in those first eighteen years of life.

But that pressure to do it all and have it all is based on a lie. Your kids don't need to have all those lessons. They don't have to be the best at a sport to be well adjusted in life. They don't have to have the latest fashions or the nicest car. In fact, they'd probably be better off without all those things.

Former First Lady Barbara Bush said it well in a commencement address several years ago: "Your human connections with spouses, with children, with friends are the most important investment you will ever make. At the end of your life you will never regret not having [acquired more things] or having closed one more deal, but you will regret time not spent with a husband, a child, or a parent."

Here are some practical tips for reining in a busy lifestyle:

First, *"be still and know that I am God."* Start by stopping. Begin by listening. Take time to stop and pray and listen to God. And then spend time thinking and evaluating. Plan a date or two with your husband just to reevaluate your schedules, your romance, and your marriage.

Second, *decide what you value.* God has made abundantly clear in His Word what He values. Make a priority list by yourself and with your husband. What will you fight for, and what will both of you fight for? My friend Linda Dillow developed a list of "resolves" and reads them at least once a year. These would be good for every wife to adopt as her own:

- "I resolve to keep my husband my second priority after God."
- "I resolve to not settle for mediocrity in my marriage."
- "I resolve to look at life through [her husband's] eyes."
- "I resolve to grow as a sensuous lover."

- "I resolve to give rather than receive."
- "I resolve to be faithful to my marriage vows, not only in word, but in intent."

Third, *set important guidelines for yourselves and your family.* One of the hard choices Dennis and I made was to limit our children's involvement in sports to one per child. Not one sport each season, but one all year. That sounds terribly confining and restrictive by today's standards of eclectic choices and the accompanying pressure to achieve scholarship-level ability. But with six children we chose to value family time, family dinners, and evenings at home over a life of fast food on the run and evenings spent in the car. As poet Dorothy Parker said, "The best way to keep children home is to make the home a pleasant atmosphere—and let the air out of the tires."

I must add that we relaxed these standards when our kids reached sixteen and could drive themselves to some practices and games. But before they were in high school, we made sure we were the primary influencers in their lives. It was a value-driven decision. We chose the important over the urgent that "everybody else was doing."

Fourth, *honestly evaluate your "need" for all the extra things in life.* I know from my experience and my love for beautiful things how easy it is to be busy with fixing my house, getting things for my kids, finding the best bargain. It's not wrong unless it leaves me stressed, exhausted, and unable to engage with my husband. It's a question of the important versus the urgent. All these things will burn someday, 2 Peter 3 informs us. Am I spending too much time on what will someday be gone in a blink of the eye?

HE HAS A HEART FOR ME

Romance demands that both husband and wife take responsibility to make it a priority. It's your marriage. You can fashion it any way you want, but keep in mind, romance is like a fire. If you neglect the importance of romance in favor of juggling the urgent demands of life, your love will grow cold. A fire must be attended, or it will die. Properly stoked and refueled, your romance can burn for a life-time. An important question for you to ask yourself is: *At the end of my life, where do I want to find warmth?*

Making romance a priority also means planning for it and building it into your schedule. I'm all for spontaneity. But romance and good sex won't happen without planning in our busy world. One of my favorite stories comes from Dan Allender, president of Mars Hill graduate school and a member of our FamilyLife speaker team, who learned that even the best-laid plans to squeeze romance into a busy schedule are subject to rough sailing. I asked him if I could share his story, and he agreed.

Dan and his wife, Becky, found themselves driven by an end-less stream of urgent needs during an ultra-busy, six-week period. Far too many things pulled at them, not the least of which were two graduations. Dan and Becky barely had moments during the day to speak to each other.

Dan decided he had to act before they ended up on opposite sides of the world. He suggested that they schedule a few hours alone to talk and to celebrate their marriage. After they compared their calendars, they found the only window of time was 5:00 p.m. on a Thursday.

When the day arrived, Dan was ready. He had carefully thought through their brief window of romance. That afternoon, he left work early and stopped at the store to pick up some fresh grapes and cheese. At home he rummaged through the kitchen and spot-ted a silver platter. With care he arranged grapes and cheese on the tray, then filled two long-stemmed goblets with juice and added them to finish the presentation.

When he reached the bedroom, he pulled back the covers on the bed and placed the tray there to wait for her. His wife arrived, and in Dan's words, "She looked gorgeous." She slipped into bed.

Dan double-checked the door to make sure it was locked. At this point, I'll let Dan finish the story:

> Standing by the closed door, I was so thrilled about the prospect of finally dining together, talking together, and making love that as I moved to the bed, all of a sudden, I found myself airborne. I had leaped into bed and just like in an accident where everything slows down to miniscule movements, I realized I was mid-air heading toward my wife . . . a naked, balding, middle-aged man propelling himself toward his wife who had a silver platter, goblets, and grapes beside her.
>
> I immediately thought, *What have you done?* Gravity always takes over, and I hit the bed like a beached whale. The goblets spewed into the air. I couldn't miss the panicked look on my wife's face. Shocked, she appeared to be thinking, *I'm looking at a land-based Shamu* [the popular Sea World killer whale].
>
> My wife was angry. I was upset. Here we were trying to have a few moments alone and I had ruined the mood of romance. We exchanged a few tense words, punctuated by tears. I apologized . . . and then I quit my efforts to romance her. After I finished cleaning up the mess, I figured we were done and started to leave.
>
> My wife said, "Where are you going?"
>
> I said, "I just figured we were done for the day."
>
> Let me tell you my wife's romantic response. She looked at me and said, "Silly man, I have intentions for your body. You're a bumbler, but you have a heart for me. Get back in bed!"

My favorite line is Becky's when she said, "You have a heart for me." She chose to overlook her husband's poor choice of diving into bed and focused instead on his heart for her. She favored compassion over anger, love over disgust, and empathy over retaliation. As husband and wife, they needed time together. Becky rescued her husband by her loving response and invested in her marriage. This woman has her priorities straight.

The key is to keep romance alive by *intentionally working at it*. Nobody does it perfectly. So don't stress over the mistakes your own "bumbling" husband makes. Give him some grace. Make romance with your husband a priority.

Your calendar can become the single most important tool to preserve your relationship and romance. You can plan times for romance, as Dan and Becky did. You can write "TS," which means "think sex" on your calendar, as my friend Linda Dillow did. You can say no to the tyranny of the urgent and yes to regular, planned private oases of love with the man you married. Why wouldn't you want to encourage him in that way?

The apostle James stated, "If any of you lacks wisdom, he should ask God, who gives generously to all without finding fault, and it will be given to him" (1:5). The Lord knows your commitment to a planned weekly romantic encounter is *vital*. He will guide you as you keep busyness and misplaced priorities from sabotaging your marriage.

Remember, the end will not be better than the beginning if you do not make sacrificial choices today in favor of your marriage. Romantic time with your husband will not just happen like it used to. Neither of you has the time or freedom you once had. A marriage that has weathered the storms of life and remains passionately alive "until death do us part" is the dream of every couple who walks down a wedding aisle. Ecclesiastes 7:8 (NKJV) reminds us that "the end of a thing is better than its beginning; the patient in spirit is better than the proud in spirit." Romance *can* get better with age if you're wholeheartedly committed to saying "no" to the tyranny of the urgent, "no" to the stream of distractions, and "yes" to romancing each other.

RESTORING YOUR RELATIONSHIP
THROUGH FORGIVENESS

There's nothing worse than lying in the darkness, back-to-back, fuming about some petty argument that has it's roots in exhaustion, pressure, or busyness. Satan is out to destroy marriages and one of his best tools is *unresolved conflict.* No wonder Paul urged believers: "Do not let the sun go down on your anger" (Eph. 4:26 NASB) and to "Be kind and compassionate to one another, forgiving each other, just as in Christ God forgave you" (Eph. 4:32).

How did Christ forgive us? By laying down His life. He didn't wait until we apologized first. He took the initiative to forgive. I should do the same, even when it feels that my husband is clearly in the wrong. Sometimes it's much easier for me to see only *what he did wrong* than it is for me to admit my part in the conflict.

I'm still called to love him. When conflict arises, I must resist my tendency to *run from* a confrontation and, instead, *run toward* forgiveness. I choose to listen, to imagine how my husband feels, and to pray for wisdom, understanding, and God's help to work it out. As Ruth Bell Graham said, "A happy marriage is the union of two forgivers." You may say, "Yeah, but you don't know what my husband did to me." You're right. I don't.

But God does. And He still desires you to seek forgiveness.

Maybe it was an affair years ago.

Maybe it's Internet pornography you discovered last week.

Or a harsh word spoken this morning.

Give it up. Seek help from a Christian counselor if needed. I am fully aware that some of the emotional and spiritual damage can run deep. I am also convinced that romance cannot grow in soil that has been hardened by unresolved conflict. So, for the sake of your marriage, forgive "not seven times, but seventy-seven times" (Matt. 18:22). Humanly speaking, this type of forgiveness is impossible. Through prayer and laying your burden at the foot of the cross, Christ will honor your brokenness. He *will* work His resurrection power to heal and restore the romance to your marriage.

Romantic Interlude

Why is forgiving each other so difficult?
Why is it so important to make forgiveness a way of life?
Name one offense that you've been harboring against your spouse—
then seek his forgiveness. If nothing comes to mind,
ask him if there's anything you've done that needs forgiveness.

Part Five

FIRE
THE DESIRE

Fire the Desire

INTRODUCTION

God loves variety.

Every corner of creation testifies to His infinite imagination and design. When He created butterflies, He breathed life into more than 40,000 different varieties. No two snowflakes or thumbprints are alike. From plants to planets, God has created a sumptuous feast for the eyes, rich with diversity.

Yes, God loves variety. His palette overflows with an endless array of color. Why, then, do some approach the celebration of romance and physical intimacy with such drab shades of black and white? As believers, you and your husband can grow in your enjoyment of each other as you trust God to expand your understanding of marital love.

From finding comfort and safety in each other's arms to spending a whole evening trying new ways of pleasing each other sexually, you and your husband have a private, intimate relationship that needs to be nurtured. After all, the pressure is off. You aren't performing or trying to impress another person as you were when you were dating. You are free to enjoy blissful variety between the sheets. You're free to explore what feels good, to experiment, and to enjoy each other's body, knowing that you ultimately are honoring God through the celebration of what He created for His glory.

Romantic lovemaking with your husband is the God-ordained playfulness and pleasure that you share with no one else. A loving Father designed the laughter and joy, the comfort and acceptance found in sex to further your relationship and oneness. The following pages represent an invitation to color outside the lines by adding some spice to your lovemaking.

Speaking of spice, it has been said that making love is a lot like making chili. Some like it red hot. Others prefer things mild—or even slightly sweet. With a pinch of pepper, you add the spice. A healthy dash of Tabasco and you're really turning up the heat. Tame, torrid, or a twelve-alarm-fire-blazin' chili, no two recipes are alike.

Likewise, when you and your husband share a bed, you share a chance to make love according to a recipe that suits your tastes. Just as any good chef understands the importance of varying the menu, the key to avoiding bedroom boredom is to mix things up a bit. These five romance starters will help expand your repertoire.

Candles, soft lighting, music, scented sheets, heated lotions, even chocolate syrup, and whipped cream are ingredients that can add variety to passionate lovemaking. Freedom plays a big part in this. The bedroom is not the place for modesty. In God's original design, "The man and his wife were both naked, and they felt no shame" (Gen. 2:25).

The bedroom is the one place to really "let go." Just as the office is not the place for a low-cut dress, fishnet stockings, and six-inch heels, neither is the bedroom the place for wearing fleece adult-sized footed sleepers or getting undressed in the dark. In the words of Linda Dillow and Lorraine Pintus: "Swing wide the gate and intoxicate your husband with delight." As Solomon showed us, God intends for sex to be a feast of oneness, enjoyed often. He said, "Eat, friends; drink and imbibe deeply, O lovers" (Song 5:1 NASB).

If the sexual expression you and your husband creatively engage in is not forbidden by Scripture, if it doesn't demean either one of you, and if you keep it exclusive to the two of you, you're free to paint with broad strokes.

What follow are creative ideas that will engage your imagination. May I give you a few pointers on maximizing your Fire the Desire experience?

1. Don't lose sight that these are for your husband, not you. You may not be all that "jazzed" or think some of these are all that exciting. The question is, What would *he* like?

2. Use these ideas to spark your imagination and creativity. One reason that we aren't more imaginative in this area is that we don't spend the time to consider what our husbands would really like. Creativity is usually a function of inspiration and perspiration—that extra effort to make a memorable romantic encounter.

3. After trying these simple romance starters (which get progressively spicy), be sure to get a copy of *Simply Romantic Nights* from FamilyLife.com for a host of additional creative dates.

By the way, Dennis will be giving your husband a few tips on how to romance *you* in ways that you'll really appreciate. Let's get started and go to class. How about a freshman level course: Fire the Desire 101?

FIRE THE DESIRE 101

Whispers of Love

You've probably heard the saying, "Behind every successful man is a woman." I'd like to amend that to say, "Behind every successful man is a woman *who loves and desires him*." Remember, one of the romantic needs of your husband is to feel *desired* by you. All day long, he competes in a dog-eat-dog world. He faces pressure and criticism from his boss and peers. His competition is constantly breathing down his neck.

He's got to get up every morning and slay the beast.

Although he might appear on the surface to be as unshakable as a rock, you'd be surprised at the doubt and insecurity he wrestles with inside. But something magical happens to his spirit when he knows you *desire* him. When you desire to be intimate with him, he is able to take on the world because he knows he *matters* to the most important person in his life.

Yes, you are the wind in his sails. More than that, you are the brightest star in his universe; your words will bring the rain or sunshine. With the right word spoken by you, your husband can climb a glacier with bare hands. A wrong, hurtful word, and he is as wounded as a hurt puppy. With that in mind, bring a little sunlight his way by spicing things up. How? You'll use your most powerful tool: your voice.

Using just your words and the power of suggestion, you're going to flirt with and tease him in ways that might just prompt a call to 911. First, decide on something creative or adventurous to try in the bedroom. Is there something you or your husband have talked about but haven't done? Is there something he especially enjoys that you don't do very often? Once you have that something in mind, you're ready to start.

When your husband heads off to work, wait a few minutes, and give him a call in the car. Let him know you're already thinking about what you'd like to do with him that night. Say something like, "Honey, I was thinking of something . . . well, something a little different I'd really like to try in bed tonight. Are you up for something a little more *creative*?"

Then pray that he doesn't swerve and get a ticket.

No cell phone? No problem. Just wait until he's at work to call. Or leave a message on his private line. In either case, around lunchtime, dial up the suspense with another call. This time, when he answers, say, "It's time for lunch, but I . . . I've lost my appetite."

He'll say, "Is something wrong?"

Pause, and then, in a whisper of love tell him, "I'm hungry for *you* . . . Would you please hurry home before I starve?" You might want to give him a description of your plan for him that night. If you've never tried anything like this before, don't be surprised to hear the phone drop or for him to ask, "Who is this *really*?"

Often, the bedroom becomes boring because we fail to fuel anticipation. So, enjoy your afternoon knowing that you've just made his day . . . and his night.

Now, as the saying goes, "Make the call." ❧

FIRE THE DESIRE 201

Drive Him Wild

The minivan is the ultimate family vehicle. There's room for the kiddos, the groceries, and a dog. What's not to like? Oh, just that it's boxy, boring, and as sexy as cold oatmeal. Adding to the minivan's bland appeal are the inevitable juice cup stains on the seats and a complete zoo of animal crackers hibernating in every crevice. Is it any wonder why a man goes through a midlife crisis?

Think about it. Your husband secretly dreads the day when he needs to switch cars and take the minivan to work. He knows he'll end up parking next to his boss (who will have arrived in a jet black BMW Z4 3.0i Roadster). Embarrassed, your husband knows to save face he must force a smile—the one that says, "Oh, this? It's a loaner while my Corvette is in the shop." Of course, the second he'd open the door, an army of dried Cheerios would leap out and ambush any chance of making a good impression.

We moms are less given to the politics of car envy.

If someone were to make a face at what we're driving, no problem. Minivans just go with the territory. We've made peace with this reality. Sure, we would prefer a snappy red Miata convertible, but right now "practical" is more important. Just the same, here's an idea sure to inflate your husband's morale, among other things.

For starters, there's a reason why the seats of a minivan are removable—a reason not found in the owner's manual. Taking out the backseat will transform that lackluster minivan into a "love nest." In its place, put a sleeping bag, a flashlight, some throw pillows, and maybe a few snacks. A portable CD player with several of his favorite tunes would be a bonus.

When your husband comes home, invite him to change into something casual. With a kiss, tell him you've got something special planned for later that evening *after* the kids go to bed. Once they're down, quickly make sure the stage is set *inside* your garage where you'll park the minivan in the dark. Keep the sliding door open and the dome light off. Turn on the CD player. Soft and inviting are best. You're all set . . . unless, of course, you want to slip into something more comfortable.

Then lead your husband by the hand to his creative date. He might ask, "Where are we going?" Tell him, "Anywhere you want, sweetie." When he reaches the minivan, hand him the flashlight so he gets the picture of what you're driving at . . . see if he doesn't shift into high gear. Best of all, you don't ever need to leave home to drive him wild.

If the thought of smooching in the garage (which is definitely a guy thing) stalls *your* engine, consider scheduling your minivan madness on your weekly date night instead. Once the sitter arrives, lead your husband, blindfolded, to the van. Then drive to a secluded overlook where you can watch the sun set and the moon rise. That is, if you're not too busy enjoying each other in back.

The next time he sees his boss's tiny sports car, he'll be thinking, *Yeah, nice car, but he can't do what we can do with* this *baby.* 🌂

FIRE THE DESIRE 301
Microwave Magic

Ingredients: 1 movie, 1 medium-sized bag of microwave popcorn, and 2 hot hands.

Forget about watching the Iron Chef. This spicy date is an original recipe that will have you and your husband cooking up a storm in no time. In fact, this recipe is sure to challenge the old saying, "The quickest way to a man's heart is through his stomach." I must forewarn you, if you can't stand the heat, better stay out of the kitchen.

First, call your husband at work sometime on Friday afternoon. Ask him to stop by the video store on his way home. Invite him to select a movie for the two of you for the weekend. Make sure he knows it's *his* choice. Don't worry. Even if he picks a boring martial arts "guy movie" with endless car chases and explosions, I doubt you'll ever get that far.

Once the kids are in bed or, better yet, away for the night at Grandma's house, it's time for the show to really start cooking. Ask him to get the popcorn going—make sure he follows the directions on the bag so it doesn't burn. Your job meanwhile will be to get *him* going. Once he hits the "start" button on the microwave, that's your cue to get him started as well. You only have three minutes and ten seconds so you've got to work fast.

Push your unsuspecting hubby against the kitchen counter, and give him a passionate kiss. As you kiss, whisper that you're hungry for him. Let your hands roam over his body. Hurry, there's not much time left. With an eye on the timer, continue getting him fired up until the microwave beeps.

When it does, immediately stop what you're doing.

At that point, give him a mischievous grin and say, "Oops. Popcorn's ready. Guess we'll have to pick up where we left off *after* the movie." Don't be surprised if he gets bored with the video . . . and never touches the popcorn.

And don't be surprised if he comes home the next day with a jumbo case of popcorn to restock the pantry. 🌿

FIRE THE DESIRE 401
The Gift Card

Your husband probably has a favorite home improvement store, golf pro shop, or sporting goods outlet. For his birthday or Christmas, I bet he might have hinted how nice it would be to have a gift card so he could get a new tool, putter, or gadget.

This romantic twist to the traditional gift card will breathe new meaning into the phrase "the gift that keeps on giving." After all, *you* are the "place to shop," and your husband is your only "customer." He won't be "shopping" for tools, jewelry, or electronic gizmos.

He'll want you!

Start by designing the gift card. Decide how simple or complex you want it to be. A no-frills approach would be to use a three-by-five-inch card and a felt tip marker. However, if you really want to impress him, give the gift card a more personalized look by scanning a photo of yourself on the front side. Using a desktop scanner, a word processor, and a printer, pick a photo that will fire his imagination: a picture of you in a swimsuit, a photo of when you were all dolled up or maybe a close-up of just your eyes.

Next, assign a total "point value" to your gift card: 50, 75, or 100 points. After you finish the design of the card, decide what's on the shelves at your "store." What does your husband really enjoy in the bedroom? Come up with six or seven "activities" for him to choose from, and assign each a relative value.

Use these suggestions as a place to start. Modify them as needed to suit your tastes:

- *Breakfast in Boxers:* Saturday morning he'll linger in bed while you fix his favorite dish. For a twist, serve it wearing a nightie (15 points).
- *The Blue Plate Special:* While his buddies clog their arteries with burgers and fries, he'll skip lunch and head home for a healthy "nooner" (10 points).
- *The Birthday Suit:* He'll enjoy a warm bubble bath where you give him a hand with the washcloth (10 points).
- *In Your Dreams:* He'll say, "Pinch me; I must be dreaming," when you wake him up in the middle of the night for some good loving (10 points).
- *Double Your Pleasure:* Celebrate your marriage twice in one day (15 points).
- *Have It Your Way:* He picks the pleasure (20 points).

He can choose any or all of the options as long as the total value doesn't exceed his gift card amount. After you've created the card and the options, you're set.

Before he heads off to work, hand him the card with a kiss good-bye. When he looks puzzled, present him with the list of options for its redemption. Tell him the card "expires" in one month and you expect it to be fully redeemed. Then nudge him out the door with a mischievous wink, and say, "Honey, don't forget, satisfaction is guaranteed." ᘒᗅ

FIRE THE DESIRE 501
Dinner and a Show

Move over Shakespeare . . . roll over Beethoven. There's a new show in town. Even if you don't have access to a Broadway play or local dinner theater, you and your husband can still enjoy "Dinner and a Show." In fact, you won't even be leaving the house for this night on the town. Dinner is take-out, and *you* are the "show."

For this date, you'll be putting on a fashion show—with a twist. Choose a night when you know you'll have some extended time to spend together. It's best if the kids are asleep or at Grandma's house. Don't fuss over dinner. Just order pizza or Chinese.

The main event is the show, not the dinner.

As you finish the meal, ask him to clean up the leftovers because you'll need to excuse yourself to get ready for the "show." If he asks what you mean, just tell him you've been looking through your wardrobe and need his opinion on a few items. Assure him that all he has to do is just sit back, relax, and enjoy the performance.

You will have previously laid out several of his favorite outfits— only your goal is to add a little heat with each one. The plan is to gradually turn up the temperature without touching the thermostat. The last outfit will be the showstopper.

Keep in mind that the sight of your body stimulates your husband's imagination. When you take the time to look attractive for him, it speaks volumes. And since he's easily aroused by sight, a certain outfit or glimpse of your body is often enough to get him going.

Slip on the first outfit—it might simply be jeans and a shirt, or maybe he prefers shorts and a tank top. Whatever it is, you might just conveniently "forget" to button the shirt or wear undergarments. You decide. Before making your appearance, take a few extra moments to touch up your hair and makeup. The extra effort will be worth it. If you have a CD player, turn on appropriate music.

Now comes the fun part.

Call him to the bedroom and have him sit on the edge of the bed as you model the first outfit. Let him see it from all sides. Ask him if he thinks the shirt goes well with the jeans or whatever. Be creative as you walk the "runway." After he's given his feedback, excuse yourself to try on the next outfit.

Make this one a little more risqué—maybe a little black dress with stockings and high heels—or just bare feet. Whatever he likes, go for it. As you model the second outfit, make sure he knows that audience feedback is important. After several minutes, it's time to excuse yourself again.

The third time out, go for the lingerie.

If your budget allows and it's been a while since you've purchased something new, surprise him with something adventurous. Steer away from the flannel; you are, after all, modeling for an audience of one, who just happens to be your greatest fan. You definitely want to wear something that will bring down the house.

Take your time modeling the last outfit. Then suggest that he follow you to the "changing room" because you'll need some help slipping out of this one.

And get ready to hear, "Encore!" ❧

REKINDLING THE ROMANCE

(for Him)

ॐ

Trading Places

(Bryan's Perspective)

Friday, 3:27 p.m.

My wife and I are in our midthirties, and suddenly for reasons I still don't quite get, she thinks we're headed for a divorce. I know we have issues. But our situation can't be this complicated. I make good money. We live in a great house. The kids are doing fine. So, what's the big deal?

The truth is, I'd rather have a stick in my eye than be here burning another perfectly good Friday afternoon with a marriage counselor. It's like the whole world has turned into one long episode of *Oprah*. We're all supposed to share our *feeeeelings*.

Don't get me wrong. While I can't stand all of this touchy-feely psychobabble, I *am* trying to be a good sport. For what it's worth, I love my wife, and I know we could use some help, you know, making sense of our differences. Our counselor, John Engle, seems like a good man. He's not the kind of guy I'd take hunting with me, but he's actually said some stuff that makes sense.

A minute ago, John gave a little speech about how the first step in maintaining intimacy is all about making yourself vulnerable.

Fine. I rolled the dice, inched out on a limb, and took a chance at sharing my feelings. I told him that I was tired of making efforts to be romantic and then being pushed away sexually.

We weren't always this way. When we first married, our bedroom sizzled. But over the years, she developed this aversion to all things sexual. I'd say probably after our second child was born was when the Big Chill froze me out. Whenever I'd go to bed and try to heat things up, I discovered that she was wearing body armor concealed under a thick blanket of snow.

What gets me is that every time I bring this up privately, she gives me an Arctic look. I happen to have an aversion to frostbite, which is why I took the risk and said something today. After I spilled my guts, she delighted in spreading my small intestines on the floor.

Rather than address our sexless marriage, she listed all of the stuff I do wrong: all of the times I failed to listen to her, failed to *be* there for her, not to mention how I failed to do a hundred things. Listening to her accusations without defending myself was like being forced to sit still while taking a pounding with a sledgehammer.

And when I, in self-defense, told her that it took a lot of courage to open myself up about our sex life in front of John, she turned away and looked out the window. Why is it so hard for her to understand that sex is important to me? I mean, *really* important. I didn't ask to be wired this way. That's just how God put me together.

I told her that when she pushes me away, she's making it difficult for me to stay faithful. She actually told me to "get over it." Nice. If only she knew. When I'm rebuffed in the bedroom, the next day there are Trisha, Marci, and Jenna in my office who think I'm brilliant and funny. I catch myself starting to flirt with them. Their attention sure feels good. There are times when I actually imagine how nice it would be to . . . well, you get the idea.

John, of course, reminded us that we vowed before God "to forsake all others" when we got married. I pointed out that I made that vow because I never thought I'd have to be celibate *in* marriage. Bad move. I could tell by my wife's reaction that I'll be in the doghouse for at least another month.

Probably sensing the friction between my wife and me, John brought a hand to his mouth and cleared his throat. "Bryan, let me ask you something."

"Fire away," I said.

"Are you willing to do *whatever* it takes to make this marriage work?" His right eyebrow inched up as he asked the question.

"Sure. I want this to work. Definitely."

Was John kidding? I never said I didn't love her. I just said I'd love it if she'd remember her side of *us*. I'd like to feel that my needs are as much of a priority to her as are the kids, her part-time job at the mall, and all of her girlfriends that she seems to have plenty of time to talk to on the phone. Look, I'm not a high-maintenance guy. Just provide me with the basics: sex, food, adventure, maybe a little TV now and then, and I'm good to go.

Even with our problems, I still love her. The truth is, she's actually more beautiful to me today than when we met back at the University of Pittsburgh. That's saying a lot. The first time I laid eyes on her, I thought I had died and gone to heaven.

It was a hot, muggy September afternoon during my sophomore year. Having just finished a grueling soccer game that somehow erupted into a rugby match, I was beat. I remember heading to the locker room drenched in sweat. That particular day I took a shortcut through the gym. The girls' volleyball team was doing its thing so I stopped and enjoyed the view. That's when I saw her. Thin. Blonde. Curves. The complete package.

She was poetry in motion. I honestly had never seen such a babe my whole life. I couldn't take my eyes off her. I must have stood there transfixed for a good five minutes. She wasn't tomboyish like some of the girls on the team. She had this quiet, mysterious confidence about her. Even the way she spiked the ball, she seemed to float through the air.

I just *had* to know her name. Which, as any guy can tell you, is a frightful proposition. It's not like I could just walk up and say, "Hi, I'm Bryan Taylor. Will you be mine?" What if I did take the risk of striking up a conversation? Then what? Stand there like a tongue-tied moron in the presence of a goddess? I think not.

So, I did what every kid learned back in junior high—I snooped around. In fact, the minute I got to the locker room I asked my roommate, Thom, if he knew who she was. You've got to know something about Thom. He and I pumped iron together, and he, unlike me, was one of those phys ed majors who basically *lived* in the gym—most days he smelled like one too. But by hanging at the gym, Thom knew the score on everyone in that arena.

After I had described her to him, we walked to the edge of the bleachers, and without being too obvious, I nodded in her direction. For a second, I was transported back in time to my junior high dance. I remember summoning the courage to ask a girl to dance when a jittery feeling, like a host of butterflies fluttering inside of my chest, stole my breath. That same, choked-up feeling plagued me as I watched this nameless beauty from the sidelines.

"So, what's her name?" I said.

Thom folded his arms together. "Dude," he said, shaking his head side to side. "Forget about her."

"Why?"

He paused. "She's taken."

"Married?" My heart dropped to my feet. The entire collection of those junior high butterflies returned with a vengeance.

"No, *taken*." He turned and headed back to the lockers.

"What's that mean?" I said, tagging along while stealing another look in her direction. "Taken can mean so many things . . ."

Thom stopped and smiled.

"Listen, slugger," he said with a punch to my arm, "rumor has it she's got someone back at Villanova in Philly, a *senior*. He's got money too."

"So?"

Thom cut me off. He reached around the base of my neck with his thick hand and squeezed. "Do yourself a favor, bro. Take a cold shower and forget about her."

"Just like that? Right."

You see, I was convinced that if I could just get on her radar, I'd have a fighting chance of winning her heart. Sure, she might tell me to go pound sand or worse. Love is a huge risk. What part of life isn't? But in my book, she was a rare exotic bird, and I just had to get close to her. And I was intrigued by the challenge. I pressed him for an answer. "Come on, Thom, at *least* give me her name."

After a long minute of grinding his jaw, he spoke. "It's Angela."

The rest you might say was history. I moved in like a sly fox, slow and steady. My plan was to make a point of just "happening" to appear wherever she was . . . the gym . . . the library . . . the student lounge. This went on for a week or so. Then late one night in the laundry room and quite by accident, it happened. We spoke.

When I arrived with my dirty clothes, I spied Angela sitting in the corner studying. Alone. This was promising. She was wearing jeans and a frumpy, oversized shirt. Her golden hair was pulled back into a perfect ponytail. As I absorbed the details, my heart made such a racket I was sure she could hear every wild thump. I did my best to play it cool. When she looked up, my heart spiked. Her eyes were even more beautiful up close. We exchanged smiles.

Angela stuck her nose back in her book, and I promptly stuffed about a year's worth of clothes into the washer. That done, I pretended to read a book while the washing machine munched away at my soiled clothes. In true foxlike style, I sat with my back to the washer so I could keep Angela in my peripheral vision. I looked down at my book, primarily to think of something witty to say.

Three minutes later, still at a loss of how I might break the ice, I heard a gasp. I looked up at Angela. Her eyes had widened, and her otherwise tanned face had turned as pale as Ivory soap.

"Something wrong?" I said, kicking myself for such a dumb-sounding first sentence.

She suppressed a musical laugh. "You might want to turn around and see for yourself," she said with a point of her delicate finger.

Not sure what to expect, I turned. An avalanche of foam was cascading out of my washer and onto the floor. I jumped to my feet, raced to the machine—feeling like a complete idiot—and started to fumble with the mess. The next few minutes were a blur. Struggling with the snarl of an angry Maytag, a tidal wave of bubbles, and a jumbled mass of jock straps and tee shirts, I watched my chances of making a good impression sail down the floor drain.

Seconds later I felt her by my side.

"Thanks," was all I managed to croak.

"How much detergent did you use?"

I blinked. "Um, maybe half the bottle?"

That produced a soft smile. "Silly—you're supposed to use no more than a cupful."

"Oops." I flashed her a cheesy grin. How was I to know? I'm a guy. I figured lots of clothes, lots of detergent, right?

I'm telling you, in spite of the rough start, that night was awesome. After cleaning up the Tide-induced volcanic flow of foam, I offered to buy her a shake. We ended up talking for *two hours*. We really connected. We had a ton of stuff in common. Not to sound too mushy, I honestly didn't want the night to end.

What's more, I thought my heart would explode when I discovered she wasn't involved with some rich dude back in Philly—contrary to what Thom had said. There was no boyfriend and no "done deal." I later learned that Thom had fabricated the whole story. He was hoping to make a move on Angela himself.

Before I knew it, one thing led to another. I was spending my every waking moment dreaming up creative ways to surprise Angela. I won't bore you with the details, but I'd put notes in her mailbox and flowers in her dorm room. I took her on a picnic.

Romance? You bet. I majored in romance for four semesters. Once, I scribbled an unsigned message on the blackboard in an auditorium where I knew she was going to have a class. I even recorded a cassette where I pretended to be a disc jockey playing her favorite songs.

Angela and I got married after we graduated.

Of course, as John helped me to see, I don't do all of those little romantic things these days. I haven't in years actually. I guess that's one reason why we're sitting at opposite ends of a sofa in John's office. But give me a healthy break. When you're in college, you have the time to do stuff like that.

These days, I love her just as much, but there's no energy for all of that. We've got three kids, you know what I'm saying? I have to make the house payment so I work long hours at a job that I don't like. Providing for my family, doing the yard work, fixing the cars, and even making pancakes for the kiddos on Saturdays are my ways of letting Angela know I love her. That's got to count for something, right?

My trip down memory lane was interrupted when John turned his attention and spoke to my wife.

"Angela," John said, tilting his head in her direction. "Are you willing to do *whatever* it takes to make this relationship work?"

I glanced at Angela, who remained silent. Her eyes seemed sad, even distant. I'm not much of a mind reader, but her expression sent a dagger of anxiousness through my heart. Was she suppressing something? I mean, what was so difficult about John's question? I thought working on our marriage—saving our marriage, as she put it—was the whole point of coming here the last few months.

I shifted in my seat, although I wanted to jump up and blurt, *Come on, sweetheart. I'm not that bad. It's not like I'm a drunken wife-beater. Tell the man yes and let's move forward. We can work this out.* Instead, I managed to bite my tongue. Her silence was almost unbearable. Instead of answering, Angela turned her head and looked out the window. I swallowed hard.

For the first time in my life I had to think the unthinkable. Was there someone else? Was that it? But who? Maybe some guy she met at the mall? A few weeks ago John said that even though we were married, I still needed to compete for her affection. Dummy me. I should have acted on his advice.

Still nothing from Angela. I shot John a look as if to say, *I could use a little help here.*

"Angela," John said, answering my unspoken plea. "Would you like for me to repeat the question?"

Wherever her mind had wandered, Angela tuned back in. "No . . . well, sure."

John caught my gaze for a split second and then looked at her. He said, "Are you willing to do *whatever* it takes to make this relationship work?"

Angela played with the cross hanging around her neck. "Yes . . ." I exhaled.

"Good," John said. With that, his entire expression changed from Mr. Mellow to Mr. Mischievous. "Now, if you folks will give me just a minute." He dropped his yellow pad and pen on the floor and got up. John walked behind me toward the cabinets. I heard him unlocking a cabinet or something, but beyond that I had no idea what he was up to.

When John returned, he carried what looked like two small Coke-shaped bottles and some papers. He put them on the coffee table right in front of us, so I figured he was offering us a drink. I started to go for my bottle. Big mistake. Angela jabbed me with her elbow—that's her idea of a hint not to say or do another thing until further instruction.

"Not so fast, Bryan," John said, holding up a finger. "You might want to know the ground rules before you take a drink of that."

"Huh?" I said. How ridiculous. Ground rules? I'm pretty sure I know how to take a drink all by myself.

Instead of giving us the green light to proceed, John sat back in his chair just checking us out. I'm not sure what game he was playing, but my patience was growing thin. I checked my watch and was glad to see our time was almost up. I really needed some fresh air.

"Here's the way I see it," John said at long last. "This might surprise you, but your marital difficulty is really not that different from what I find in most couples who come to me for help. You both want to make this work—you said so yourselves a moment ago, right?"

I glanced at Angela and then nodded in unison.

"And you both recognize things aren't what they should be. Now, correct me if I'm wrong, Angela," John said. "I hear you saying that you wish Bryan were more romantic, more attentive, more communicative, and more responsive to your needs. You'd also like for him to be more of a spiritual leader. Is that a fair summary?"

She crossed her legs. "Yes."

Me? I'm wondering what in the world his question had to do with the two bottles.

"While you, Bryan, wish Angela would agree to and enjoy sex more often. You'd like for her to be open to greater creativity in the sexual expression and occasionally initiate physical intimacy," John said. "You'd also like for her to put a little more effort into looking attractive when you come home at the end of the day, right?"

I was already in the doghouse with Angela, and here John was making sure I never got out. But what could I say? He was right on the money. "When you put it that way, those things sound so shallow, but, yes. What guy wouldn't?"

John ignored my question. It might be nice if he validated my point. Instead, he said, "And it's clear you both feel as if you've reached an impasse. The walls you've built in your marriage over the years appear insurmountable, and you're unsure of how to turn back the hands of time."

John stopped and looked us over. This was getting old. I wished he'd just cut to the chase. I was getting thirsty, and I started to remember all of the stuff I needed to do over the weekend. Plus, with a Steelers game, I had to figure a way to convince Angela the Iceberg into letting me go out with the boys.

John started to talk, this time just above a loud whisper. "I know a surefire way for you to reignite the passion in your marriage. Are you interested?"

"How's that?" I said, probably a little too enthusiastically.

"By walking a mile in each other's shoes for just one week." John's eyes narrowed like a hawk. "*Literally.*"

Angela and I swapped puzzled looks. Even she, with all of her intuitive insight, didn't appear to know what John was driving at.

"I know this might sound far-fetched," John said. "But, please, hear me out. Those bottles in front of you contain a highly sophisticated medication, recently approved by the FDA. It temporarily changes what we call 'your emotional set.' Upon drinking the contents, you, Bryan, will experience life through the emotional set of your wife, and you, Angela, will see and feel life the way your husband experiences it. After one week, you'll return here, and I'll serve you the antidote to reverse the transformation."

John leaned back in his chair and fell silent. My eyes drifted from him to the bottles. I've heard of some far-out stuff, but that had to be the wildest thing I've ever been told. Sounded like something out of a sci-fi movie. I cracked my knuckles, and ever ready to take the plunge into uncharted waters, I said, "You're serious?"

He nodded. "So, what do you think?"

What did I have to lose? Either the medication worked as advertised, or it didn't. I couldn't imagine John offering us something illegal—or immoral. Besides, the stuff was probably just glorified cough syrup or something.

"I'm game if she wants to," I said, turning to Angela. I could tell by the way she chewed on the right side of her bottom lip that she wasn't quite ready to jump in with both feet. Big surprise there. The next few minutes as John worked to assure her, I only half listened to the exchange. Teetering on the edge of frustration, I said, "Come on, sweetie. Let's go for it."

John checked his watch. "Our session is just about over. Now, if there aren't any other questions and if you're ready to see how the other half lives," John said, pointing to the table, "please sign the waiver."

I snatched the page; I gave it the once-over as John rambled on. He said, "This is just a formality that indicates you voluntarily agreed to participate in the study." He handed me a pen. "Afterward, drink from the bottle in front of you. You should feel the initial effects in thirty minutes or less. Full potency will be reached in a matter of a few hours."

I figured I could do anything for a week. No problem.

I signed and passed the form to Angela. For a split second, I felt my action was somewhat like Adam and Eve in the Garden, only in reverse. You know, taking the forbidden fruit and giving it to your mate. Anyway, the whole thing was probably nothing more than one big trick of the mind. On the other hand, what if it actually worked? That's when a crazy thought surfaced: *If she has my emotional set, then she'll want to have sex every day.*

This was too good to be true.

I reached for the bottle.

Friday, 4:54 p.m.

There's nothing worse than rush-hour traffic in Pittsburgh. I've always thought that whoever designed this maze of bridges and tunnels must have been drunk. Now we're stuck on the Fort Pitt Bridge heading into a jammed tunnel.

I managed to maneuver into the middle of this sea of bumpers and exhaust, feeling the heat of Angela's displeasure at my side every inch of the way. She's ticked because we didn't get the jump on traffic. I'll admit that was my fault. And I'd like to talk it out, but it's as if she's erected the Great Wall of China between us.

Meanwhile, I'm itching to tell her about the bizarre metamorphosis that happened to me back at John's office. Five, maybe seven minutes after dumping that liquid into my system, I became overwhelmed by this euphoric connectedness to my surroundings. It's as if I had stepped out from under the shadows and into a warm light. The world suddenly felt like a fragile, beautiful place, rich with an endless array of colors and possibilities.

The best way I can describe the sensation is that it's what a caterpillar must feel on the day she breaks free of her cocoon and discovers she can fly. Don't ask me why. But something within me longs to embrace life at a much deeper, emotional level. Take this odd episode.

We were saying good-bye to John in the reception area when I saw a child of maybe three staring at the fish tank. His dad was conducting business on a cell phone. Every time the kid wanted to point out a fish, his dad waved him off. I found myself empathizing with the child's disappointment. I wanted to come alongside him, get down on his level, and share in his wonderment.

That was my first clue John's prescription was more than a placebo. Since then, every sensation, every conversation draws me like a magnet—which is so *not* like me. I am a card-carrying type A personality. I strive to stay on task. I take charge. I budget my time. I get things done. I definitely don't make time for small talk.

But today, rather than dashing out of John's office to beat the traffic as I normally do, I got caught up in this really meaningful conversation with the receptionist. She's probably in her mid-twenties; you could say she's one of those perpetually happy, "Have a nice day" bubbly types, even when it's pouring rain.

Anyway, I didn't plan to linger. I just sensed *intuitively* that something was troubling her. I was making our follow-up appointment when I had this feeling that I ought to probe a little. So, I asked her about her day. One thing led to another. Turns out her mother, who lives in Chicago, fell and broke a hip, and she doesn't have the money to go see her. I pictured my own mom as she confided in me. My heart filled with compassion for this woman. I wished there was something we could do to help.

Weird. All of a sudden I'm thinking like Mother Teresa.

Plus, I wasn't flirting. As attractive as she was, I didn't view her as some piece of eye candy to feast on while waiting for an appointment. I'm embarrassed to say, I've been guilty of that in the past.

In fact, here's a real eye-opener. Over the last hour it felt as if a thick fog of sensuality has been lifted from me. I no longer spend endless energy dodging sexual thoughts. Talk about freedom. I mean, ever since the sixth grade when, out of curiosity, I stole a glimpse up Holly's skirt, it's been a battle. I figured when I got married, my struggle with impure sexual thoughts would end. Not so. At least not until now. This is seriously different.

I always assumed Angela struggled with the same deluge of sexual ideas that I battled. Come to think of it, we never really talked about this. I pressed lightly on the accelerator and glanced at Angela as we inched forward. I started to say something, but stopped. I've been watching her out of the corner of my eye, and for the last two minutes, she seemed distracted by the driver in the UPS truck next to us. I wondered if she thought he was attractive.

I leaned my left elbow out the window, braked, and scanned the traffic jam for a way to merge. That's when I heard a sharp heave from Angela.

"Babe?" I said. I lowered the radio.

"Yeah?"

"Is something wrong?"

Her face flushed. "No . . . why do you ask?"

"You gasped."

"I did?"

"Yeah. Just a second ago."

I studied her face. Maybe she was checking out Mr. UPS. I

leaned slightly forward to scope him out. He was my age, trim, and wearing shorts. Don't ask me why, but I caught myself comparing his sideburns to mine. His ran down past his earlobe, forming a point mid-jaw. I glanced in the rearview mirror and decided I might just look good in longer sideburns. But in the very next second, I became self-conscious of my slight double chin. What's that about? Why should I care what I look like compared to him?

"I, uh . . ." Angela pulled her hair back over her shoulders. Shifting in her seat, she pointed to the car ahead. "I thought you were going to bump the car in front of us."

That made no sense. We were at least five feet away, and the traffic was stopped. Which must mean she *was* ogling him. "Babe, we weren't moving."

"Oh. Gee." She started to fidget with the hem of her skirt. "Well, maybe that stuff John gave us was playing tricks on my mind."

I looked straight ahead. Who does she think she's kidding? Frankly I felt hurt—and a little betrayed. Wasn't I good enough for her? Sure, compared to that guy, I could stand to lose a few pounds. Still, I'm not exactly pudgy . . . or am I? Come to think of it, why, all of a sudden, am I so obsessed with my looks?

๑ ๑ ๑

Twenty minutes later, we pulled into the driveway. I was so hacked with Angela; I marched for the door and headed to the kitchen. My mom, who had been babysitting our kids, would be dropping them off in a few minutes, and they'd be hungry. Friday was usually pizza night, but tonight I felt the need to make sure the kids had something healthy. Go figure. Most Fridays I'm planted in front of the TV while Domino's delivered. Instead, I opened the refrigerator and foraged through the bins. I spied a plate of leftovers: a couple of chicken breasts and some pasta. It was a start.

"What's for dinner?" Angela said, sneaking up behind me. She added, "*You*, I hope, big boy." I grabbed the dish, turned, and faced her. She stole the plate from my hands and set it aside on the center island. She reached for my waist with both hands and drew me to her. I'd have to be blind to miss her bedroom eyes.

"Angela, in your dreams," I said, startled by my reaction. For reasons that I can't explain, I found her sexual advance . . . unappealing. "The kids will be here *any minute,* and I'm in the middle of making dinner, in case you've missed the obvious." I brushed past her and headed for the pantry for some pasta, sauce, and a can of corn.

"Come on, Bryan, how about a little appetizer?" She gave a light swat to my behind. When I didn't respond, she chased me around the island to the stove. "Or we could always skip ahead to the main course."

As I placed a pan on the burner, I could tell Angela was already red hot. She had unbuttoned her shirt and started to tug at my belt. Strange. Usually this would be my dream come true. I'd lock the doors in a heartbeat and get down to business. For reasons I didn't fully grasp at first, there was something about her attitude that bothered me. A minute later, it finally dawned on me: *How could she expect me to have sex when she had been so obnoxious just minutes ago?*

Truthfully I might warm to her if she'd set the table or made some effort to show me she was aware of my priorities to get things ready for the kids. But she was absolutely clueless. I went to the freezer and scooped a cupful of ice cubes.

"Here," I said. "You need to cool down, babe."

"Huh?" she said, refusing to take them.

"The kids will be here any second—"

"Exactly. Right *now* the house is empty, we're alone . . . you've always wanted to do it in the kitchen—"

Emotionally conflicted, I cut her off. "I don't know who put the tiger in your tank, babe, but look around. The laundry is piling up, the house is a mess . . . plus, I've got to cook dinner and set the table before the kids come, get it?"

"No, I don't *get it.*" She raked a hand through her hair. "What's your problem? It's pizza night—"

"My problem?" I yanked a sponge from under the sink and started to wipe down the kitchen table. "If you don't know, I'm *not* about to tell you."

Angela shot me a look that could fry bacon. "Ooh!"

"You know what? You really take the cake." In my mind, her offenses were as obvious as her partially exposed bra. Number one, she never admitted drooling over that guy in the truck; two, she had been rude to the receptionist at John's office; and, three, she ignored talking to me the whole way home. Now she wanted my body? Still fuming, I plunked down the plates, napkins, and silverware while she sulked, arms crossed, by the sink.

The doorbell rang and I felt a wave of relief.

"Saved by the bell," I said with a snicker.

She threw a wet kitchen towel at me.

Saturday, 8:16 a.m.

Saturday morning the kids love it when I make green pancakes with sprinkles. It has become a family tradition. Today was no different, with one exception. As I flipped the flapjacks, I kept replaying the disaster in our bedroom last night. I've never been so confused; I wished I could call a buddy to talk about it. But who?

You see, after dinner, I gave Angela the night off to go to the mall or a movie. I figured maybe she'd chill out and I'd get some time to think things through. After all, I'm a guy. For years I could have sex at the drop of a hat. Anywhere, anytime, for any reason . . . or no reason. Trust me, all my wife had to do was give the green light and I'd be raring to go.

Yesterday, something changed inside me.

When Angela came home from the mall and joined me in bed, she was even more fired up than the episode in the kitchen. She was all over me like an octopus. And yet I honestly couldn't bring myself to make love to her because we hadn't resolved the issues of the day. Even when I asked her to apologize, she either couldn't see or refused to see how important it was to me to iron things out before I could respond sexually.

That sounds nuts, right?

The truth is, last night I could think of a dozen other things I'd rather do than have sex. Like sleep. That scared me. I used to fight sexual temptation all day long. Now, it's just not such a burning priority. I mean, there's a part of me that would be more open to sex if Angela tried to be *somewhat* aware of my needs.

I served the kids their pancakes and poured a cup of coffee. As I watched the steam casually waltz around in my cup, I remembered the note John had handed us as we left his office. He told us to open it only in an emergency. I'd say the loss of my interest in physical intimacy qualified as one. I found the note and tore it open.

John had typed three words: *Now you know.*

Staring at the meager sentence, I felt my forehead bunch into a knot. What in the world? That's it? Was he kidding? Here my emotions feel as if they've spent the night in a blender and that's supposed to help? Of all the raw deals.

I read it again. *Now you know.*

Now I know *what?* That I resented my wife's sexual advances? That I felt betrayed by her ogling other guys? That I spent time comparing myself to the way other men look? Or that I wished Angela would try to connect with me emotionally? I gulped my coffee and secretly wished John was nearby so I could dump the whole pot of hot liquid in his lap. What kind of prank was he pulling? The nerve.

I had half a mind to drive over to his house and give him a piece of my mind when, like a bolt of lightning, a new idea struck me. I stared at the words on the page as the thought crystallized.

Last night, after I had cleaned up from dinner, I had bathed the kids, I had tossed a few loads of dirty clothes in the washer—and actually used the right amount of detergent—and I had picked up around the house, while Angela was out having a good time. Naturally I was exhausted when I got to bed. Being intimate with Angela was the last thing on my mind. I just needed some downtime. *Now you know.*

It dawned on me: this is what it must be like to be Angela every day. I never fully appreciated how hard she works and how much she needs my affirmation. I never valued the way she thrives on conversation and shuts down if I don't connect with her. I could see how important it was for her to know I'm tuned in to her world.

Now you know . . . how selfish I had become.

Truthfully Angela is even more of a mystery *now* than before I drank that crazy medicine. I mean, it's amazing that we *ever* had sex, considering how little I did in the past couple of years to warm her up or whatever. Don't get me wrong. When we were first married, our communication and our physical intimacy were great—maybe because I was still romancing her.

But I had lost sight of the fact that God, for whatever reason, really had wired my wife entirely different from me. While I didn't need the same depth of a relationship that she needed in order to thrive in our marriage, she did. She needed me to perform those day-to-day kindnesses that showed her how much I still loved her.

Now what?

I poured her a cup of coffee, thankful that John's little experiment had shed new light on our relationship. As I reached for a spoon and a napkin, I smiled. Ever the prankster, I also knew our present situation presented the perfect chance to pull her leg. You see, since this was such a struggle for *me* to be *her*, then Angela must *really* be wrestling with what it's like to be me.

Interesting.

For the fun of it, I decided to suggest that we leave things the way they were . . . *permanently.*

That would get her.

Part One

The Power of Romancing Your Wife

Let him kiss me with the kisses of his mouth—
for your love is more delightful than wine. Pleasing is the
fragrance of your perfumes . . . Take me away with you.
—Song of Solomon 1:2–4

Chapter 1

THE GLORIOUS MINEFIELD

s Bryan was beginning to grasp, guys spell romance with one of the shortest words in the English language: *sex*. His wife, Angela, used a different dictionary and language. Like most women, she spells romance: *relationship*. While Bryan and Angela are fictional characters, their inability to speak each other's language, appreciate each other's perspective and needs for romance, caused them to *survive* rather than to *thrive* in their marriage.

Worse, they had no game plan that would enable them to appreciate their differences. Instead of turning toward each other and complimenting one another, they were tempted to turn away from each other.

What about you? Have you reached a point where romance sometimes feels like a clash of the titans because your definitions and your needs are so different? Are there days when, sexually speaking, you feel you're the offense and she's the opposing defense; when your goal is to score and hers is to prevent it? Have you been rebuffed so many times in the bedroom, you've quit trying?

Are you tempted to do an end run around your vows by looking to pornography or flirtation with other women? Have you begun to entertain the thought that someone else—anyone else—*must* be better than the woman you married?

Your marriage doesn't have to settle for mediocrity. There is a plan that delivers hope. The God of the universe who created a billion galaxies and flung them into space created romance for you and your wife to enjoy. I'm convinced God wants your romance to blossom and grow, not shrivel up and become nonexistent; He wants you to experience great sex, satisfying oneness, and a whole new level of intimacy you never dreamed possible.

That is why we wrote this book.

In the pages ahead you'll discover just how passionate God is about passionate marriages. Think about it. He put the Song of Solomon right in the center of the Bible so we wouldn't miss this feast of love. In fact, two chapters unashamedly depict the love-making of Solomon and his bride.

In the bite-size chapters that follow, I'll help you learn how to fluently speak your wife's language of romance. I'll also take on some thorny subjects that zap the romance from a marriage. We'll look at how a wife's repeated rejection of a husband's sexual needs affects his soul; how masturbation and fantasy rob many married men of the energy to pursue their wives relationally; and how a man can have an honest dialogue with his wife about her needs and his needs. Plus you'll learn how to move your marriage out of the romantic doldrums and experience a new adventure.

You might be thinking, *No way, Dennis. You don't know my wife. Our relationship is colder than frost on the tip of an Eskimo's nose.* You might be right. Perhaps you are in a highly unusual situation. However, we've watched God thaw the hearts of those who didn't have two sticks to rub together. Take, for example, this note from Tonya whose marriage was on the rocks. She was one of more than 15,000 who attended FamilyLife's *Rekindling the Romance* arena event in Orlando. In just one day she watched God revolutionize her marriage. She writes,

> We've had nothing but difficult times in our marriage. I can't think of any particular time when I felt SAFE and SECURE and really felt LOVED and NEEDED by someone. My husband constantly puts everything else before our

family. All we get are his leftovers. Frankly, I had the divorce papers just about completed the day we went to this event. But, when we arrived home that night, our Covenant Ceremony consisted of letting our children throw the divorce papers into the fire on the backyard grill while we watched the joy on their faces as they did it!

God is still in the business of breathing new life into dead marriages. And when He makes a promise, you can take Him at His word. As Jesus promised, "All things are possible with God" (Mark 10:27).

All things? Yes, including revitalizing the romance in your marriage. The initial step begins by *forgetting* a few things. Forget what you may have seen in the movies or on TV; forget the promises offered by the endless stream of "male enhancement" pills that clog your e-mail inbox. Maximum romance is the by-product of a man who knows *how* and *what* to sow in the garden of his wife's heart.

That's God's design, and I'll show you how to do it.

I WANNA HOLD YOUR HAND

At the same time, let me be clear. I can't think of anything more difficult to write about than the subject of romance. Especially in marriage. Sounds odd, doesn't it? You'd think that to write about love, sex, and romance would be a breeze. A walk in the park. A joyride with the top down on a sunny day. Not so.

I hate to break this to you, but when you married your wife, you stepped into the middle of a *glorious minefield*. How so? Marriage, when firing on all cylinders, is truly *glorious*. You might say that marriage is the Rolls Royce of all earthly relationships. No other expression in life rivals the indescribable ecstasy of romance and sex shared between a husband and a wife in the covenant of marriage. But marriage is a glorious *minefield*.

You see, there's a cosmic battle raging around your romance. Satan, the enemy of your soul *and marriage,* doesn't want you to succeed. He's relentless in his attempts to discourage you, to confuse you, and to draw you away from honoring your vows. He works overtime to wreak havoc in your marriage.

Toss in kids, overwork, underpay, your free will, your wife's free will, an unhealthy dose of selfishness, false expectations, old tapes filled with past failures, the echo of slammed doors, raised voices, and harsh words—not to mention constant sexual temptation—and you've got a minefield of epic proportions. Far too often, what was supposed to "complete us" has cut us in half.

As I worked on this book, I invited a group of fifty men to answer a number of intimate questions about romance in their marriages. Some had been married two years, others more than thirty. Across the spectrum, I found painfully honest statements describing their minefield. Consider these:

- We've been married five years, and on average, we do not have sex. She won't even talk about sex with me. Yes, most of our married life I masturbate every chance I get when I'm home alone.

- We've been married twenty plus years and have sex less than once per week. It's routine: same old, same old each time. How can I get my wife to have and enjoy sex more often?

- In the past ten years, I have resigned myself to not engaging in sex with my wife as often as I would like. We have sex once every two or three *weeks.* To deny myself is a sacrifice I must make in our relationship. But the longer we go between times of intercourse, the more I am tempted to fantasize.

- When my wife turns me down, I feel rejected, hurt, and unattractive. I get so very angry.

It's incredible to consider the depth of the hurt, the vast disappointment, and the private sufferings these men face in their marriages. Trapped, burdened, and alone, the God-given masculine spirit has been crushed by a wife who, in most cases, probably doesn't even realize how much her rejection has cost her man and her marriage.

And I'm gonna write about this?

You bet. While it would be much easier to talk about deer hunting or putting the engine in a pickup truck, I'm convinced beyond a shadow of a doubt that if you use the principles we'll discuss to fight for your marriage with bulldog persistence, and if you determine right now to stand by your vows no matter what the picture looks like at the moment, you *will* rekindle the romance.

Romantic Interlude

How often do you enjoy an unhurried walk after dinner?
Or initiate a date night with her—minus the kids? When did you
last lock the bedroom door, light the candles, and celebrate your
marriage for a full hour or two? Take the first hour just to talk.
And if it's been a while, why not take the lead tonight?

But be forewarned: you have a leading role to play in this mysterious dance of biblical romance. If I may be so bold, I bet your wife is longing to see you lead the way by demonstrating that you are connected to her world. Far too many men are like the guy who bench-presses 250 pounds, but can't lift a finger around the house. Or the guy who can dismantle a rifle in thirty-seconds flat, but have difficulty replacing the toilet paper when it runs out.

Remember, you reap what you sow.

There are no shortcuts to a romantic relationship. The more fluent you become in speaking her romantic language and thus meeting her needs, the more your marriage will thrive. By the way, as I share what I've learned about romancing one's wife, you might feel as if I'm just trying to trick you into extended foreplay. You may wish I said more about your desire for physical intimacy. Don't worry.

While you're discovering how to cherish and treasure your bride through a relationship, Barbara will have a little chat with your wife about your needs for romance and sex. (If you care to take a peek, read Barbara's Chapter 5 on the power of a woman in her man's life.)

"Can't we just quit fighting and have sex?"

Whether you've been married three, seven, or nine or more years, I'm convinced that the best is yet to come. I've been married since 1972, and without question, we are more in love today than at any point along the way. Why? We learned that the deepest romantic connection actually began to blossom *ten or fifteen years into our commitment.*

Where do you start? How can you rekindle and enjoy the *glorious* aspects of marriage while, at the same time, not lose a limb in the minefield? The first step is to understand what Bryan learned: a woman views romance in the context of a relationship. The key to her heart is giving her access to *your* heart. I'll give you specific tools on this a little later.

The second step is to understand that there are actually three phases of romance in marriage. To help you instantly apply what you're learning, each chapter includes "Romantic Interludes." Each offers a powerful tip to immediately experience romance with your wife.

Now, if you can stand the heat, turn the page, and start loving the love of your life.

Husbands . . . live with
your wives in an understanding way.

—1 PETER 3:7 (NASB)

Chapter 2

THE THREE PHASES
OF ROMANCE

 f you're like me, you had no idea what you bargained for when you got married. On the surface you thought your wife-to-be was flawless. She'd walk into a room, and your heart would dance inside your chest as if answering the call from African drums. The smell of her hair and the softness of her skin captivated your spirit. You wondered how God could create some-one so beautiful; you knew without hesitation you'd do anything to win her hand.

You laughed and lost sleep together. You likely stayed up well past midnight talking in person or on the phone. You showered her with flowers and perhaps a card with a clumsy attempt at poetry. And every time she walked into a room, Roy Orbison's song "Pretty Woman" started to play inside your head.

This is the *new love* phase of romance. From your first date, your engagement, and through the wedding, you walked around in a cloud of delight. She was, after all, your queen, and she could do no wrong. Your world was a brighter place with her at the center of it.

The *new love* phase in marriage is characterized by an intense puppy love attraction, excitement, and frequent physical intimacy. For most couples this romantic state where the planets are perfectly aligned lingers a year, maybe two.

When Barbara and I were married, those first years were a

fun-filled delight. Sure, we had our adjustments, but it was a season marked with little responsibility and a lot of time to develop our relationship. We lived in Boulder, Colorado, and took advantage of the Rockies. We explored together, went ice fishing together, and hiked together.

One weekend on a whim, we drove all the way to Yellowstone National Park, just in time to see Old Faithful erupt, and then we turned around and came home. Our lives were marked by adventure, discovery, and romance. She had plenty of relationship time with me, and we enjoyed regular times of sexual intimacy together.

But guess what we found out?

New love is 90 percent unsustainable. Why? We tend to date and mate based upon an *illusion*. It's only after we are married that life has the chance to peel back the layers that mask the tarnished reality. Love may be blind—for a while—but marriage quickly produces 20-20 vision.

Author Elisabeth Elliot once told me: "Something happens to change the dynamics after the wedding ceremony. This person that you thought was a *prize* package turns out to be a *surprise* package." In the end, depending upon how much of an idealist you are, some or much of what you imagined or believed to be real about another person turns out to be a mirage.

Nearly every husband at some point in his marriage finds himself waking up next to his wife, wondering if he has made the biggest mistake of his life. Which brings us to the second phase of romance, the *disappointed love* phase.

Here, as we saw in the story of Bryan and Angela, a couple wrestle with the fact that marriage wasn't what they expected. Day after day, a cold, hard reality hacks away at their mutual illusion. Privately the partners start to entertain these thoughts:

Why can't she ever be ready on time?

Why doesn't he help me clean up after dinner anymore?

Can't she balance a checkbook?

Why can't she cook as well as my mother?

Can't he pick up his clothes for once?

Why does she talk on the phone so much?

Why does he spend so much time watching stupid ball games on television?

Why doesn't she want sex as much as I do?

Doesn't he like going to shop with me at the mall?

Does she always talk this much?

Why has he stopped talking to me?

With time, and out of utter frustration, this once inseparable couple sleep back-to-back. Neither understands where the joyride went off the road and into the deep weeds of isolation. Although they might not know it, what they're experiencing is actually a good thing, for it *can* put them on the road to the third phase of romance, *cherishing committed love*. More on that in a moment. But first, let's get our hands around what happens when reality grinds away the illusion.

BLUE MOON

Picture a guy in his thirties. Let's call him Stan. His life's dream is to own a 1963 Corvette Sting Ray—the only year Corvette made a rear split-window coupe. Stan is convinced he'd be happy if he could just get his hands on one of those rare beauties. He knows only 21,513 Corvettes were made—of which 10,594 were split-window coupes. His odds of finding one in decent condition are like finding a needle in a haystack.

But that doesn't stop him from pursuing his dream.

After years of searching Stan stumbles upon a classic car auction offering what appears to be the perfect Sting Ray. This baby has been garage kept, and it comes with leather seats. Talk about a real crème puff. Never mind the fact that the winning bid will approach $55,000. It's a *classic*, and he'll do anything to become the proud owner.

Stan wins the high bid and brings home his prize. As he drives the Corvette around the neighborhood, heads turn and people stare. It's everything he thought it would be: true happiness on wheels. And then something happens. Stan notices a puff of blue smoke from the tail pipes. *Hmm. What's this?* Several days later, a faint tap-tap-tap from the engine compartment catches him off guard. *Lifters?*

Concerned, Stan takes the dream machine to his mechanic. That's when he learns the ugly truth. The engine rings are shot; the lifters need replacing; the head gasket is leaking fluid; and there is more rust on the frame than he was led to believe.

A painful burst of reality, like a front-end collision, slams the illusion. The car, which looks good on the surface, has serious internal issues. As the mechanic itemizes the cost to repair the car and replace the parts, poor Stan is only half listening. Extensive engine work wasn't what he had bargained for, was it?

In a moment like this, a wise man would step back and realize it was still a 1963 'Vette. In spite of the flaws, she was nonetheless a one-of-a-kind treasure. She'd be worth every ounce of effort and every last penny to get her firing on all cylinders once again.

And so it is with marriage.

Once you get past the *new love* stage, reality edits your illusions as you get under the hood and *disappointed love* sets in. You might discover that your bride has been abused (sexually or verbally), or that she suffers from low self-esteem. She might have had an abortion—and never felt safe enough to share that while dating.

Her dad might have walked out on her when she was young, and now she has difficulty trusting another man.

Those heart issues weren't evident at first. Her unique needs demand extra patience, love, understanding, and care. Make no mistake. These pressures threaten to douse the romantic fires to the point that maintaining intimacy feels like building a fire in a downpour. Imagine the shock that Steve, married fifteen years, faced in the wake of his reality check. This *FamilyLife Today* listener writes:

> Dennis,
>
> My wife and I have sex once a week—if that. Why is it that before you get married, your fiancée is just as interested in sex, she enjoys physical touch, gets easily aroused, and has to resist temptation. But, after the ceremony, everything changes. Sex is no longer important. She'll do it for me, but she makes me feel bothered when all I'm desiring to do is what we both wanted to do before the ceremony.

It sounds as if Steve might feel tricked or lied to—or both. His reality screams, "You got a raw deal, buster!" Now what should he do? What should you do if you're in a similar situation? Do you keep one eye on the door? Do you storm off of the field and take your football home? Or do you roll up your sleeves like the proud owner of a classic car and put in the sweat equity to make your marriage a thing of beauty?

Romantic Interlude

Take your wife out for coffee one night this week, and rehearse for her the day you first met. Include plenty of details: what she was wearing, what her hair looked like, the glow in her eyes, and how she made you feel. Ask her for her rendition of the story.

STUCK ON YOU

When Barbara and I are faced with our disappointments, we remember this: *God is the One who brought us together.* God created the institution of marriage in the first place, with Himself at the center. He works in our hearts to draw us together in a relationship that ultimately brings glory to Him.

Yes, God uses my wife and the conflict in our marriage to reveal the condition of my own heart. Whenever I'm stubborn, clueless, arrogant, controlling, rude, prideful, or selfish, Barbara's voice calls me back to Him. Is that fun? No. Am I a better man for it? Absolutely.

I'm a better man because she's committed to loving me as no other person on the planet can. Now, God could have made marriage to be as predictable as gravity. He could have enabled Barbara and me to kick it into neutral so that we could coast for fifty years together. He certainly could have wired marriage so that we didn't have to work at loving, caring, and meeting the needs of another person.

But He didn't. God created marriage to be both romantic and redemptive. His desire is to help us rid ourselves of selfishness. As the writer of Hebrews put it, "Let us throw off everything that hinders and the sin that so easily entangles, and let us run with perseverance the race marked out for us" (12:1).

Once the illusion has been stripped away, every man is faced with a crossroad. He must decide whether he's willing to occasionally put aside his hobbies, his agenda, his sports, or other desires and *commit* to loving his wife no matter what comes and, in turn, enjoy the fruits of that investment, or he can take the pathway of least resistance, which ultimately leads to the dead end of isolation or a divorce.

If you're tempted to take the easier pathway, listen to me: the romance you desire will never occur without your commitment to cherish your wife. Start with you. Begin with your commitment to care for her and meet her needs. Then, begin to gently address those hard issues that weren't evident when you first married.

KEEP THINGS ROLLING

Remember Stan? If Stan deals properly with the surprises he found under the hood of his Corvette, he's in for a great ride. If, however, he ignores the needs that surfaced in his dream machine, it won't be long before he'll be off in a ditch. The same is true in marriage. That's what the *cherishing committed love* phase is all about. One of the best illustrations of what our wives need in this phase was sent to me in a letter from a woman who had heard her husband compare their marriage to a pair of "rusty old cars." Michelle writes:

Sweetheart,

In the counselor's office yesterday you used an analogy of us being two rusty old cars in need of restoration and I do need restoration. I think when you first met me, you thought I was in mint condition inside and out, but as time went on, you discovered hidden damage and became less enchanted and maybe thought, "Oh, well, it's not too bad that I can't fix it, and maybe the purchase price will be cheaper if I point out the defects to the Manufacturer."

So you got the Bargain Deal you made with the Manufacturer as reflected in our Prenuptial Agreement and your lack of commitment. You took your new car possession and began to be challenged to make it into the car of your dreams. Well, as you soon found out, you couldn't come up with all of the parts you needed to make her into your dream car. You became frustrated and began to try to force parts that really didn't fit. Now here you are today with your rusty old car, feeling you got gypped.

Maybe the Original Maker and Owner of this old car can

help you. I understand He was involved in welding and molding together every intricate piece of her . . . maybe He purposefully left out a few parts because He wanted her to be completed by the buyer . . . and maybe the buyer has only to look to the Original Maker to acquire the parts and instructions needed to complete her. Who knows what potential this old rusty car has if the buyer will complete according to the Manufacturer's instructions?

Following is a list of authentic parts needed and are available only thru the Manufacturer and His Authorized Agent:

> Your love, your respect
> Your spiritual leadership
> Your trust
> Your patience
> Your encouragement
> Your faithfulness
> Your commitment
> Your acceptance

> Expectantly Yours, Michelle

You see, the disappointed love phase is the real test of every marriage. Anyone can handle the new love phase; that's like paddling a canoe downstream *with* the current. But reality is like a swift current *against* your marriage. If you aren't careful, the powerful currents will not only dump you in the river but endanger your marriage as well. How you and your wife handle the disappointed love phase determines the ultimate success of your marriage.

Since Barbara and I married in 1972, I suppose we have encountered this phase hundreds of times. In fact, most of our marriage has been lived not on a romantic, tranquil canoe ride in the moonlight, but slipping in and out of the current. On a couple of rare occasions it felt like our marriage could be in danger.

I remember hitting the rapids about fifteen years into our marriage: Six children, leadership of an organization growing at 40 percent a year, and several health issues that Barbara faced had taken their toll on our marriage. In the midst of these swirling waters, several emotional issues surfaced in Barbara that surprised both of us. The difficulty and emotional complexity of parenting teenagers had nearly overwhelmed her. The pressure on her was relentless. And, despite my best efforts to protect her, as a mom of six, the external demands and expectations placed on her by a growing ministry was relentless. The bottom line: My wife was stressed, discouraged, and emotionally confused.

In typical male fashion, I tried to fix her, but I found that I couldn't fix what she was struggling with. While Barbara went to a counselor over the next two years, I went through a time of tremendous temptation. Even now as I look back, it's difficult to describe that temptation. But it was real. I was being tempted not by another woman, or pornography, but by the opportunity to escape the weariness of the pressure on our marriage and family.

As an act of my will, not because of my feelings, I reaffirmed my commitment to Barbara. In short, I told her, "If I had it to do all over again, I'd marry you again!" Those words of commitment brought safety and security to Barbara and gave her the freedom and strength she needed to take on the emotional giants she was facing in her life.

You see, the highway of new love always hits the potholes of reality. At that point in a marriage, a couple can shift into the third phase of romance, cherishing committed love, or stall out in disappointed love. Those who build upon the bedrock of commitment (I'll show you how in the next chapter) are positioned to experience passionate romance the way God intended.

The kind of commitment I'm talking about is as solid and as unmovable as granite. There are no escape clauses and no threats. When a man threatens to leave his wife, he is sending her all kinds of signals that he's not really committed to her. Those signals create fear and insecurity in her heart. There is no way a woman can be romantic or will open herself to a man if he punishes her with such threats of abandonment.

Now, let me ask you some tough questions:

- Have you ever threatened to leave your wife?
- What about the *D* word? Have you ever thrown it at your wife in a heated moment?
- How secure does she feel right now with your covenant of commitment to her? Tightly secure? Or a little loose and insecure?

Listen to 1 John 4:18: "There is no fear in love. But perfect love drives out fear, because fear has to do with punishment." A husband's assignment is to love his wife in a way that purges fear from her heart. He must grow a hedge of protection around his marriage. And he should treat her "with respect as the weaker partner" (1 Peter 3:7).

In my early years of marriage, I confess I was not much more than a boy struggling to become a man. It wasn't until our second decade of marriage that I finally felt I could look back and say, "You know what? I'm kind of getting the picture now of what this commitment thing really looks like." Why?

Romantic Interlude

Keep a three-by-five-inch card in your nightstand by the bed.
Begin to keep "tabs" on your wife's favorite things.
What does she like to read? What's something you heard her say
she wished she could see, do, have, experience? Write it down.
Then in the weeks ahead, pick something from the list and surprise her.

For the first ten to twelve years, most couples, including Barbara and me, are primarily working through the relational baggage they lugged with them to the altar. So, when a woman sees her man unconditionally seeking to understand her and know her and be involved in her life, she is free to trust him with her most intimate thoughts, dreams, and, yes, her body.

Do you need skill to better understand the romantic needs of your wife? Read on. We'll start working on a romantic tune-up to get your relationship revving again.

What you want, baby, I got. What you need,
do you know I got it? All I'm askin' is for a little
respect when you come home (just a little bit).
—"RESPECT," ARETHA FRANKLIN (BY OTIS REDDING)

Chapter 3

Becoming the Man
of Her Dreams

hat do Sean Connery and Harrison Ford have in common? Whether playing James Bond or Indiana Jones, these actors have been Hollywood's idea of a manly man for decades. They're rough and tough, and can fight, shoot, punch, or drop-kick their way through a crowded alley of bad guys . . . while barely cracking a sweat. They're unstoppable. Unflappable.

And they usually get at least one girl in the end.

After all, jumping in the sack with any available warm body just goes with the action hero territory. They reach for the thrill of sex without paying the price of intimacy. Take James Bond. Give him an adventure, and he'll be in and out of more beds than a mattress salesman.

In the absence of models who know how to love, cherish, and relate to one woman over a lifetime, is it any wonder that for the last few decades boys have grown up to be men who are equally clueless about how to give themselves to a lifelong love? Taking their cues from Hollywood they enter into marriage with guns blazing, thinking that their tough guy routine will save the day. But the show barely gets started when they find out how woefully ill-equipped they are to give a woman what she craves most.

A relationship.

I'm convinced we have a generation of married men who are confused and lonely; they're stuck in a lifeless marriage because they never learned how to cultivate a relationship with a woman that speaks to her romantic need for intimacy. Sandy, who attended the *Rekindling the Romance* arena event, described her relationship with her husband this way:

> Dennis, I'm afraid that I am losing respect for him as a man. He is not really contributing to our marriage or even to his own life, so it's like having a dependent rather than a husband, a partner.

If Sandy's husband is ever going to become the man of her dreams, the best place to start is by meeting her relational needs. Unfortunately the media reinforce the notion of experiencing sex devoid of a relationship. Men have been led to believe that great sex, like fresh fruit, is hanging off every tree, ripe and waiting to be picked. All they have to do is reach out and grab some. They've been duped into thinking the same should be true in a marriage.

However, great romance is the *by-product* of a relationship.

SIMPLE GARDENING TIPS

The secret is learning *how* and *what* to sow in the garden of a woman's heart. When you sow the seeds of respect, kind words, acts of tenderness, and thoughtfulness, you reap a reward from your wife in abundance. As God said through Hosea, "Sow for yourselves righteousness, reap the fruit of unfailing love" (Hos. 10:12).

On the other hand, if you fail to cultivate this relationship, or if you sow seeds of criticism, neglect, or rage, sex becomes little more than a cold, physical act in which your wife feels used and unloved. That's because God hard-wired a woman to desire relationship. Just as your wife has the power to affirm you sexually, you have tremendous power to provide her with the relationship she longs for, namely, a connectedness to your heart and soul.

When you withhold a meaningful relationship (I'm speaking about her need for conversation with you, her desire to see you plugged into family life, her thirst to hear words of affirmation), she finds it difficult to give herself totally to you. Think with me for a moment: Do you sometimes feel your wife is not excited about your sexual advances? Step back and consider how much of an investment you've been making into her relational bank account. Her heart can be like a bank account where you make deposits and withdrawals. Far too often as men we can make withdrawals and disregard making deposits or investments. We'll talk more about these three investments in the next chapter, but every wife needs you to invest *security, acceptance,* and an *emotional connection* in her life.

Romantic Interlude

In his book *Pure Sex,* Ed Young reports that the typical couple spend four minutes per day in "meaningful conversation." This week, carve out fifteen uninterrupted minutes each day. Take a walk and ask your wife, "How was your day?" As she shares her heart, listen without checking your watch, trying to "fix" her, or watching television. In fact, say, "Tell me more."

Let me give you an example of what happens when a man squanders his power to validate and romance his bride with a relationship. Pam, a listener to our radio program writes,

> My husband Keith has called me almost every low-life name that he could think of. He's called me "fat" and said that I'm "bad in bed." Although it has been almost eight years ago that Keith said these things, I can't forget them. We've been married seventeen years and the TV is still more important to him than me. Recently, while staying in

a hotel, I purchased a new nightie. When I changed clothes in front of him, his look was one of *disgust*. Keith didn't have to say a word. The look on his face told me exactly how he felt about me.

I feel so rejected physically. I can count on one hand in the last two years the times Keith has told me that I look nice. He's never at home in the evenings to help me with the children. On weekends, Keith usually finds something other than his family to keep him busy. When I've tried to talk about this, I get yelled at or spoken down to. I hate living like this. I don't know where to turn for help.

Now, I don't know Keith's side of the story, but from what Pam has said, Keith has all but abandoned his role as the provider of a safe relationship—at great cost to his marriage. By calling Pam names, Keith failed to accept her. By ignoring her in favor of the television, he failed to make an emotional connection. And by refusing to involve himself with his family, he undermined her sense of security. His marriage is a divorce waiting to happen unless he recognizes that "love is patient, love is kind . . . It is not rude, it is not self-seeking . . . It always protects" (1 Cor. 13:4, 5, 7).

A woman's need for relationship carries into the bedroom too. While a man is usually able to engage in sex almost instantaneously (*almost* anytime, anywhere), a woman needs the context of a relationship if she is to freely and playfully respond to physical intimacy. Sometimes a man will meet the relational needs of his wife during the day, but doesn't nurture their relationship in the bedroom. And men wonder why women resent their sex drive.

When a man pressures his wife to perform sexually without regard to the relational aspects of such intimacy, sex becomes shallow. Physical intimacy becomes a battle of the wills or a manipulative game that ultimately dies a slow death.

HAVE I TOLD YOU LATELY
THAT I LOVE YOU?

Just as your wife might wonder why sex is so important to you, you might be wondering why relationship is so crucial to her. You might even be scratching your head about why God wired men and women so differently. Look at it this way. As you know, God created Adam first. But did you know that Adam never asked for a wife?

It was God who said, "It is not good for the man to be *alone*. I will make a helper suitable for him" (Gen. 2:18, emphasis added). God, in His wisdom, created Eve to be the companion that Adam didn't even recognize he needed. She was created to remove Adam's aloneness. No wonder God placed in Eve an intense drive toward relationship.

God knew that man's tendency was to be alone. He gave us a gravitational pull in marriage—our sex drive—so that we would pursue our wives who, in turn, would call us to *know and be known* in the context of a relationship.

Romantic Interlude

Do you have a regular "date night" when you and your wife get time alone? If not, start this week. Pick a time that works for both of you, and let the fun begin. Beat the movie rut by browsing at Barnes & Noble, slurping at Starbucks, racing at the rink, or having fun bowling.

For a man, achieving relational intimacy is both a mystery and a challenge. I believe God wants to knock the edges off me, as a man, so that I learn to love my wife in a way that communicates love to her. During more than thirty years of marriage, I have repeatedly learned (emphasis on *repeatedly*) that Barbara needs me to pursue a relationship with her—not just when I want romance, but as a way of life. When a man pursues a relationship and gives his wife compliments only when he's interested in sex, his wife will feel used.

For example, Barbara and I have a family of eight. As you can imagine, there are quite a few responsibilities that I've got to tackle on a typical weekend. As a man, I tend to count up the "points" that I've racked up over the weekend. You know what I'm talking about: I think if I just knock off about a half dozen items on her "honey do" list—cooking breakfast, weeding the garden, helping put the kids to bed, and so on—then Barbara will feel romantic when we go to bed at night.

"I'll be right here whenever you're ready, Sugarlips"

But points are irrelevant to Barbara if she feels disconnected from me. In my way of thinking, a little sexual intimacy will connect us. But that may not even be on her radar screen as a woman. Romance for her begins heart to heart and is consummated body to body. In her way of thinking, she wants me to be her friend first, then her lover. Giving her a relationship first is how I become the man of her dreams. In other words to her there's a big difference between *doing* things for her and *being* involved *with* her. Sure, she appreciates what I do for her and for the family. But connecting on a friendship level with her is what she dreams of. I do *not* score points when I reverse the process and try to be her lover without the friendship.

Have you neglected or ignored this area of nurturing a relationship with your wife? Are you willing to get off the bench and become her hero? If so, what's your game plan? In the next chapter I'll let you in on three secrets that even James Bond doesn't have up his sleeve, secrets that will put you on the road toward *becoming* the man of your wife's dreams.

*By wisdom a house is built, and through understanding
it is established; through knowledge its rooms are filled
with rare and beautiful treasures.*

—Proverbs 24:3–4

THE IRRESISTIBLE MAN

he next time you stop at McDonald's, try this. At the counter, say, "I'd like to have a hamburger, fries, and a Coke, please." Then listen carefully to the cashier. If she's worth her salt, she'll ask you, "Will that be *large* fries and a *large* Coke?" You see, a well-trained cashier would never ask, "Will that be *small* fries and a *small* Coke?"

What's the difference?

Just millions of dollars. Changing one word—*large* instead of *small*—is called "suggestive selling." That's no accident. McDonald's intentionally places a positive thought in your mind about buying the large size. Why? The company's research shows that customers will more often than not sink their teeth into the larger order if presented with the larger option.

Understanding customer behavior isn't small potatoes.

When multiplied by millions of orders a month, tens of millions of extra dollars a year flow into hungry cash registers—all because the company took the time to know the customers. McDonald's is so committed to understanding its clientele, it even knows most customers prefer to bite into a hamburger and taste the catsup *before* the mustard.

What does this have to do with romance? Plenty.

McDonald's success as the world leader of fast-food franchises came about because the company became a careful student of the customer. In the same way, one key to thriving in your relationship is to *understand your wife*. This is not to suggest that you should try to manipulate her. Rather, as you invest time and effort to understand your wife, you'll discover how to define romance using your wife's dictionary. I have to admit that I defined romance for years using my *distinctly male dictionary*. There's nothing wrong with my distinctly *male* dictionary—as men, we spell romance: sex. However, I've learned when I want to communicate romance with Barbara, I'd better understand how she defines the word! As I noted in the last chapter, an irresistible man becomes a student of his wife. As he does, he understands the three nonnegotiables for a romantically satisfying relationship: *security*, *acceptance*, and an *emotional connection*. Let's unpack these one at a time.

SECURITY

If a man heard somebody breaking into his house in the middle of the night, what guy wouldn't grab a baseball bat and defend his wife and his children against the intruder? That's a given. But did you know that your wife is, in many ways, under assault every day? Look carefully, and you'll discover there are all kinds of forces that have already broken into her life; they've already compromised the security of your home life.

Who are these intruders?

Often they come in the form of unresolved issues from the past—wounds from abuse, from family abandonment, from poor choices in the past, or from a divorce. These trespassers might not be obvious to you on the surface, but they can rob your wife's sense of well-being *years* after the fact.

For example, when Barbara and I were first married, I had no idea that she had experienced some painful things growing up. Some of those wounds began to surface about *fifteen years* into our marriage. I'm going to purposefully be vague because *what* she had experienced was not as important as *how* I responded. When the persistent invaders finally came out of the shadows, I did my best to comfort her and express the love of Christ to her. Although I didn't always know what to do, I didn't run from her wounds. I didn't deny she'd been hurt. I tried to let her know that she was loved and that our relationship was a safe place for her to begin to heal. And I asked God to give me wisdom to know how to love and encourage her. God does answer prayer.

Even as I shouldered the burden with her, I knew we could use some added help from a counselor, so we made arrangements for counseling. Barbara would say today that those days were very challenging, but going through the experience *together* enabled her to be liberated ultimately.

Past issues are not the only unwelcome guests that threaten a wife's security. She desires to know her husband is committed to providing financial security in the home. Do you take the lead in establishing a family budget and pay off bills in a timely manner that creates security, or do you create fear with reckless financial decisions? She wants a relationship built upon the bedrock security of a husband who refuses to follow his temptations. Are you a man in control of your passions, or do you lack self-control? And when she is subjected to a cruel or emotionally abusive coworker, family member, or friend, she needs a husband who will defend her. Do you protect her emotionally from any person who is trying to take advantage of her by going to that person and verbally shielding her?

What about your wife? What vandals threaten her security? Does she struggle with the memory of an abortion, sexual abuse, or her parents' divorce that robs her joy today? Are there unhealthy influences or relationships in her life? Does she fear the future: growing old, children leaving home, the loss of parents and friends? If so, how do you plan to evict these home invaders?

Allow me to suggest that you do *not* try to "fix" it or "fix" her. Most importantly, I'd encourage you to pray with and for her. Do not underestimate the power of praying with and for your wife. Pray simply, but pray out loud. Take her by the hand and ask God for wisdom and help with the task. Proverbs 2:6 (NKJV) assures you that "the LORD gives wisdom; from His mouth come knowledge and understanding." Ask God to guide you.

For example, if you know that your bride had a mean-spirited father, you might pray something like this: "Lord, my wife has been deeply wounded by comments her dad made years ago. Help me to know how to be a good listener and friend to her the next time we talk about this. Guard my tongue from saying anything that would add to her pain. Give me insight and, above all else, a heart of unconditional love for my bride."

Secondly, I'd encourage you to repeatedly verbalize your love and commitment to her. Your wife may be about to take on an emotional giant in her life, and she needs to know that you are standing with her and for her. Remind her that you promised "for better or worse."

Thirdly, give her the freedom to process what she is experiencing emotionally with you. This kind of conversation means that you become a safe haven in an emotional storm. Let her talk without offering a solution. Comfort her with words of understanding that create hope.

It's a wise husband who can look back into his wife's life and evaluate how she has been affected by past events rather than sit back and be critical of how she was raised, or make negative comments about the parents who raised her. Instead, the prudent husband will serve as a healing ointment, a salve of love, one that fosters an environment where healing takes place.

Romance thrives in a secure relationship.

ACCEPTANCE

When it comes to acceptance, every man should take a page from the Song of Solomon and apply it to his marriage. You see, Solomon knew the importance of elevating his wife's beauty, her appearance, her dignity, her worth, and her value as a woman. As you'll see in a moment, he carefully chose *his words* to communicate how beautiful she was to him. Such praise and affirmation are *essential* for a woman to hear. Acceptance begins with *an understanding of what your wife is feeling about herself.*

Does she feel good about the way she looks? Her hair? Her clothes and shoes? Her weight? Her skin tone? Her body image? Her teeth? Her overall attractiveness?

Chances are good that she compares herself to the airbrushed models of perfection she sees every day. From the covers of the magazines in the checkout line to the advertisements she watches on television, your wife is constantly made to feel inferior, unworthy, and unacceptable.

In Solomon's case, he understood that his wife struggled with her self-esteem because of her physical appearance. She said, "Do not stare at me because I am dark, because I am darkened by the sun" (Song 1:6). Keep in mind that she said this at a time when getting a Coppertone tan was *not* attractive. In fact, women in those days preferred a milky white complexion to the sun-kissed look.

Solomon recognized her need for affirmation and didn't hesitate to go beyond mere acceptance. He lavished praise on her. He said, "I liken you, my darling, to a mare harnessed to one of the chariots of Pharaoh" (1:9). Now, before you try that line on your wife, keep in mind the context. The picture was of Solomon's finest mare, most likely an Arabian beauty, a dark creature of unquestioned magnificence. It was the finest horse that money could buy. This exotic creature would have turned heads— maybe even caused a stampede because of her exquisite beauty. In other words, Solomon used poetic language to tell his wife that she was *magnificent.*

But that's not all.

Solomon quickly added, "Your cheeks are beautiful with earrings, your neck with strings of jewels. We will make you earrings of gold, studded with silver" (Song 1:10–11). He not only accepted her and saw her as a woman of great beauty, but he lavished jewelry on her. When was the last time you sprang for a new bracelet? A necklace? A ring? With something extraordinary, like Solomon, let your wife know you esteem her greatly.

When Barbara and I were first married, I realized early on that she needed to be cherished for her beauty. When we started to have children, her body began to change. She wondered if she was still physically attractive to me. I worked at praising her beauty at that stage in our marriage. And now that we've moved into the empty nest years, I can't coast. I understand how important it is for me to continue to praise her. The truth is, I think she's spectacular!

In the same way, your wife longs for unconditional acceptance. She secretly hopes you'll notice and commend her various qualities—her receptivity and obedience to God, her personality, her faithfulness in raising children and making a home. Because you are the most important person in her life, your affirmation and acceptance unleash an inner beauty and a confidence that radiate.

EMOTIONAL CONNECTION

Marriage is a partnership that takes teamwork. Some men fail in their partnership because they don't make an emotional connection with their wives. Heidi, who attended a *Weekend to Remember,* writes,

> My husband does *nothing* to help me around the house. I am just plain tired. I do all the laundry, dishes, cooking, cleaning, everything after working all day . . . oh, we'll stay married, but I just know we could be happier.

Did you know that when you participate in family life by sharing in some of the daily duties, you connect with your wife on an emotional level? Remember, she's spelling romance r-e-l-a-t-i-o-n-s-h-i-p. Working together around the house or in the yard (Barbara's other domain) is a great way to communicate your love for your wife.

> *Romantic Interlude*
>
> When you come home from work, here are four of the most
> romantic words to say to your wife: How can I help? You'll never
> go wrong asking this question any time of the day or night. Those words
> are music to her ears because they demonstrate that you desire to
> connect to her world. Why not try it—and mean it—tonight?

Another way to connect emotionally is to *compliment your wife*. Proverbs offers this pointer: "Pleasant words are like a honeycomb, sweetness to the soul and health to the bones" (16:24 NKJV). How often do you praise your wife for what she does? Consider a few of these compliments to brighten her day:

- "Dinner was great! Thank you for always making creative meals, even when you're tired of cooking."
- "I love the way you read books to our kids. That's so much better for them than watching TV."
- "I'm grateful that you carefully budget our paycheck each month."
- "I admire the way you handled yourself with that rude salesman—you have such a winsome approach."
- "The flowers you planted make our home so much more inviting. I appreciate your hard work."

As you work to make an emotional connection with your words and actions, go below the surface to the real issues of life. How? Start to *talk with her*. For some, this involves a conscious choice. Share with her, for example, what goes on at work—what you're doing well, where you're struggling, the people you're working with, the people you encounter. Most women love hearing all of the details. You'll also discover that she can provide wise counsel on different issues you're facing.

Finally ask your wife questions about what *she* is feeling, and then listen to her. One way I do this with Barbara is to ask questions that can't be answered with a "yes" or "no." For example, I might ask her, "How did that exchange with our teenage son make you feel?" Making the effort to know specifics about her background, her favorite things, and her dreams all communicate to her, "I want to *know you.* I want to be your *soul mate.*"

A favorite question of mine is, "What is the most courageous thing you've ever done in your life?" Try that question on a date night with your wife, and give her time to think about her answer. You might consider sharing how you would answer the question.

Here are several other questions to help you make the connection:

Her Background

1. What is one of your earliest childhood memories?
2. What is one thing from your past that you struggle with?
3. What was one of your proudest achievements before we met?
4. What was your relationship with your dad like? How about your mom?
5. At what age and what were the circumstances when you placed your faith in Christ as your Savior?

Her Favorite Things

1. What restaurant do you enjoy going to the most?
2. What is your favorite clothing store?
3. What is your favorite food, beverage, and dessert?
4. What would you say was our best family vacation, and why?
5. What is your favorite book in the Bible? Hymn? Why?

Her Dreams

1. If money was not an issue, what kind of car would you love to drive?

2. If you could live anywhere in the world, where would you like to live?

3. Did you finish college? If not, do you dream of completing your degree one day?

4. What dreams do you have for our children?

5. What do you long to experience with me in our marriage?

6. What do you want to accomplish after the kids are grown?

We've looked at three keys to unlocking a romantically satisfying marriage: security, acceptance, and an emotional connection. As you study your wife and learn how and when to use these keys, you will become an irresistible man. If you're hungry for more, and if you're ready to supersize your order, in the next chapter I'll give you thirty more ways to love your lover.

Her children arise and call her blessed;
her husband also, and he praises her: "Many women
do noble things, but you surpass them all."
—Proverbs 31:28–29

Chapter 5

THIRTY WAYS TO
LOVE YOUR LOVER

eet Don. Don is a basketball "nut." He's the kind of
sports buff who can talk nonstop about his favorite basketball teams with anybody who'll listen. One evening,
Don's wife took a seat next to him on the couch. She placed her
arms around his neck and asked him point-blank: "Do you love me
more than basketball?"

Puzzled, Don considered her question for a long minute before
answering. He finally said, "College or NBA?"* While most of us
men would never make a blunder of that magnitude, we often miss
the opportunity to affirm our wives. Marriage is not a spectator
sport. Nor is it a place for verbal jabs or cynical put-downs. Those
male digs might work in the locker room with the boys, but they're
out of bounds with our wives.

What do Don's wife, your wife, and my wife need? Affirmation.
Lots of it. Soft, tender, thoughtful, unexpected, meaningful, heartfelt affirmation delivered with *no sexual demands attached*. That's
difficult for a man, I know. A man usually sets goals and generally
acts only when he is after something. When it comes to romance,
he's tempted to give affirmation only because he hopes to "get sex"
in return.

*See "Loving Her More Than the NBA," *Reader's Digest*, October 1997, for more on this.

As we look at showering our wives with affirmation in this chapter you and I will score big when we make our goal unconditional affirmation—no strings attached. My aim is to make my wife feel loved, valued, cherished, and affirmed as the love of my life.

We all would do well to watch Solomon in action. Solomon, by contrast, referred to his wife as "my beloved" forty times in the Song of Solomon. That choice phrase is packed with affirmation. It's a romantic expression, a call to rich friendship. Each time Solomon said, "My beloved," his words clothed her with dignity and value.

What woman wouldn't flourish under such a constant stream of loving affirmation?

Here are thirty nonsexual ways to cherish your bride through words and acts of affirmation. And by the way, these are nonsexual so that *you speak her romantic love language.* It's important to remember that you are *not* doing these things to get something in return. Perhaps she will reciprocate in your language back to you, but that's not your goal. Are you ready?

THIRTY WAYS
TO LOVE YOUR LOVER

1. Hug and kiss her *every morning* before leaving the house. Research indicates that marriages that practice this simple discipline are much healthier than those that don't. If she's sleeping, leave her a note, or gently kiss her forehead and whisper, "Have a wonderful day, sweetheart."
2. Reach across the front seat of the car when you drive and hold her hand, even for a few moments. Allow your fingers to become entwined.
3. Write, "I'm crazy about you, honey. You're the best!" or another personal message on a yellow sticky note. Attach it to her bathroom mirror.

4. Call her from work and say, "I've been thinking of how good I have it with you in my life. Thanks for all that you are as a woman and all that you do for me and our family."

5. The next time you get a pair of tickets to a ball game, theater, or concert that she'd like to go to, make a sacrifice. Instead of going with a buddy, tuck them in her purse with a note saying, "You deserve a night off. Have fun with a girlfriend."

6. Go an entire day without criticizing anything about her. Instead, try to notice her doing something that you really appreciate, and tell her how much you value her.

7. Go to bed at the same time with her for a week; just talk or read a book and share the quietness together. Or play a card game that you used to play when you dated or were just married.

8. Brush her hair and compliment her hair and eyes.

9. While she studies her face in the mirror, come up behind her and gently kiss the back of her neck. Say, "God broke the mold after He made you. You are so beautiful."

10. Evict Leno and Letterman from your bedroom. Cart off the TV, and when she asks what you're doing, tell her you'd like to start making a habit of listening to *her* rather then a couple of middle-aged men in pancake makeup.

11. Call her or send her an e-mail midafternoon and ask her how her day is going.

12. Try your hand at making breakfast on Saturday morning. Tell her she deserves a break and should feel free to sleep in.

13. Take her car to the gas station, fill the tank, vacuum the floor mats, and clean the windows. When you park it at the house, leave a note on the dash with just a heart and the words, "Thinking of you."

14. Write her a short love letter in which you list several ways that she has blessed you this year.

15. Resurrect common courtesies. Start opening the car door for her as you did when you dated, pull out her chair for her at the dinner table, offer your arm while walking down stairs, and help her put her coat on.

16. If she's doing the laundry, pull yourself away from whatever you're doing and offer to bring the hamper.

17. Put the toilet seat down when you're finished, and wash your hands. I'd estimate that 40 percent of men don't. Our wives do know. Stroking her face *after* you've been to the bathroom suddenly loses its romantic appeal!

18. Put down the newspaper or turn off the computer, and say, "Why don't we go for a walk and talk? I'd love to hear about your day."

19. If you overhear her engaged in a difficult situation on the phone or with a child, compliment the way she handled the conversation.

20. Initiate daily prayer with her. This one spiritual discipline has transformed millions of marriages. Make a commitment, and then begin to pray together every day. Begin by giving thanks for her and your family, then pray with her about her worries and challenges. Ask her to pray for you about a challenge you are facing.

21. Say, "Thank you," after every meal she serves. Then help her clear the table or offer to do the dishes with her.

22. If she has wrestled with a specific spiritual issue (such as gossip, envy, a lack of compassion), tell her how much you appreciate her desire to handle it in a godly manner.

23. Express appreciation for her doing the laundry and folding your clothing.

24. Each day try to say, "I love the way you _____," and fill in the blank with something you've observed.

25. When your wife irons your shirts or picks up the dry cleaning, say, "Thanks, honey, for taking such good care of me."

26. When the alarm goes off in the morning, wrap your arm around her, press your body next to hers, and cuddle for several minutes. When you leave, say, "I wish I didn't have to go."

27. The next time you go to dinner, say, "You've had a tough day, sweetie. Why don't you pick the spot tonight?"

28. When you are together in a crowd, find a way to brag on her. Say, "My wife is such an amazing cook," or "I've got the best wife—her _____ never ceases to amaze me."

29. The morning after making love, touch her tenderly, and tell her how wonderful it was to be with her.

30. With your wife in the room, tell your kids, "You've got the best mommy in the world. Isn't she great? I just love her so much."

31. Bonus for those with young families: Help her put the kids to bed each night.

For some men, the thought of affirming their wives sounds like a lot of work. Others are anxious about being so vulnerable with displays of affirmation. Whatever the reason, they hesitate to step out and pursue the call to love found in Ephesians 5:25 (NKJV): "Husbands, love your wives, just as Christ also loved the church and gave Himself for her."

If you've hesitated affirming your bride, or if you've been slow to praise her qualities, trust me on this: just do it. Affirming your wife through even just three or four of these ideas will do wonders for your romance. Is that too difficult to believe?

You'll never know unless you try, right?

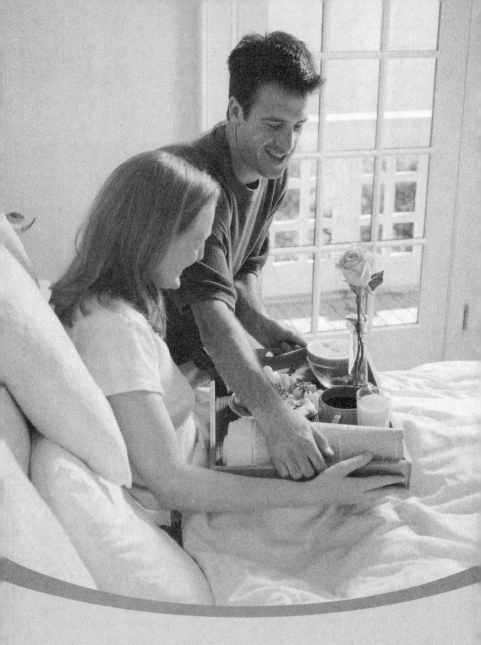

Tell her about it.
Tell her all your crazy dreams.
Let her know you need her.
Let her know how much she means.

—BILLY JOEL

Chapter 6

How to Reach Out and Touch Her

hen cell phones were introduced in 1983, the early models were as practical as holding a two-pound brick to the side of your head. They cost more than $1,000, and coverage was spotty at best.

Today, cell phones are as light as three ounces and are offered free. By the end of 2003, the United States alone had more than 154 million cell phone subscribers, with a new customer signing up every two seconds. One report predicted that annual cell usage in the U.S. would top 450 *billion* minutes by 2007. (I bet 20 percent of those minutes will be used by my teenage daughter!) Without question, we are the most "connected" generation in history.

So, then, what could possibly be wrong with this picture?

American culture has become increasingly *high tech* but *low touch*. We're e-mailing, faxing, paging, cell phoning, instant messaging, voice mailing . . . you name it, we're doing it. One problem. We're talking more but communicating less. Or if you will, our communications are more frequent but highly superficial. If the thousands of letters in our mailbag at FamilyLife are any indication, rarely do we dig down and connect with the soul of another human—especially a spouse.

In marriage there is nothing as easy as talking and yet nothing as difficult as communicating. The bottom line: if you want to be a romantic man, then be a great friend to your wife. Romance is, after all, like a friendship that has been set on fire. To ignite the passionate fires in your marriage, the fine art of conversation is essential.

REAL COMMUNICATION

This *illusion* of being connected by cell phones is not a substitute for the real thing: face-to-face conversation.

Don't get me wrong. I own a cell phone and love the convenience it provides. But the communication that takes place when I'm talking to my wife on the phone doesn't compare to what happens when I take her face into my hands and look into her soul as we share our hearts.

When Solomon spoke about the woman he loved in Song of Solomon 4, he spoke of her eyes, her hair, her teeth, her lips, her temples, and her neck. In other words, Solomon was focused on the "communication center" of his wife. He knew that all of these features have much to do with where the souls of two people are ultimately linked together. Further, he knew that a passionate relationship and a soul-to-soul connection happen best when we stop, linger, and *look* at the person we're talking with.

Think with me for a moment: When was the last time you really *looked into the eyes of your wife?* I mean really looked? And smiled?

Romantic Interlude

If your wife has small children at home, she's probably starved for adult conversation. Tonight, why not put the kids down early, turn off the TV, and make her a cup of tea? Then invite her to sit with you in a quiet spot and give her a real treat: your undivided attention.

One of the most powerful principles for romance that any man could apply to his marriage is: *Words spoken face-to-face, heart-to-*

heart, to your wife are powerful. If you want to touch your wife deeply, do what Solomon did. Look into her soul through her eyes. She's longing for that kind of intimate conversation. Touching base by phone is fine. But for a woman, that's like watching an old black-and-white TV. It lacks color.

You see, one of her top romantic needs is to be heard and understood by her man. She longs for an openness, a sharing of dreams, hopes, desires, and even disappointments through *focused* conversation. I imagine you might be thinking, *Time out, Dennis. A conversationalist? I'm a man of few words.* Funny, that's what Moses said when God asked him to be His spokesman.

Listen to this: "Moses said to the LORD, 'O Lord, I have never been eloquent, neither in the past nor since you have spoken to your servant. I am slow of speech and tongue" (Ex. 4:10). What did the Lord tell him? "Who gave man his mouth? Who makes him deaf or mute? . . . Now go; I will help you speak and will teach you what to say" (vv. 11–12). If you, like Moses, are wondering how this is going to work, I'd say, it's easier than you may think.

Start by praying and asking God to help you. Then practice answering your wife's questions with more than one sentence. For example, if she asks, "How was your day, honey?" you have a choice. You could say, "Fine," and leave it at that. Or you could offer specifics: "I had a good day, honey. I finished my report for the boss. He absolutely loved it and even hinted at giving me the ABC account."

I have found that when I go into some detail about my life—what happened at the office or what's on my mind—Barbara feels included in my world. She doesn't want the thirty-second "news" sound-bite version of my day; she wants to know the details. She doesn't expect the *Gone with the Wind* version, but she'd sure appreciate a little more than a grunt and a one-word response of "fine."

Detailed conversation signals that Barbara matters to me as a friend. That's an important first step. Moving from a *friend* to a romantic *confidant* happens when I engage her *emotionally* in the conversation, which means sharing not just *what* happened, but how I *felt* about it. Using the above example, I might add: "When he mentioned the ABC account, I felt a mixture of excitement and fear. I mean, could I really handle such an important client? I'd hate to blow it. Do you understand what I'm feeling here?"

Sharing worries, failures, and dreams draws her into the interior of your life. Many women don't feel needed by their husbands because they are rarely invited "inside" through this kind of communication. When a wife is left on the outside looking in, she feels like a mere acquaintance. This is why connecting conversationally is essential to romancing your wife. *Please hear me on this: when a woman doesn't have that opening to her husband's soul, she ends up feeling like an object rather than a partner when he pursues romance and sexual intimacy.*

Now, let me ask you several pointed questions.

How much time did you spend in focused conversation with your wife today? Should you turn off the TV or the computer, or put down the newspaper, and spend quality time talking with her? When you talk, are you sharing "just the facts," or do you remember to communicate your feelings?

I want to give you the courage to experience what Barbara and I have come to enjoy: the depth and satisfaction of a true friend and mature romance. By working on our communication together, Barbara and I have become so much more than pals who share a house, a bed, six kids, and a last name.

We are truly soul mates. We *know* what's going on in each other's life. Neither of us can imagine going through life without the other. Even after thirty plus years of marriage, I'm still captivated by her. All of her. Her heart, soul, mind, and body. Our love runs deep because we have practiced, and continue to practice, regular, intentional, focused, face-to-face conversation. I haven't done this perfectly, but I have done it repeatedly.

I'd suggest that you take a personal "communication" inventory by asking, "Am I fulfilling my wife's romantic need for conversation?" Your inventory should include the following questions for her:

1. On a one to ten point scale (ten being the highest), how would you rate our communication/conversation?
2. What's the best time of the day and place for us to talk?
3. What is one thing I could do better when it comes to communicating with you?

Not only will your romance benefit, but regular communication acts as a protective hedge around your relationship.

We've heard from many conversationally-starved women who have gone *outside* their marriages and into a relationship with other men in order to fulfill their hunger for conversation. Carol is one such woman. She writes,

> I came across an article entitled "Avoiding Emotional Adultery." It touched me deeply because either I had done, or was thinking of doing, everything that was written. For example, I have a friend at church. He and I started to tell each other *everything* and we consider each other best of friends. I am married; he is not.
>
> He started to tell me how much he likes a young lady from our church. Then we started to talk about my marriage. I made the mistake of telling him things were not going great. Before I knew it, he and I were spending more time together, talking on the phone, and wanting to be together when we were apart.
>
> This is not the first time I've committed emotional adultery. While I love my husband very much, when he does what *he* wants to do and doesn't spend time with me

and the family, I go and get the attention from someone else. This has been going on for years.

I had stopped being unfaithful to my husband for a while now—at least two years. But every time I meet someone new, someone who takes the time to listen and spend time with me, I start to fall back into this pattern. I know that I need to pray more because, while I got out of the last friendship on time, what might happen with the next person who comes around?

Carol's last question is haunting. Her words should burn a hole through our tendency toward complacency in conversation. We must resist depriving our wives of such life-giving conversation, or we run the risk of sending them into the arms of other men.

Romantic Interlude

Place a sound machine in the bedroom or home office to mask your more intimate conversations. Barbara and I have one, and it was a lifesaver with a house full of kids.

There's another aspect of intimate conversation that we can glean from Solomon's example. It's one thing to talk about the "stuff" of life with a spouse. It's quite another thing to use the face-to-face time to speak in romantic terms. As I read Song of Solomon, I can't help noticing how he praised his wife for her beauty, her kisses, her purity, and the sexual love that she gave to him. *He didn't just take the gift of her love; he cherished the treasure she gave to him as her husband.*

Cradle her face in your hands and tell her that she causes your heart to beat faster . . . that you love making love to her . . . that you can't get enough of her voice. Praise her for the "little things" she does as your wife—and be specific. Then with a twinkle in your eye, tell her that you would marry her all over again.

Of course, you could say all of this to your sweetheart on your cell phone while cruising down the highway . . . or standing in line at the grocer . . . or while you are at the office. You just won't be in the room to savor her reaction.

It's your call.

Our struggle is not against flesh and blood,
but against the rulers, against the authorities, against the
powers of this dark world and against the spiritual forces
of evil in the heavenly realms.

—EPHESIANS 6:12

Chapter 7

LEAD ME ON

 t the outset of this section I described marriage as a *glorious minefield*. God designed marriage to be a place of passionate, electrifying oneness shared between a man and his bride. When this heavenly union is firing on all cylinders, there's no earthly experience that comes close. That is God's glorious divine design.

The minefield is this: *what God has created, Satan seeks to corrupt*. Whether you realize it or not, Satan has your marriage in his crosshairs. From the moment you said, "I do," he started taking aim. He hides in the shadows taking potshots with his black darts of doubt, mistrust, anger, pride, lust, and a host of other twisted munitions in hopes of neutralizing you and your wife.

His greatest pleasure would be to alienate your relationship with God and annihilate your marriage in the process. Does that sound like an overstatement? Just look what he did to the first couple. The devil slithered his way into the Garden of Eden and planted the first seeds of doubt in the heart of Eve: "He said to the woman, 'Did God really say . . . ?'" (Gen. 3:1).

The rest is history.

Look carefully at what happened: "When the woman saw that the fruit of the tree was good for food and pleasing to the eye, and also desirable for gaining wisdom, she took some and ate it. She also gave some to her husband, *who was with her,* and he ate it" (v. 6, emphasis added).

Why didn't Adam speak up? Why did Adam fail to protect Eve from this enemy? After all, he couldn't plead "ignorance." He knew what God had said, and he was there watching the entire hellacious dialogue between his wife and the deceiver. Could it be that Adam was tricked into dropping his guard? No. Adam *passively watched* what was going on and *still* left Eve to fend for herself.

Why is this important? What does this have to do with the topic of romance?

I believe your wife carries around a *wound of betrayal* in her spirit that has its roots all the way back to the mother of humankind—which might explain why *spiritual security* is one of a woman's top needs today. Adam betrayed his obligation to protect Eve *spiritually* from the evil one. In like fashion, far too many men today are failing to spiritually guard their wives. As a result, both their relationship and their romance suffers.

Romantic Interlude

If you don't do this already, ask your wife, "How can I pray for you today?"
Then later on in the day let her know that you prayed for her.
Better yet, pray for her aloud right on the spot.

A poll conducted by Barna Research Group in 2004 for Promise Keepers found a mere one-in-eight Christian men surveyed viewed spirituality (as defined by reading the Bible and becoming a better Christian) as important to focus on in marriage. In the absence of spiritual leadership, is it any wonder that the divorce rate, the number of broken lives, marital infidelity, and listlessness within Christian homes are no different from those in the general public? You and I have been charged with the high and noble calling of spiritually protecting and nourishing our wives.

So, how do you become the spiritual leader?

The best place to begin is to align *your* heart with the heart of the Father. After all, you can't be a leader in the home unless you are a follower and imitator of Christ. So, start by putting "on the full armor of God so that you can take your stand against the devil's schemes" (Eph. 6:11). In fact, why not take a minute to get reacquainted with the details of this spiritual armor (Eph. 6:14–18)?

Trust me. I'm not suggesting that you enroll in seminary to become fluent in Greek, Latin, and Hebrew with the ability to memorize the original ancient texts. But you and I would do well to walk onto this spiritual battlefield properly equipped. Assuming that you are in a relationship with God that is growing, and that you are spending "face time" with Jesus, that is, time in His Word, prayer, and fellowship with Him, here are four specific ways to provide the spiritual leadership for your wife and family.

1. Taking the Lead in Daily Prayer

I believe it is so important for a man to put his hand on his wife daily and say, "Father God, I ask You to preserve and protect and keep my wife from harm and evil and temptation this day." Whether you pray with her in the morning or at the close of the day, be assured that there is real power when a husband and a wife bow before the Almighty God and ask for His protection and blessing. James observed, "The prayer of a righteous man is powerful and effective" (5:16).

As I was working on this book, Bob Lepine (co-host of *FamilyLife Today*) shared with me this interesting exchange with his wife, Mary Ann. Apparently as Bob was leaving for work one morning, he put his arm around Mary Ann and prayed, "Lord, I pray that You would stretch Mary Ann today, that You would challenge her spiritually and cause her to grow in the image of Christ."

When he finished praying, Mary Ann looked him in the eye and said, "Would you just pray that I have a nice day and that the kids would behave? None of this spiritual stretching business!" I can understand Mary Ann's desire. At the same time, I recognize the importance of praying for my wife, Barbara, to grow spiritually—even if that requires some stretching.

The key is to know *your* wife and to pray for *her needs*. There are clearly times when you should pray that your wife has a fun, playful, relaxed day, filled with things that bring her joy. There are also times when it's appropriate to pray that the Lord deepens her faith or expands her view of God, or she tastes the thrill of victory over a crisis or sin in her life.

If you are unsure about what she needs, ask her.

And when you pray, don't worry about saying all the "right" words. The Holy Spirit will help you pray. Paul explained, "The Spirit helps us in our weakness. We do not know what we ought to pray for, but the Spirit himself intercedes for us with groans that words cannot express" (Rom. 8:26).

If you want to truly love your wife, then make a commitment and pray with and for her daily.

2. Taking the Lead in Spiritual Growth

A great way for you to provide spiritual safety and security is to encourage and make it possible for your wife to grow spiritually. I wish an older man had told me early in my marriage how important this responsibility was for me as a husband. I didn't help Barbara as I should have years ago when our children were little. I didn't help her make her spiritual growth a priority and execute that plan.

Here are several suggestions—some that I did, others that I wish I'd done for Barbara:

- Encourage your wife and give her the freedom to get involved in a weekly Bible study such as Bible Study Fellowship, Precepts, a Beth Moore study, or a similar exploration of Scripture. If it's in the evening, *you* take care of the children so she can go. Or provide extra money in the budget for Mother's Day Out so she can go during the day if she doesn't work outside of the home.

- Help her find a woman who is ahead of her in life, and encourage her to establish a mentoring relationship. Doing this is *very* important for newlywed wives and new mothers, although a spiritual mentoring relationship is beneficial at every life stage (Titus 2:3–4).

- Come alongside her in assisting her to find the time to read the Scripture and pray daily. Such nourishment for her soul is one of the best investments you can encourage her to make. Look what happens when a person marinates in the Word of God. David wrote, "Oh, how I love your law! I meditate on it all day long . . . I gain understanding from your precepts; therefore I hate every wrong path. Your word is a lamp to my feet and a light for my path" (Ps. 119:97, 104–105).

- Consider participating with her in a *Homebuilders* study group or a small group Bible study. (For details on starting a Homebuilders group, visit FamilyLife.com).

- Be courageous and lead her in finding and plugging in to a church that feeds her, you, and your family the Scripture, one that meets your family's spiritual needs.

- Read the Bible to her daily. I know a woman whose husband has read the Bible to her daily for nearly all of their fifty years together. Not only have they been through the Bible nearly forty times, but the Bible has been through them many more times.

- Take her to a Weekend to Remember marriage conference. (Go to FamilyLife.com and click on *events* for more information.)

Nourish your wife spiritually and she will feel loved and cared for.

3. Taking the Lead in Spiritual Defense

There are certain influences that we should *not* invite into our homes. I'm speaking specifically of the movies rented, the television shows watched, the music and the magazines or books purchased, and the choice of video games played. Paul was clear about this issue: "Whatever is true . . . noble . . . right . . . pure . . . lovely . . . admirable—if anything is excellent or praiseworthy—think about such things" (Phil. 4:8).

We receive many letters from women who long for their husbands to set a high standard in this arena. Far too often Satan gets his toe in the door when a family neglects the application of biblical discernment to its entertainment diet. And it's usually men who want the satellite dish that gets hundreds of channels. What sense does it make to pray for revival in your marriage and home and then give hostile, spiritually bankrupt ideas a free pass?

In the words of Solomon, "Above all else, guard your heart, for it is the wellspring of life" (Prov. 4:23). Early in our marriage, I sought to guard our family's heart by not subscribing to cable television, by establishing standards for video rentals (no R-rated movies), and by canceling a free subscription to *Sports Illustrated* (I like the magazine, but I don't like the swimsuit edition). Whether or not you agree with my actions, the question remains: What are you doing to protect your wife and family spiritually? I challenge you as a man to deny yourself the indulgence of entertainment that is marginal. It wouldn't hurt to ask your wife for her thoughts on this. Or maybe it would!

4. Taking the Lead in Forgiveness

Absolutely nothing paralyzes romance like resentment. Look at Ephesians 4:31 (NASB): "Let all bitterness and wrath and anger and clamor and slander be put away from you, along with all malice." The Scripture commands us to literally stop the attacks on our spouses and stop trying to take out our resentment toward them.

Instead, forgiveness calls us to be "kind and compassionate to one another, forgiving each other, just as in Christ God forgave you" (Eph. 4:32). A Christian marriage is a marriage full of grace, a relationship that says, "Honey, I choose to forgive you even when you aren't acting like you deserve it."

Keep in mind that humility is at the heart of forgiveness. Being humble means being teachable. It's a spiritual receptivity that says, "I am willing to learn what God has for me to learn." It's being quick to admit a mistake or an error and ask for forgiveness. Humility fuels self-denial and puts to death arrogance. There is no greater turnoff for a woman than a man who is arrogant, stubborn, and rebellious, one who is self-centered and refuses to admit fault and seek forgiveness.

Romantic Interlude

Why not set your alarm ten minutes early tomorrow morning?
Slip out of bed, get on your knees in the quietness, and pray over your wife and family. Ask the Lord to rekindle your love for each other.

Remember, Satan would like nothing more than to divide your marriage, to have you become embittered and withdraw from your wife and leave her unprotected. The Scriptures warn that we should not give the enemy a "foothold" in our lives or relationships. We give Satan "leverage" when we allow resentment and bitterness to grow in our hearts. Romance cannot grow in the toxic soil of an embittered heart. Instead, as a spiritual leader, you "must seek peace and pursue it" (1 Peter 3:11). When you do, it's evidence that Jesus Christ is at work in you.

Indeed, when you step up and take your place as the spiritual leader using these four initiatives, you are creating the environment where romance can flourish. Think about it. Your spiritual leadership serves as the first line of defense against the number one enemy of your relationship. What wife wouldn't thrive and respond to her husband when she knows she is spiritually protected?

Awake, north wind, and come, south wind!
Blow on my garden, that its fragrance may spread abroad.
Let my lover come into his garden and taste its choice fruits.

—Song of Solomon 4:16

Chapter 8

SAILING OUT OF
THE DOLDRUMS

t the age of forty-one, Christopher Columbus set sail in 1492. Against the advice of those who thought he'd sail off the edge of the world, he left Spain and headed for the New World. Under favorable winds and a full sail, he could cover a mere 180 miles a day. Not exactly jet speed.

As he sailed across the ocean, his sails went completely limp in a section of the sea near the equator that was void of wind. Columbus and his crew sat like fish in a bucket—going nowhere fast. In fact, the current of the ocean caused him to drift backward.

Desperate and running out of options and supplies, he feared for their lives. What he didn't know was that they were trapped in what is now understood as a regular phenomenon in that part of the ocean called the "Doldrums." It's a section of ocean where the winds die out for weeks at a time. Thankfully, after eight long days, a southeast trade wind began to blow, filling their sails, and off Columbus went to Trinidad and finally the New World.

In many ways, his experience is a picture of what I call the "marital doldrums"—that place where romantic winds cease with no passionate currents to pull us along. We remain listless and wonder why in the early days of marriage we were sailing along just fine, only to find ourselves stagnating as the years roll by.

Any couple can get caught in the doldrums. Sometimes it lasts for a few weeks or months . . . and there are times when the winds *feel* as if they are gone for years.

Many marriages sail into the doldrums and never come out. Over the years Barbara and I have found ourselves with little or no wind in our sails, just like Columbus—but with one difference. Columbus was powerless to "put" wind in his sails. He was stuck until the winds came along. We, however, can be proactive in our marriages to ensure that the winds of romance continue to blow. As we've repeatedly navigated through these times, we've discovered five fresh "winds," five essentials for a marriage to fill its sails and begin cruising again: focus, time, creativity, adventure, and anticipation.

FOCUS

Barbara knows many things are pulling at me on any given day. Demands at the office, personnel issues, my travel schedule, my involvement at church, issues with the children—you name it, my mind is filled with meeting these needs—just as her mind swirls with an extensive To-Do list relative to her activities. When I'm with Barbara, however, she needs me to focus—to concentrate on her needs: her priorities, her challenges, and her dreams.

Focus is undivided attention. I win in my relationship with Barbara when I turn my focus from my list of priorities to zero in on her and to enter her world; when I listen without staring at the television or going through the mail as she talks; and when I respond and dialogue with what she has said.

A great way to focus on your wife is to go on a regular date night. Or consider heading to bed early and asking her how her day was. Focus fosters communication and a connection.

Focus also understands her needs when it comes to romance. Do you recall how she spells it? *Relationship.* Spend energy prayerfully thinking about how you can meet her needs for romance/relationship. Take a sheet of paper, and craft a highly romantic day and evening *for her.* Spell out the specifics of how you intend to focus on her—a love letter, a gift, flowers, a walk, a picnic or a nice meal, a drawn bubble bath, scented candles and a massage. If she likes surprises, then surprise her. And if you don't know what would speak romance to her, ask her and take notes.

TIME

The gift of time is almost as valuable as diamonds to my wife. *Almost.* She knows there might be other things I need to do rather than sit and talk, go for a walk, or take a drive in the country. So when I give her my time, I'm saying to her, "You mean so much to me, of all the things I could do, I want to spend time with you."

Men, hear me on this: romance and relationships will never flourish without time together. I spent the first ten years of our marriage learning and relearning that lesson. One of the best things we did was to take the television out of our kitchen where we ate and out of our bedroom—that TV used to compete for our time together.

Evaluate your schedule. Where can you find time (fifteen to thirty uninterrupted minutes) to try to connect with your wife on a daily basis? For some, that might be early mornings. Others will find that taking a walk after dinner or doing the dishes together is the best option. Jim, married eighteen years, wrote me after attending a *Weekend to Remember*. He said,

> We had a pretty good marriage, but then things sort of leveled off. I decided that I'd try washing the dishes with my wife for just one week. That was seven years ago and we're still doing the dishes together every night. I wouldn't have thought that sharing in the mundane task of conquering the mountain of dishes would actually bring us closer. I cannot think of a better investment of my time than those precious, suds-filled moments.

If that doesn't sound very romantic to you, find what works for you and your wife. When we had teenagers, we used to take a walk in our garden after dinner. The teens cleaned up while we caught up with each other. Whatever activity you choose, the key is to do something that gives your wife the gift of time together.

CREATIVITY

Think back to the things you did when you were dating. You probably invested in cards, flowers, balloons, poems, maybe a picnic or two. A woman responds to creativity because your resourcefulness signals that you expended the energy to think about her, woo her, charm her, and love her in a new way.

When did you last do something *romantically inventive?* Something that she didn't expect? There's nothing like the fresh winds of creativity to fill the sails of your marriage again.

- Like using FedEx to send a love letter or poem.
- Like leaving notes of love and affirmation all over the house or in her car.
- Like giving her a coupon book filled with things you'll do for her.
- Like tenderly touching her hand or face with no sexual strings attached.

Or how about writing five love letters, addressing each to your wife at your home address, and then sending one to the postmaster in each of the following post offices with a note asking him to hand stamp the postmark and mail it back to your wife? You may want to find a special "love" or "romance" stamp to affix to each letter. Send your love letters to the postmaster at these places:

- Romance, AR 72136
- Valentine, TX 79854
- Kissimmee, FL 34741
- Loveland, CO 80537
- Bridal Veil, OR 97010.

ADVENTURE

Your marriage will never outgrow its need for adventure. I'm not suggesting you scale Mount Everest or hang-glide across the Grand Canyon—although there *are* some women who thrive on edgy stuff. While *you* might enjoy that, your wife will probably prefer an adventure that allows for relational time. Barbara really enjoys it when I make all the plans for us to take a weekend trip to a cottage in a remote location not far from home. Our favorite place is by a stream in the woods. No television, no phone, no e-mail or Internet, no newspapers, and definitely no malls. Of course, you could really keep things interesting if you had to hunt or fish for your meals, too. For others, a trip to a big city like New York, Chicago, Washington, D.C., or Los Angeles would present a plethora of adventures—a world class museum, going to the theater, ethnic restaurants, or window shopping at famous stores.

On the front end, whether you "rough it" or not, make sure she knows that on this trip you will avoid the sporting events and all of the distractions that clutter your lives most of the year. We've found that we do better by not scheduling much of anything. She reads while I cook. With no distractions, a couple of nights away have given Barbara and me a relational and romantic oasis. And on a couple of occasions, these getaways gave us the opportunity to encourage each other during some pretty discouraging days.

I believe every couple should plan two or three of these *adventure* weekends a year—away from the routine, the kids, and the house. Rediscover your spouse and what would spell adventure and romance to her. Then make it happen.

ANTICIPATION

Perhaps the most forgotten ingredient to eliminate boredom from a marriage and to maintain the winds of passion is the power of anticipation. When you were dating, you used anticipation frequently.

For example, you might ask her if she's available for a "special" dinner three days in advance. When she says yes, for the next three days you're both anticipating that special time alone—you're thinking about what you'll say and how you can impress her, while she's thinking about how she'll fix her hair and what she'll wear. Anticipation fuels imagination and refocuses you on the relationship, which can ignite romance and passion.

When you marry, you may think the prize is won and the quest is over. You and your wife live under the same roof, and every day begins to look like a carbon copy of yesterday. When there's nothing to anticipate, the relationship can become routine. You stop creating the thoughtful encounters that build excitement.

For example, what would happen if you were to say, "I have a surprise for you next Tuesday at lunch"? All week your wife would be wondering about that surprise. Anticipation adds energy to a relationship and the fun of romance.

Romantic Interlude

When was the last time you took your wife on a picnic?
Why not surprise her this week by arranging for a picnic at the
local park or in the backyard? It doesn't have to be fancy.
Just use a tablecloth and serve sandwiches, grapes, and bottled water.

OKAY, GUYS . . . BARBARA DOESN'T WANT YOU TO MISS THIS

As a man, I like equations and formulas. I like them because the logic rings true. For instance, you can always count on the fact that 2+2=4. The problem is that equations and formulas work in mathematics and science, but they are not always reliable when it comes to romancing our wives. Let me explain.

Let's say that you brought your wife flowers with a nice note and let's say that your thoughtfulness resulted in some nice romance (sex) between the two of you. In a man's way of thinking the next time he is looking for romance, he tries to reduce their relationship to an equation. He reasons, "If flowers resulted in passion and romance the last time, then why not try it again?"

I've done this. Trust me, it doesn't work the way you and I wish that it would.

Here's what's happening. Your wife doesn't want to be "figured out." Barbara once told me that just because $A + B + C = D$ last week, that doesn't mean the same equation works this week. There's a certain mystery to romancing your wife; she's a puzzle that doesn't want to be pieced together, solved and framed on the wall.

Your wife wants you to be a student of her, willing to pursue her in different ways on different days. Why? Because if she feels that she's been "solved," there's no mystery and no reason to pursue her.

Instead, part of the intrigue and the mystery is for you to know what communicates love to her at any given time. Does she need to get out of town for the weekend or just to have a break for an hour? Does she want a full body massage or just a foot rub? Would breakfast in bed make her day, or is taking her to lunch on her menu?

Sometimes she likes a planned surprise—that's when you tell her you've got something special planned for the weekend, but that she'll just have to wait to find out what it is; other times she's impulsive. Sometimes she's in the mood for a soak in the tub; other times she'd prefer a walk in the rain. Focus on what *she* enjoys doing. Make her feel special. Beware of thinking passion and romance are an equation: $A + B + C = D$!

Whenever I don't know what Barbara needs, I ask, "Cookie, what can I do to communicate that I love you?" Usually she'll share some of her needs, or something she needs me to do for her. Sometimes she does not have an answer right off the bat, especially if she hasn't had time to be in touch with her feelings that day. I've learned that her needs change and that I must flex with this mystery of romance and not to take it personally if I don't always get it right.

I've found that when a man invests in focus, time, creativity, adventure, and anticipation, he will enjoy a real relationship with a real person who knows and loves him in ways he never dreamed possible. As I've pursued this kind of relationship with Barbara, she has affirmed me as a man in ways that I never expected.

One example will suffice.

In 1997 we had our 25th anniversary. I spent a year to *focus* on our *time* together. I decided that I was going to be *creative* and really WOW her with an *adventure*—a surprise trip at Christmas time to New York City. I planned it all out—a couple of Broadway shows, a carriage ride in Central Park, shopping at Macy's, plus all the glitz and glitter of New York City at Christmas. Then, in order to surprise her, I told her that we had a "ministry fund raising event" to go to—*that was a big mistake!*

ONE CAUTION: When surprising your wife, make sure the time of the year is a good time for a surprise. I should have just told her what I was doing and given her a year to *anticipate* the celebration of our 25th.

Our time in New York City was a romantic time because of all we did together. I was able to truly surprise her (in a good way) while we were having lunch at Tavern on the Green just on the edge of Central Park. At the end of our meal, the waiter (who wore white gloves) brought a plate with a silver cover. He lifted the silver cover off revealing two roses and a new diamond ring. A friend had given me a special deal on a nice diamond and two sapphires that nestled on either side of the diamond—quite spectacular. There were tears, laughter, more tears, and an embrace. It was an unforgettable lunch. And a very romantic getaway.

You don't need diamonds to hit a home run, but you do need these five essentials—focus, time, creativity, adventure, and anticipation.

Part Two

THE ROMANCE ROBBERS

Catch for us the foxes,
the little foxes that ruin the vineyards,
our vineyards that are in bloom.

—Song of Solomon 2:15

Chapter 9

The Fantasy Foxxx

hink back to the story of Bryan and Angela. One complaint that Angela expressed to Bryan was his lack of attentiveness to their romance. He, in turn, pointed to the busy pace of life, his work, and the kids, which prevented him from making romance a priority.

Like Bryan and Angela, far too many couples find themselves blindsided by jammed schedules, a mountain of bills, over commitments, petty conflicts, the endless needs of the children, and a host of other things that zap marriage of the romantic vitality God intended.

Solomon gave these romance robbers a name: foxes. You see, in Solomon's day foxes presented a real challenge to agriculture. The foxes would sneak in and eat the blossoms while they were still tender, eliminating the possibility of a fruit crop from the vineyard.

Here's the connection to romance.

Solomon used this metaphor to warn couples about the "foxes" that inevitably sneak into our marriages and nip love in the bud. Of course, both husband and wife have a responsibility to maintain the fruitfulness of their marriage by going "fox hunting." However, I believe it is the man's role to take the lead as the protector of the romantic "vineyard" by setting "traps" to eradicate these destructive pests.

In this and the next four chapters, we'll take a look at four of the more tenacious foxes: sexual counterfeits, passivity and indifference, sexual greed, and romantic conflict. There are other foxes, but these bad boys are at the top of the list for us as husbands. By the way, you might want to go on a date with your spouse and come up with your own prioritized list of foxes. Then compare your list of foxes—her list might be a little different from yours.

The first fox in the romance vineyard is *counterfeit pleasure*. This seductive creature lurks in the darkness hoping to ensnare you with pornography, masturbation, or extramarital affairs. This fox nips you when you're tired, alone, angry with your spouse, discouraged . . . and especially when your defenses are down.

His goal? To lure you away from your vow of fidelity to your wife by dangling the carrot of instant gratification before your eyes. This enemy whispers, "Why work so hard to romance your wife? Why wait for her to respond? Why risk rejection—again? If she's not meeting your needs, take care of yourself." Literally.

Romantic Interlude

If you have been unfaithful to your wife through either an affair or pornography, may I encourage you to find a man that you can confide in and seek counsel from? The men I know who have taken this step and the step of confessing this to their wives have found the process painful, yet healing.

We are enticed with the tempting notion that sexual fantasy is harmless—it's our "private business." While these lies are echoed by our sex-crazed culture, nothing could be farther from the truth. Just ask Amber. Her "fiercely loyal" husband of twenty-two years embraced this falsehood with devastating consequences. Amber writes,

> Unbeknown to me, my strong Christian husband, Chris, began a diet of pornography while traveling on business trips. His personality *totally* changed from being kind and

soft-hearted to arrogant, rude, and disrespectful. As always, sin is progressive. I discovered dozens of telephone calls on his cell phone to a number that said, "This is Felicia, please leave a message."

His pornography habit led to his frequenting "happy hours" and singles bars with Felicia, a young divorcee (fifteen years my junior). Chris showered her with flowers, special birthday dinners, and only God knows what else. When I confronted him, he said, "I was tired of not having fun. I deserve to be happy." Chris has now moved out of the house, splitting up our family in the process.

There's a reason why Jesus warned, "I tell you that anyone who looks at a woman lustfully has already committed adultery with her in his heart" (Matt. 5:28). He knew that fantasy and lust were traps for men. When we entertain sexual thoughts about strangers in the theater of our minds, *we give ourselves to those images.* When we invest our sexual energy with others, we will have little or no sexual energy for our wives. Like Chris, we can be led down the pathway of poor choices and, ultimately, devastating consequences, one compromising thought at a time. Or, we can take pleasure in our wife's embrace. Solomon said, "May you rejoice in the wife of your youth . . . May her breasts satisfy you always, may you ever be captivated by her love" (Proverbs 5:18–19).

The trouble with us men is that we underestimate our vulnerability in this area. We tend to think that we're bulletproof. We forget the words of 1 Corinthians 10:12, which warn, "If you think you are standing firm, be careful that you don't fall!" We're seduced into believing that a "little bit of porn" . . . or lingering over the Victoria's Secret catalogue . . . or the swimsuit issue of *Sports Illustrated* . . . or visiting a "marginal" Internet site is no big deal. We can control it.

We also underestimate the power of sin. Someone has said, "Sin would have fewer takers if its consequences occurred immediately."

Sin and death are synonymous. Sin destroys romance and is deadly in a marriage.

But remember Amber's words? "Sin is progressive." Listen to this story from Tom. At fifty-six, this married man of thirty-three years began to dabble in pornography "on the side." Tom wrote me after listening to a broadcast by FamilyLife on the effects of pornography. Tom said,

> Two years ago, I started to use pornography mostly for masturbation. That led to some acting out. I was ultimately arrested for a sex offense. When I didn't come home that evening, my wife and daughter were alarmed and called the police. The next morning as the charges were read against me, my daughter was in the courtroom witnessing the whole shameful event. I wished I were dead.

Imagine how different things might have been for Tom had a friend come alongside him and asked, "How are you feeding your sexual appetite throughout the day? What do your eyes focus on when a woman walks by? What are you watching on TV? What are you permitting your mind to feast on?"

Early in our marriage I made an important discovery about my sex drive. If I spent even an hour in front of the television during what used to be a safe harbor, the "family hour," I noticed that by the time we went to bed, I was ready to be intimate with Barbara, but she was not ready for me! I had to learn to guard my mind from "feeding" on these images which were only serving to prime the pump. Proverbs 4:23 became a life-and-death verse for romance in my marriage: "Guard your heart, for it is the wellspring of life."

If I don't guard my heart, who will?

Solomon's words couldn't be any more relevant than they are today, given the way pornography fuels the Internet. Even with filters, the simple act of checking e-mail can be like walking through an adult bookstore or a red-light district.

Unfortunately rather than guard our hearts against this fox, we're quick to offer a host of "reasons" to justify a well-developed fantasy life. Listen to these candid comments by Christian men I surveyed:

- "I regularly masturbate to relieve stress, tension and to compensate for a lack of sexual satisfaction in my marriage."
- "We've been married fifteen years. I masturbate primarily to deal with the rejection and loathing of my wife."
- "How else can I stay happy with no sex from her? I hate rejection. What, do I smell bad? Why can't we have a great sex life?"
- "It's difficult to see the payoff in putting this sin of masturbation away, since it serves as a pressure release keeping me from 'bothering' my wife."

Their feelings of desperation and pain are evident, however, their self-serving solution is unhealthy. The growing trend today is men who are escaping to the safety of a fantasy at the expense of lost intimacy with their wives.

Now what I'm about to share with you is controversial. But based upon the feedback from our radio listeners and a number of groups that we have informally surveyed: Thirty to forty per cent of married women *desired sexual intimacy more often than did their husbands.* I believe what is happening in many marriages is that the husband becomes tired of being turned down and turned off. Rather than discuss and work through this rejection with his wife in a healthy way, he finds other outlets for his sex drive. I believe many get into pornography and begin masturbating to relieve the sexual tension and pressure.

The result is a vicious cycle: with his sexual energy siphoned off and being drained away, there is little or no compelling reason to pursue his wife as God designed. She begins to wonder why he's not interested in sex as much as he used to be. She doesn't ask. He doesn't tell. Most wives have no idea that married men avoid rejection by taking the "safe" way out and masturbating.

She, in turn, concludes he's no longer interested in her. Which makes her even less responsive to him . . . and so goes the cycle. In the end, the romance dries up, and two lovers become stale mates.

Most wives have no idea how compelling the sex drive is to a man. How could they? Have you ever tried to explain what it's like to your wife? Try finding words to help her understand how much it defines us as men. By the way, if you attempt this in your marriage, there should be *zero* shame in sharing with her how God made you.

How will you handle lust, fantasy, pornography, and masturbation?

Do you want to pursue a relationship with your wife, or retreat to the safety of chasing fantasies? Do you want deep intimacy with a real person, which has its risks and rich rewards? Or do you want the no-risk variety relating to a digital, airbrushed swimsuit model when nobody is looking? Have you wandered off the straight and narrow path, but now desire to win in the real relationship? If so, let me suggest some stepping-stones to get back on track.

DOCTOR, MY EYES

First, I'd start with the understanding that "if we confess our sins, He is faithful and just to forgive us our sins and to cleanse us from all unrighteousness" (1 John 1:9 NKJV). Yes, *embrace God's grace.* Seek the cleansing that comes from a heart that has been touched by forgiveness. Ask Him to renew your mind and to set you free from sin and the bondage of counterfeit pleasure.

I know this sounds like a giant risk, but the second step is to *come clean with your wife.* James urged, "Confess your sins to each other and pray for each other *so that you may be healed*" (5:16, emphasis added). Impossible, you say? Listen to Greg. He writes,

Sixteen years ago I was involved in an adulterous affair with a woman. I was involved with her for over a year. My wife never found out about my sin, although she suspected I was lying to her about the whole affair. My sinfulness has hurt many people, and it has robbed my wife and me of our intimacy.

Last night, I was convicted to confess my sin to my wife. It was one of the hardest things I've ever had to do. She did not respond at all like I had feared she would. She was loving and understanding. She told me she suspected all along and that she had been waiting sixteen years for me to tell her.

I've been in my own prison for the past sixteen years. My unconfessed sin has haunted my dreams and has held me in bondage. Ironically, I am a Prison Guard at a maximum-security prison, yet I've been in my own prison cell for the past sixteen years. Last night I was set free.

Not every woman will respond as graciously as Greg's did. I've known men who have found great "relief" in confessing their sin, however, the husband's betrayal now becomes his wife's burden. Regardless of your wife's response, it would be wise to seek the help of a godly counselor.

Whether you've engaged in an actual affair as Greg did, flirted with an affair of the mind, or escaped to pornography, now is the time to come clean. Jesus said, "If the Son sets you free, you will be free indeed" (John 8:36).

My third encouragement would be to *share your feelings about your sexuality with your bride.* I know that sounds risky. Most men never talk with *anyone* in their lifetimes about such a personal issue—especially not their wives. Still, your marriage will grow as she comprehends the importance of her response when you initiate intercourse.

The best vehicle might be to write a letter to her about how you feel about your sexuality. Include any anxiety you may feel, whether it's about the risk of performance or the fears associated with initiating physical intimacy. Let her know how you feel when she turns you down—not in an attempt to manipulate her, but to bring oneness and further her understanding of your needs. Will this feel awkward? Perhaps.

But don't let that stop you.

The rewards are well worth the risk.

Romantic Interlude

To beat the battle of lust, remove the sources of sexual temptation from your home, including offending magazines and novels, premium cable services, and unfiltered Internet access. Consider reading Stephen Arterburn's *Every Man's Battle* or Randy Alcorn's *The Purity Principle* for encouragement.

Finally, as I can personally attest, *never, ever, drop your guard*. For many years FamilyLife could not afford to send our wives with us as we men traveled and spoke at our *Weekend to Remember* marriage conferences. One Saturday evening in Kansas City, I was exhausted after a full day of speaking. I decided to head back to the hotel and call it a night. Alone inside my room, thankful for the break, I turned on the television and kicked off my shoes.

After I'd been watching the movie for a few minutes, my hotel phone rang. I glanced at the clock, wondering who would be calling so late. *Maybe it's Barbara*, I thought. I answered and heard the sultry voice of a female at the other end. She said, "Hi . . . how are you doing?"

Puzzled, and not wanting to be impolite, I said, "I'm doing fine."

"What are you doing?"

"Watching a movie."

She lowered her seductive voice a notch and said, "Can I come up to your room?"

Although I was alone, tired, and away from my wife, immediately my guard went up. I said, "I don't think that would be a good idea."

She persisted. "Are you sure? Why not?"

"Well, two reasons. Number one, I'm happily married and have been for over ten years. Number two, the movie I'm watching is *The Ten Commandments!*"

Never let down your guard. Peter wisely wrote, "Be self-controlled and alert. Your enemy the devil prowls around like a roaring lion looking for someone to devour" (1 Peter 5:8). Whether it's the advances of another woman or another siren call of temptation, "God is faithful; he will not let you be tempted beyond what you can bear. But when you are tempted, he will also provide a way out so that you can stand up under it" (1 Cor. 10:13).

Yes, temptation is powerful, and it lures us by promising counterfeit pleasure. The following letter I received from a listener to *FamilyLife Today* demonstrates the *real cost* of caving in to sin:

> Our problem is intimacy. My husband is strongly into pornography and that takes up his sexual energy. The more he succumbs to the calling of his sinful nature, the less hope there is for us. You see, he's already reached a point where the only satisfaction he gets is self-satisfaction. I find myself ashamed and defiled by my husband's actions. His spiritual walk has been a yo-yo because of his inability to give up his life of sin. He won't seek help and now, when we try to be intimate, he cannot complete the act.

What about it? God has given you and me only a certain amount of sexual energy to pursue our wives romantically and intimately. Will you turn away from the imposters and turn toward a real relationship with a real person? If so, why not do as Job did? He said, "I made a covenant with my eyes not to look lustfully at a girl" (Job 31:1).

May God enable you to catch this fox and keep him caged.

There is no fear in love.
But perfect love drives out fear.
1 JOHN 4:18

Chapter 10

WHEN SHE'S INTERESTED AND YOU'RE NOT

L et me make something clear up front.

You might be tempted to think that there would *never* be a time when you, as a man, would turn down the sexual advances of your wife. Or, if for some reason you did, your rejection would be as rare as the appearance of an albino zebra. I understand that feeling. If such is the case with you, feel free to move on to the next chapter. On the other hand, you might want to read on to better understand what is becoming a growing phenomenon among men. Some estimates I've seen place this lack of interest in sex by men at upwards of twenty-percent or higher. While this represents a minority position, it's one problem we continue to hear about from those who get in touch with FamilyLife and, as such, worthy of our attention.

Take, for example, Svetin Gulisija, a twenty-six-year-old man living in Croatia. Not long ago, he came home from a hard day on the job. For reasons I'll never fully understand, Svetin decided the last thing he wanted was sex with his wife, Oleandra. As the story goes, she was in the mood to spark a little romance. He, however, was too tired and wanted to be left alone.

His solution?

White hot with anger, Svetin stormed out of his house and started a fire in the woods behind his home. Pause with me to consider the irony of this true story. Here's a guy who was too tired to be physically intimate with his wife, and yet he had enough energy to launch a fireball in the backyard! It boggles the mind.

As you might imagine, the flames quickly blazed out of control. Local firefighters had to race to their home and evacuate the couple. When police asked Svetin what inflamed him to do such a thing, he explained that he was fighting fire with fire. He did it so he wouldn't have to have sex with his wife.

Talk about a burned-out lover.

Granted, most men don't go to such drastic measures to avoid intimacy in marriage. And while Svetin's method of communicating a lack of interest in sex is an extreme case, male passivity toward physical intimacy is a very real problem in 20 to 30 percent or more of the couples we hear from. I'll give you three examples. Casey writes,

> It seems like every article I read talks about a man's high sex drive and how women are typically tired and not interested in sex. The opposite is true of my husband and me. I try to get him aroused and interested in sex, but he is never really in the mood nor is he affectionate to me.
>
> He expects me to let him know when I want to be intimate, and I need to do the seducing. This is really hurting our marriage, and I am resentful of his lack of interest. I try to be as attractive and sexy as I can, but nothing seems to work. Do you have any advice?

Likewise, Laura, the mother of three children, feels abandoned by a husband who leaves the loving to her. She writes,

> I fear that my husband and I have reversed roles in our marriage. I am always the one who initiates intimacy and

sex. He is the one who doesn't have the time or energy to be with me. He doesn't ask me out or make special plans for us to be together. His list of "reasons" is endless. This leaves me feeling unloved, undesirable, and rejected. I don't think that my husband looks at our physical intimacy as a gift from God that should be celebrated.

The following letter reveals how devastating such rejection can be for a woman. After attending a marriage conference, Amy included this note in her evaluation:

My husband and I have been married for 8 months. I am 38 and he is 44—both first time marriages. However, intimacy in our relationship is almost non-existent. He seems pretty much disinterested and 99 percent of the time rejects me when I try to initiate lovemaking. I have tried to talk to him about it but he says there is no problem. I, on occasion, will arrange a "special evening" to get him in the mood and then it seems to be okay. But this is few and far between. The rejection I am experiencing has become almost too much to bear.

While it is much more likely that you are the one experiencing the rejection, if you have been rejecting the advances of your wife, my intention is not to heap guilt on you, but to help you understand what may be going on in you and in your marriage. When a man shows little or no sexual interest in his wife, she will experience several emotions. First, she's going to feel she is undesirable as a wife and a woman. She's going to wonder, "Am I attractive?", "What's wrong with me?", and "Does he love me?" A woman whose husband is usually disinterested is going to profoundly feel rejected (just as a man feels rejected when his wife shows a disregard for his sexual needs).

Romantic Interlude

One way to signal sexual interest while minimizing verbal rejection is to light a candle on the nightstand. If you're interested, light your candle. If she's interested, she lights her candle. If the desire is mutual, both will light their candles . . . and let the sparks follow you to bed.

God's design is for a man to "be united to his wife, and they will become one flesh" (Gen. 2:24). God created sex in marriage to be shared, not withheld. And when romance, tenderness, and sex are not shared, a sense of loneliness sets in that can ultimately result in emotional and sexual temptation. As Barbara mentioned earlier in this book (in Chapter 8 for women), there's a reason why so many women read romance novels—they are vicariously looking for what they are not getting at home.

Physical intimacy is not optional in marriage. When you ignore this God-given command to cultivate intimacy and romance with your wife, she is left with a void in her soul. Your romantic and sexual advances have tremendous power to set her apart as a woman and affirm her value. But rejection in the bedroom places her on emotional quicksand. Carla, a listener, writes,

> My husband has no desire to make love to me. I have to initiate all of the encounters, most of the time unsuccessfully. I felt rejected on a nightly basis so I took a night shift job so I wouldn't cry myself to sleep each night.

You see, Carla's femininity is really on the line. Often, a woman like Carla will struggle to try harder to be the "perfect wife." She'll spend hours, even days, trying to understand why she is so undesirable. As she spins her wheels, there may come a point where she will be tempted by an extramarital affair.

I can't stress this strongly enough: *a marriage devoid of romance and sexual appreciation with each other is not how God designed marriage to function.* God gave us romance in marriage so that we could frequently celebrate our love—spiritually, emotionally, and physically. As you discover ways to romance your wife and learn how to serve each other, you grow together as a couple. You and your wife "become one."

As a man, if you are not initiating on a regular basis, let me encourage you to take an honest inventory of what may be causing your lack of sexual desire. Since the sales of drugs like Viagra, Levitra, and Cialis (all of which address erectile dysfunction) may approach $2 billion in 2004, many men may think the problem is physical.

But a physician I interviewed while researching this book told me the problem for most men is not inadequate desire or erectile dysfunction. It's often a dysfunction of the heart—anger, resentment, and bitterness.

What kind of kiss do you want: sweet, spicy, or "Whoa, Nellie!"?

YOU'VE LOST THAT LOVIN' FEELING

Let's look inward for a moment with a series of questions to see if something is short-circuiting what is a normal, God-given drive. *Are you angry or bitter at your wife? Is there a reason for your anger?*

Has she wronged you? Has she disappointed you? Mocked you? If so, consider Colossians 3:13, "Bear with each other and forgive whatever grievances you may have against one another. Forgive as the Lord forgave you."

Is your sexual desire being siphoned off and satisfied by a regular diet of pornography and masturbation? For many men, as we discussed in the last chapter, pornography has become the preferred expression of their sexuality because it represents a "no risk" and "no failure" approach to sex.

Are you driven at work to such a point that you are totally spent when you get home? Some men are out of touch with their emotions simply because they're working too hard. Like Svetin the "burned out lover" I mentioned, they are so spent by sixteen- or eighteen-hour days, they have nothing left to invest in their marriages.

Are you in denial about some other type of sin in your life? Sin can suppress our most powerful appetites.

Do your wife's past sexual experiences before marriage anger you or intimidate you?

Did someone touch you inappropriately when you were a boy? Past sexual abuse can truly inhibit healthy sexual expression in marriage. Did you grow up in a family where you were made to think sex was dirty? Were you made to feel shame for your interest in sex? Were you caught viewing pornography or masturbating?

Are you hiding something from your wife? Perhaps a previous sexual encounter, an affair, or the practice of homosexuality.

Could it be that you tried to initiate at a point early in your marriage and you failed to perform or your wife rejected you? Is the risk of failure simply too great now? Or are you withdrawing from her sexually as a strategy to protect yourself?

If none of these questions raises an issue that applies to your situation, there may be a possibility that your body produces a lower-than-average amount of testosterone. There are a host of reasons why these levels may be reduced, including the use of certain antidepressant or blood pressure medicines. Your doctor can measure your body's testosterone production and perhaps prescribe a treatment to return it to normal levels.

Whatever the reason, *a man who refuses to address his low libido and meet his wife's needs is putting his marriage at great risk.*

If you are wrestling with this issue, and if talking with your wife about it is too difficult, seek help. Find a pastor, a counselor, or another godly man in whom you can confide. Do it for the sake of your marriage and family. Step out of the shadows of isolation and into the healing from the One who gives "every good and perfect gift" (James 1:17).

He can and will help you rekindle the sexual side of romance with your wife. And for the record, starting a fire in your backyard is not what God has in mind.

Each of you should look not only to your own interests,
but also to the interests of others. Your attitude should be
the same as that of Christ Jesus.

—Philippians 2:4–5

Chapter 11

WHEN LOVE TAKES A BACKSEAT TO SEXUAL GREED

ou might be tempted to think this is one chapter you can skip. Hold on. Before you jump ahead, let me ask you a few questions. Does your wife have the freedom to say no to your sexual advances without fear of experiencing your displeasure? If she says, "Not tonight, dear," what will you do?

Will you get angry? Seethe? Withdraw? Pout? Sulk?

Do you pressure her and insist that she "do the deed" because that's what she is "supposed to do" as your wife? Do you play the "submission" card because you think God is on your side? Do you use your words to manipulate her or heap guilt on her just to get your way in the bedroom? Do you find yourself making her "pay" for her rejection the next day or two by giving her the cold shoulder?

Or do you ask her for a romantic rain check and find a non-sexual way to love on her in spite of your disappointment? And will she still feel safe in your love after she's said no several times?

You see, sexual greed occurs anytime a man *demands or insists* on using his wife's body for his selfish purposes. Such greed is never mutual because greed makes no provision for the feelings of others. Take, for example, this gritty letter I received from Velvet, a thirty-year-old woman. Even when she attempted to satisfy her husband, his greedy, self-absorbed behavior devalued their intimacy and her. Velvet wrote me a pretty pointed letter:

> I went out of my way to please my husband sexually and he enjoyed it. But he didn't return the affection or the passion. After he was aroused, we proceeded with intercourse which left me unsatisfied when it was over. I tried to encourage him to touch me and kiss me—he would for a few seconds, but then it was back to business. It's as though my body parts are switches and if the switch doesn't go on at the flick of the wrist, well, that's my problem.
>
> Needless to say, over the years this has made me draw back. I've lost my playfulness. I now know what women mean when they say they just feel like a hole for their husbands to use to masturbate. It's a crude way to explain it, but that's exactly how I feel. I feel as if I am not worth the effort.

Do you see how a woman could feel? Rather than feeling like the cherished focus of his affection and a partner in rich lovemaking, Velvet has been reduced to an object. When a man like this insists on "taking what's *rightfully* his" without regard to the relational or sexual needs of his spouse, he damages his wife and his relationship.

Just getting married does not give a man total freedom over his wife with no regard for her feelings and desires. Marriage does not give him a free pass to use his wife as an object. A man was always intended to love his wife with a *sacrificial love*: "Husbands, love your wives, just as Christ also loved the church and gave Himself for her" (Eph. 5:25 NKJV). That means to care for her, nourish her, and cherish her with love, giving her the dignity with which God created her.

WHEN THE SHOE
IS ON THE OTHER FOOT

I should point out that sexual greed and sexual selfishness are not just male problems. Women are sometimes guilty of them too. The most irresponsible and destructive example of sexual selfishness I've seen is found in this letter from Nicole, a listener to *FamilyLife Today*. Nicole has been married a number of years, and her husband desires physical intimacy, which, as we've discussed, is his top romantic need. She has zero interest in sex. In no uncertain terms, she has selfishly drawn a line in the sand.

This is not a conflict—it's not even a skirmish. It's an all-out war. Nicole writes with a scorching pen:

> Your programs about "marital intimacy" make me mad. Here is a news flash: After the first few years, married women do not want sex. *DO NOT WANT IT.* Men, on the other hand, believe they are ENTITLED to it. So what do you do? You quote Scripture out of context to try and validate what is men's lack of self-control and an unwillingness to grow up.
>
> You also recruit a couple of insipid Southern belles [a reference to two radio show guests on *FamilyLife Today*] to give credence to your notions and to try and make women second-guess their instincts. About thirty years ago, the columnist Ann Landers surveyed her readers about marital sex. Overwhelmingly, married women said, "No thanks." She repeated the survey about ten years later. Same response. Men freaked out, of course assuming something was wrong with the women instead of accepting that it is normal for the spark to die a natural death.
>
> Listen, fellows, there are more important things in life

than keeping your britches happy. The time comes when you must tuck it away. Accept it. Try. Don't "guilt trip" women into something they do not want just because you can't control your hormones.

My heart goes out to Nicole. I have to wonder how she has been "damaged" sexually at the hands of men. But she has no idea how much damage she's inflicting on her husband. Her cold, harsh, selfish attitude belittles him as a person and his manhood.

Just as Nicole's attitude of rejection is damaging to a marriage, the same could be said when a wife feels pressured to perform against her wishes. How do we guard against such greed from either side of the bed?

One antidote to sexual greed is a recommitment to love your wife with a love that is *not* focused on your needs as a man.

A man who loves his wife as Christ loves the church sets aside his sexual agenda and is sensitive to the needs of his bride. He gives her the freedom to respond rather than forcing his desires on her. (I'd encourage you to read how I came to grips with "giving my wife freedom" when we experienced an unforgettable night in Mexico. See page 51 in the women's section). That's a lesson Andrea's husband hasn't learned. This hardworking wife home schools five children under the age of fourteen. In spite of the fact that she suffers from rheumatoid arthritis, her husband puts intense pressure on her to perform sexually without regard to her physical limitations. Worse, his idea of physical intimacy appears to have its roots in pornography. Andrea, one of our radio listeners, writes,

My husband wants to have sex *every* night. We usually have sex about once in every three nights. Sometimes we'll manage every other night. My problem is that he wants me to be very aggressive and sluttish. Please put me with someone in my same situation so I can talk to them and find out how to make myself do this. I like romantic, soft, and happy. He wants dirty, hard, and angry.

A man should never pressure his wife against her will into engaging in acts that make her feel threatened, violated, or demeaned. Such behavior really should have no place in a marriage. The apostle Paul wrote, "Among you there must not be even a hint of sexual immorality, or of any kind of impurity, or of greed, because these are improper for God's holy people" (Eph. 5:3).

Look, I'm all for creative sexual play in the bedroom. I encourage fresh ways to be intimate . . . just as long as both husband and wife agree and the practices don't violate Scripture.

Man to man, if you haven't already done this, I'd like to challenge you to do something radical: formally give your wife the freedom to say no to your sexual advances. Pledge to her that you will not manipulate her, control her, or get angry at her.

You know what those words of self-denial will do for her? They'll unlocked her heart. They'll remove the pressure of performance from her. They'll valued her. In that moment, she'll know that you treasure her as a whole person—not just for what she can do for you in bed. Self-denial is an additional way to defeat sexual greed in your marriage.

Romantic Interlude

One of the best questions a man could ask his wife regarding their sexual intimacy is, "Sweetheart, when I make love to you, do you feel loved by me?" If she says, "Yes, sometimes," or "Yes, most of the time," ask her, "How can I do a better job of loving you?" If she answers, "No, I don't feel loved," ask her, "What can I do to help you feel loved by me?"

I want to make one more very important point about this because I am a man—I *do* understand what it is like to *need* to be with my wife. Nevertheless, you and your wife *must* discuss what she wants you to do with your sexual desire for her. Help her understand in a loving way that there is no other person on the planet who can meet your need. This does not have to be a repeated point of contention in your marriage. You *can* talk it out. If you find this too difficult to tackle one on one, or, if she appears to be immovable in her understanding of your sexual needs, seek godly counseling. Do *not* allow this problem to persist. Seek help.

As you work toward this understanding, know this: self-denial is the basis for a great marriage and great romance. A man practicing self-denial on behalf of his wife tells her that she is valued and loved as a partner. If you have difficulty practicing self-denial, pray that you'll become a man who knows how to deny himself for his wife. Does this sound like a downer? Be encouraged. I am personally aware of a number of men who had to practice self-denial for several years but who are now enjoying the fruits of their patience.

While you're at it, pray for your wife that she'll feel loved when you initiate sexual love with her. If you and your wife are believers in Jesus Christ, the Holy Spirit will guide you into becoming better lovers. Invite the Holy Spirit to come into your bedroom and bless your marriage with passion and romance. Remember, the God of the universe created and designed romantic love in the first place.

You may think, *The Holy Spirit wants to help us be better lovers?* Absolutely. Paul said, "My God will meet all your needs according to his glorious riches in Christ Jesus" (Phil. 4:19). He didn't say, "All of your needs *except* sex." The Holy Spirit can teach us to better understand each other's needs. He can empower us to defeat selfishness. He comforts us when our needs may not be fully met. And the Holy Spirit can bring peace and harmony where there are discord and frustration *if* you both submit to Him.

The Top Ten Most Romantic Things to Do for Your Wife

FamilyLife surveyed nearly one thousand couples to identify the top ten most romantic expressions a man can offer as he pursues his wife. Keep in mind, your wife is uniquely created by God. She has her own idea of what is romantic to her. Use this top ten list as a place to start. Consider going on a date and giving her this list and asking her to personalize it according to her priorities.

10. *Holding hands.* Whether for a moment or much longer, hold hands while driving, walking, sitting in church, or talking in bed.

9. *Massage.* Give foot rubs, back rubs, neck rubs, or a body massage. Don't miss the feet—the Chinese have suggested for centuries that certain areas of the foot are connected to every organ in the body!

8. *Acts of service.* Remember the common courtesies: opening the door, serving her, pulling a chair out for her, offering your arm while walking, or giving her a break from the kids.

7. *A kiss.* Give her a kiss. Nibble on the back of her ear or her neck, or just kiss each other before leaving for work or at the end of the day when coming home. Or, try locking lips for a full ten seconds—many couples have forgotten the power of a nice, gentle, prolonged kiss.

6. *Walking together.* Early morning, after dinner, or as the sun sets, walking *just as a couple* is best.

5. *Something written.* Leave notes, letters, poems, cards, messages on the bathroom mirror, or creative written reminders of affection somewhere she'll find them.

4. *Going out on a date.* A weekly date without the kids can be a lifesaver for your romance. Take her to dinner and/or the theater; go on a drive, antiquing, window-shopping, or some special place she's been talking about.

3. *Meals.* Have a quiet meal together with candlelight, linger over breakfast, or go on a picnic. Get dressed up and go to a nice restaurant. Definitely not fast food!

2. *Touch.* Use nonsexual touch: holding her, hugging her, cuddling with her, or placing an arm around her in public. Cradling her face in your hands and looking into her eyes, and gently rubbing her back can communicate tender love to your wife.

1. *Flowers.* Deliver, hand-pick, or bring home a single rose. It's the gold standard, men. You can't go wrong. Tulips are a great second choice.

*For if you forgive men when they sin against you,
your heavenly Father will also forgive you. But if you do not
forgive men their sins, your Father will not forgive your sins.*
—MATTHEW 6:14–15

Chapter 12

OUTFOXING
THE FOXES

Barbara and I surveyed more than a thousand couples and were stunned to learn that more than 50 percent *never* discuss the romantic conflict in their relationship. Romantic conflict occurs for a variety of reasons, including when one person desires sex and the other doesn't; when one person desires to try something new in the lovemaking, but their idea is rejected; or when something special is planned, but those plans have to be abandoned because of a miscommunication. Most couples don't start out this way. When they are first married, couples may attempt to discuss their romantic differences, even argue or have emotionally heated quarrels. However, after repeated disappointments, misunderstanding abounds, and they stop trying.

Rather than try to talk it out, they give up and retreat. They might bury it or give in to placate their mates—anything to avoid dealing openly with it. Romantic conflict occurs in all marriages. The problem is that we are not handed a manual when we get married that helps us to deal with unmet needs and disappointments—especially regarding sex.

The truth is, based upon our twenty-eight years of experience with training almost a million couples at our conferences and events, we now know that most couples don't have good skills in resolving general conflicts in marriage. No other area of marriage, with the exception of money management, begins to approach the intensity of romantic conflict.

Romantic Interlude

If you have a difficult time expressing your feelings or disappointment about the bedroom, try writing out your thoughts in a card, a note, or even an e-mail. Consider using phrases like "I feel . . . , I think . . . , I hope . . . , I'd like . . . , I choose . . . , and I dream . . ." Avoid using phrases such as "You always . . ." and "You never . . ."

Andy, who attended the *Rekindling the Romance* arena event in Orlando, Florida, said, "Romantic conflict is the elephant in the living room that we don't talk about. In twenty-two years we haven't figured out how to resolve it." How about you? When conflict in the bedroom wrinkles your sheets, do you get angry? Do you fight? Withdraw? Retreat? Or have you decided to ignore it?

In a moment, I want to get real practical and give you four disciplines that will equip you to catch this fox *together*. But first, let's pinpoint the six primary causes of romantic conflict:

1. *Wrong timing.* He initiates, but she's too exhausted. She takes the lead, but he's got a deadline to meet at work. Maybe both plan a romantic evening, and then something unexpected comes up. Allergies, a crisis with a child or family member, or a phone call can put a chill on the evening.

2. *Different needs.* Frequency, variety, and creativity in lovemaking are constant sources of conflict. One wants more sex; the other desires less. One is content with vanilla; the other wants thirty-one flavors . . . all in one night.

3. *Different expectations.* When they finally get alone, she has relationship on her mind. She wants to cuddle, talk, and share dreams for an hour, but it's been some

time since they've been together sexually, and he wants to go for the goal. Or, when both are anticipating sex, perhaps he wants a five-course feast, and she wants a quick snack.

4. *Selfishness.* She needs to warm up, but he's already fired up. Or he's given all day to meet her relational needs, yet she selfishly withholds physical intimacy. In some cases, it boils down to a simple unwillingness to be responsive to meet the unique romantic needs of a spouse.

5. *Fear and insecurity.* Many couples don't trust each other with such intimate longings. Maybe they've been abused emotionally or sexually, they've been hurt in a previous relationship, or they're afraid the spouse won't give respect when honest feelings are shared.

6. *Wrong attitude about sex, passion, and romance.* Some may have a twisted view of romance because of past abuse; they may think God doesn't want a couple to enjoy sex. Others may have developed a warped picture of intimacy from their obsession with porn or romance novels. Some women wrongly use sex as a "reward" for performance when he, for example, does something on her honey-do list rather than as an expression of love and oneness.

No matter what the reason for the romantic conflict in your marriage, your bedroom doesn't have to resemble a battleground. I believe God desires for you and your wife to experience pleasure that is downright *thrilling.* How? For most it begins as we address and resolve our romantic conflicts. For others, they may need help from a skilled biblical counselor. They may be dealing with such serious scars and problems from the past that it's going to take a wise, godly counselor to help them get out of the ditch.

But most couples who practice four disciplines in marriage will begin to resolve romantic conflict in the right way: (1) they pray, (2) they talk, (3) they listen, and (4) they forgive.

1. Fight Back on Your Knees

Ephesians 6 tells us that our struggle is not against flesh and blood, but against the spiritual forces of evil. The apostle Paul made it very clear: your wife is not your enemy. In fact, as I pointed out in an earlier chapter, the devil has your marriage in his crosshairs. His goal is to isolate you from each other. He wants you detached, especially in the area of sex and romance. It's never a matter of just trying harder. Regardless of your situation, the hope we offer for your marriage begins and ends with God.

The spiritual discipline of daily prayer together invites God into your marriage. And when God is there, He is *the* One who can change things. He enables you to defeat selfishness. He can give you an understanding heart. He can cleanse resentments and replace them with forgiveness.

There is nothing more powerful in a marriage than a couple addressing Almighty God together. Bringing your needs before Him. Praying for each other that you may not be tempted. Confessing your sins to Him together. Giving thanks for your circumstances together.

The reason I encourage you to pray is that the Holy Spirit knows *exactly* what you need. No friend or advisor knows you better than God Himself. He will lead and guide you as you approach your wife. He will give you the words and the right attitude as you love her, pursue her and lead her spiritually.

I can assure you there have been many times when I have fervently asked God to know how to better love Barbara and understand how to resolve conflict with her. As I have asked for wisdom, I've watched God heal hurts, replace strife with peace, and enable us to keep on loving each other for more than three decades.

2. Talk Respectfully to Her

Ephesians 4:15 (NASB) offers a great command to apply in every marriage: "Speaking the truth in love, we are to grow up in all aspects into Him, who is the head, even Christ."

For some, it's easy to speak the truth but more difficult to do it in love. For others, it's easy to love but not so easy to speak the truth. For a relationship to grow, truth and love must be held in proper tension with each other.

"Hey Gorgeous, why don't you slip out of that nightgown? It just makes you look fat anyway."

Early in our marriage I had a tendency to use the truth like a jackhammer. Imagine being married to a person who in a rat-a-tat-tat manner keeps driving his point home. I've had to learn to ask God to help me measure my words with Barbara and sift them through love. You can ask her. It's a whole lot easier to hear what's being said if it's being said "in love."

You may want to do what I did: Ask the Holy Spirit to put a muzzle on your mouth. Ask Him to grab hold of your emotions so you can speak the truth in a loving way. If you have a hot temper, learn to remain silent and cool down before speaking. Learn the art of speaking respectfully to your wife.

The goal is not to win the argument or assign blame. Rather, the goal is to experience a rich, passionate, fulfilling marriage. Just being polite to each other when you talk goes a long way toward experiencing love. As Peter said, "Above all, love each other deeply, because love covers over a multitude of sins" (1 Peter 4:8).

Romantic Interlude

Disagreements and misunderstandings are inevitable in our conversations. The next time things heat up, rather than sniping at each other or avoiding contact, try saying, "Honey, you may be right. Help me understand why you feel that way."

---

3. Now Can You Hear Me?

It's been said that God gave us two ears and only one mouth because we ought to be listening twice as much as we speak. In the heat of the conflict, my tendency has been to formulate a defensive response while Barbara was still expressing herself. I've learned I'm *not* a good listener when I am crafting my defense.

To avoid this, I've found it helpful to recap what Barbara has said. For instance, I try to say, "Honey, let me see if I've got this right . . . ," and then repeat back to her what I think she said.

This demonstrates that I received her message or, if necessary, gives her an opportunity to clarify her point of view. Doing this was especially helpful during the first few years of marriage when we were trying to get on the same wavelength. Over time, my ears have been tuned to better receive her message. If the reception was still fuzzy, I'd ask God to help me better understand my wife.

Just as we saw in the fictional account of Bryan and Angela, it also helps to try to "feel" what the other is "feeling." Take a moment and think about the context of her life: Is there stress? Exhaustion? Illness? Is she discouraged? In need of a break? Weary of meeting everyone's needs? What exactly is going on in her life? In other words, good listeners do more than hear the words their spouse is saying; they *feel* what their spouse is feeling.

It always helps to ask your wife questions to gain an understanding of her feelings. For example, say, "How could I have worded my comment in a way that didn't feel like a put-down to you?" Being a good listener is a prerequisite to becoming a great lover!

Romantic Interlude

When possible, avoid late night romantic approaches. If you watch the evening news or check your e-mails late at night, don't expect to repeatedly slide into bed at 11:30 p.m. and have a wonderful time of passion. Try turning off the television and the computer, locking the bedroom door, and going to bed at 9:00.

---

4. Forgive and Forget

As I've pointed out, romance and resentment cannot exist in the same heart. Resentment will extinguish the embers of romance. That's why forgiveness is such an essential discipline in marriage. Forgiveness says, "By forgiving you, I give up all my rights to punish you for how you've hurt me. I no longer hold it against you, expecting you to pay for your transgressions." When you forgive your spouse, you choose to relinquish your rights to hold it against her.

Be specific as you do. Say, "You know, last night I'm sorry that I was not sensitive to your needs for space and that I didn't deal with you honorably. Will you forgive me?"

If you've wronged your spouse by pressuring her for sex or by acting rude and hurting her feelings, don't rest until you've apologized. Saying, "I'm sorry you feel that way," or "I'm sorry you felt hurt," is *not* seeking forgiveness. Instead, try saying, "I was wrong to pressure you. Will you forgive me?"

On the other hand, if she's wronged you, once she's understood how she's hurt you, *release her*. Don't hold her hostage. In both cases, we ought to act compassionately with one another. After all, we are a forgiven people called by God to forgive others. How did Christ forgive us? Repeatedly. Generously. Freely.

NOTHING BUT BLUE SKIES AND SMOOTH SAILING

Does resolving romantic conflict sound like too much work? Or are you waiting for her to take the first step? Justin, who attended our *Rekindling the Romance* event, once felt that way. He wrote,

> When we experienced conflict, my tendency was to clamp down and go inside of my shell. I had to learn to be brave and go in there and be the first to say, "I'm sorry . . . I was wrong" and remind my wife how important she was to me. I'm glad I did. When I didn't find the guts to do that quickly, I just ruined our future romance and prolonged the discord.

Romantic conflict can be, as Andy put it, the "elephant in the room" that nobody talks about, or it can be used by God to help you grow closer to each other. The choice is yours. You can be like Andy who, after twenty-two years of marriage, still doesn't address romantic conflict. Or, you can do as Justin did by taking the lead when romantic conflict arises—after all, making up is half the fun!

Love Like a Man

What does it take to become the romantic man of your wife's dreams? As you'll discover in the pages ahead, the key is learning to be fluent in her romantic love language.

- *A romantic man* engages his wife in a living and growing *relationship* without losing sight that physical intimacy is an important part of that relationship in marriage.
- *A romantic man* commits to learning nonsexual ways to love his wife while nurturing in her the freedom to be sexually responsive.
- *A romantic man* can kiss, hug, touch, and cuddle without a sexual agenda while helping his wife embrace the joy of sex at the right time.
- *A romantic man* does not pressure his wife into having sex, nor does he retreat from the pursuit of sexual oneness.
- *A romantic man* connects to his wife's world, supports, listens, and shares his heart with no sexual strings attached while being confidently aware that sexual intimacy is vital to the survival of his marriage.
- *A romantic man* will do all of these things even when his spouse is sexually unresponsive, knowing that he is called to love his wife as Christ loved the church.

As a man, you can learn to speak your wife's language of romantic love and still be fully a man, a sexual man whose sexual desires were blessed by God and created for His purposes. Remember: There is no shame, no condemnation, and no apology for fully being a man.

Part Three

Fire
the Desire

FIRE THE DESIRE

INTRODUCTION

For years I viewed myself as a very romantic man.

I planned a number of surprise trips for Barbara. I wrote her notes of love and endearment. I committed to going on a weekly date night with her to give us a chance to connect. I've bought a boatload of flowers, cards, gifts, and keepsakes. As I shared earlier, I even swept her off her feet with a modest upgrade of her wedding ring after our silver anniversary. Indeed, I was feeling pretty good about myself as a romantic until I met the Kings of Romance, Mark Montgomery and his crew of truly romantic men.

At forty-two, this pastor in Toledo, Ohio, blew me out of the water with what has to be the ultimate romantic gesture. Mark was enthralled with love for his wife. And yet he was convicted that he hadn't demonstrated his affection appropriately. Wanting to publicly honor his bride, Mark gathered fifteen men who felt they were in the same boat.

They called themselves the Men of the *Titanic*. For six months, this band of brothers carefully and secretly planned to re-create dinner on the *Titanic*. The meal, served at a local hotel, was to be an exact replica of the meal served in the first-class dining hall the night the *Titanic* sank. It was the night that courageous husbands gave up their lives for their wives.

They decorated the hall in nautical themes. They took lessons in how to properly serve the meal. They practiced a Victorian-style courtesy bow. Each table setting included a corsage, and the napkin was embroidered with a ship, the date, and the lady's name.

On the night of the main event, the women were picked up by a chauffeur who handed them personalized invitations from their husbands. As the women entered the banquet hall, their names were formally announced. A harpist played as each of the eight meal courses was marked by the sounding of a ship's bell. The men took turns singing songs or demonstrating a preplanned act of affection throughout the unforgettable night.

As the evening sailed to a close, each man offered his bride an elegant love letter printed on parchment, rolled into a scroll, and tied with a red ribbon. After dessert was served, the Men of the *Titanic* stood and sang "Nearer My God to Thee" and then shared the story of how the band on the *Titanic* played that song on the bow as the ship sank beneath the waves.

But wait, there's more.

Four years later, Mark and the men were inspired by the biblical idea of a woman of "noble character" found in Proverbs 31. This time the men decided to go on "quests" for their wives, much as the knights of old did for their queen. Each man planned his quest according to what he knew his wife would cherish. One man gave up smoking. One wrote a love letter every week for several months. Another journaled to his wife every day. Several banded together and delivered food to the homeless in the names of their wives.

Behind the scenes, they made arrangements with the Lucas Soil and Water Conservation District, near Toledo, to transform a muddy field into an "enchanted forest." There they planted 1,325 trees in honor of their wives and placed a plaque with the names of their wives. Meanwhile, as they carried out their quests, they planned a grand finale—an entire weekend at the Sawmill Creek Resort in Ohio.

When the weekend arrived, they served the women a banquet once again, this time with a medieval theme. As they served, they sang songs, described their quests, and honored the women as if they were great queens of history. Each man stood and paid homage to his wife. The Tommy Dorsey Band provided music and dancing (complete with lessons).

If you're like me, hearing such inspiring stories of love, valor, commitment, and service might start to feel a bit overwhelming. Keep in mind, these were not superheroes. These were average men who decided to exert above-average effort to cherish their wives with what we call "event romance." There is definitely a place for such mountaintop romantic experiences, and you might one day feel up to the challenge to create your own Men of the *Titanic* experience.

But there's another side to this coin. I call it "everyday romance."

There are endless ways to communicate affection and to spark romance in the heart of your wife that can be done on a shoestring budget. Need a few suggestions? The following five chapters provide you with everything you need to get started. Keep in mind that these five ideas *speak the romantic love language of your wife*. You'll be romancing her with relational-oriented projects.

Meanwhile, Barbara will be offering your wife a few tips on how to romance *you* in ways that you'll really appreciate. After trying these ideas (which get progressively more involved, but certainly nothing on the scale of the *Titanic*), get a copy of *Simply Romantic Nights* or *Simply Romantic Secrets* from FamilyLife.com for a host of additional creative dates.

These resources won't sink your boat, but they will help you sail out of the marital doldrums!

FIRE THE DESIRE 101
The Love Letter

Napoleon Bonaparte provoked strong feelings among his contemporaries. British poet Thomas Campbell once said of Napoleon, "He is the sworn foe of our nation, and, if you will, of the whole human race." Ludwig Beethoven declared, "He would trample on all human rights and become a tyrant." Love him or hate him, his military genius was unmatched. "I considered Napoleon's presence in the field equal to forty thousand men in the balance," stated the Duke of Wellington.

Indeed, Napoleon served several roles. A warrior, a statesman, and the emperor of France. He was also a hopeless romantic.

In 1795 Napoleon sat at his desk in Paris and, gazing at a picture of his love, drafted a letter to Josephine Beauharnais, a woman who had captured his heart. He wrote,

> I wake filled with thoughts of you. Your portrait and the intoxicating evening we spent have left my senses in turmoil. Sweet, incomparable Josephine, what a strange effect you have on my heart! *Mio dolce amour*, a thousand kisses; but give me none in return, for they set my blood on fire.

Tell me Josephine didn't enjoy receiving that letter. She didn't throw that love letter away. That's why we have his words today.

What woman wouldn't love to hear those words from her husband? You may not be as eloquent as Napoleon, but your wife longs to hear what's in your heart. Writing a love letter to her can be one of the most romantic things you'll ever do. Here are a few ideas to get you started.

Presentation Is Important

Handwrite the letter. Although typing it on a computer and printing it on plain white copier paper is convenient, it won't have the same impact as a letter penned by your hand. The choice of paper matters too. Look around at a gift or an office supply store for nice, elegant stationery. Think flowers, pastel colors, and softness. When in doubt, ask a female clerk for direction.

Content Is Everything

Set aside time when you can be undistracted. Find a picture of your wife, and set it in front of you—a picture you find particularly attractive will help. Take a moment to pray for your wife and ask God to give you the words for your letter—words that will stir her soul.

Then make notes. Begin by listing the qualities that you most admire in your wife. For example, you may admire her love for God, the way she cares for your children, or a specific talent she exhibits. You may appreciate the way she's supported and encouraged you during a tough time. Pay particular attention to physical attributes: her eyes, her hair, her complexion, or perhaps the way she always tries to look nice.

Feelings Matter

The most critical element of your letter is your feelings. Far too many men express admiration and perhaps their hopes for the future, but miss sharing from the heart. Get in touch with how you feel when she walks into a room, when she cares for you and the family, when she goes the extra mile.

With your notes in hand, it's time to write. Don't settle for bland, familiar words. Dust off your thesaurus, or if you don't have one, go to one of the many free reference resources online. You may want to consider crafting your draft on the computer where you can edit easily, and then once you have it all down, copy it onto the nice paper.

Deliver It Creatively

After you have written your letter, take her to dinner at a romantic restaurant and read it aloud to her. You might leave it on her pillow or on the dash of her car for her to find. You could surprise her by coming home at lunch to read it to her or have it delivered by FedEx.

Writing a love letter should not be a one-time thing. Put it in your calendar to write her something personal at least once a year. You might even buy her a nice little box in which to keep your letters.

Napoleon knew the power of words. He said, "We rule men with words." He modeled how we *romance our wives with words*. So, take a page out of history, and do as Napoleon did—fire her desire through the power of your words. ✌

FIRE THE DESIRE 201
Picture Perfect

Before describing this romantic idea, I realize you might think that I've gone soft—that this is just not a "guy thing" to do. I understand. But that's what makes this one especially romantic to your wife. She is, after all, the focus of these creative romance ideas.

It's been said that a picture is worth a thousand words. In this case, your collection of pictures will speak volumes. After work, stop by a drug, grocery, or office supply store and buy a small, blank photo album. You'll find a wide variety of shapes and sizes in the stationery department. Some are inexpensive plastic flip books; others incorporate thick paper and tasteful binding. Pick something that fits your personality and budget.

Next, raid your wife's unused photo stash. Many woman stockpile unused photos in a shoebox, a drawer, or a file cabinet. Spend a few minutes picking out some of your favorite pictures of just her, you and your wife as a couple, or even a few family shots. Depending on how extensive the collection, you might be able to pinpoint photos from a season of life together (when you first met, your honeymoon, a special vacation, your first Christmas, or a favorite memory).

Then, place your choices inside the photo album. Using a felt tip marker, write an appropriate caption for each picture. It can be as simple as "I love your smile!"; "I'll never forget our first Christmas"; or "Isn't it time we went back to the beach?" You might consider putting a favorite Scripture verse at the beginning or the end of the album along with a very short dedication, such as, "For the most wonderful wife a guy could ever have. I thank God He brought you into my life."

It's not the size of the album that matters. A short, ten-photo collection can be just as meaningful as a more elaborate notebook. If your wife isn't a photo-bug and doesn't have a collection of pictures lying around, no problem. Take a few candid shots of your own.

For a twist on the photo album idea, take twelve of the very best shots to Kinko's and have them made into a calendar. At the beginning of each month, write one thing about her that you love, and then pencil in a weekly date night. You might also want to pencil in a special surprise weekend getaway. Remember, anticipation fuels romance and adds spice to your relationship. She'll get the picture of how much you care for her long after you've given her this Kodak moment. ❧

FIRE THE DESIRE 301
Kiss 'n' Tell

On December 5, 2001, Louisa Almedovar and Rich Langley qualified for the *Guinness Book of Records* by engaging in the world's longest kiss. These New Jersey lovebirds locked lips for 30 hours, 59 minutes, and 27 seconds. To qualify, they were not allowed to sit, eat, drink, rest, use the bathroom, or in any way separate their lips.

Who said a kiss was just a kiss?

The fact that they were just dating might explain their ability to go the distance. Far too often, married couples don't make time for this romantic expression. If you need a few creative lip-smacking ideas, try these different types of kisses over the next week and experience a deepening emotional connection with your wife.

Long and Lingering: Hold her in your arms, and give her a long, slow kiss. Don't hurry it. Count to ten before releasing. When you're finished, whisper a "sweet nothing" followed by a second kiss.

Windows to the Soul: Hold her face gently in your hands, and slowly move your face toward hers. If she starts to close her eyes, tell her to keep them open. Gaze into each other's eyes as you share an intimate kiss. Try this one the minute you walk in the door.

Face Time: Kiss her forehead, her cheeks, her nose, her chin, her eyelids. Take your time lightly kissing every inch of her face. Be careful not to drool. She shouldn't feel like she was just licked by a large dog. End with a rainbow kiss that is a series of kisses that start near her ear on one side of her face, go all the way to the other ear, and end with a soft kiss on her lips. Then say, "I love you."

Cookin' in the Kitchen: With the kids around, take her in your arms and kiss her on the lips. Make it a good one. Then turn to your kids and tell them you're madly in love with their mother.

Good Morning: While she's still sleeping, gently roll over, and kiss her cheek. Now use your fingers to caress her face and ears and lips. Alternate between using your lips and fingertips. Tell her how beautiful she is to you. (To avoid having morning breath, you might want to quietly slip out of bed to brush your teeth before beginning this one.)

The Blessing: Kiss her forehead, then say, "May the Lord bless you and keep you." Then kiss her right cheek and say, "And make His face to shine upon you." Finally kiss her left cheek and say, "And give you peace." At that point, follow the blessing with a gentle embrace.

Bubble Bath and Beyond: Draw her a warm bubble bath. Light candles, and place them around the bathroom. Pour her favorite drink. Ask her about her day, her desires, and her dreams as you gently wash her all over. When she's almost ready to get out, slip out and get the hot robe that's been tumbling in the dryer. Then as she slips into her robe, stand behind her. Wrap your arms around her and kiss her just behind her ear. Ask her if there is anything else you can do for her.

Remember, your goal is not to have sex. It's connecting to your wife on an emotional level. Savor these moments. Slow down. Surprise her with your focused attention. You might not win any world records, but you're sure to be a hit in her book. ℃&

FIRE THE DESIRE 401
The Web We Weave

Don't take this the wrong way. But I think it's safe to say that our wives will never win a Grammy or an Oscar, or see their names in lights on a movie theater marquee. That's just a fact of life. That doesn't mean your wife can't experience the thrill of seeing herself celebrated by her biggest fan—you.

For about the cost of a pizza, you can build a simple yet elegant Web site tribute for your wife. Website Tonight, for example, is an online package that allows you to build a Web site from your home computer. From a five-page site with hosting for a month to a more complex twenty-page package, your options are limited only by your creativity, imagination, and budget.

Best of all, you don't have to be a computer genius or a graduate from Harvard to pull this off. Templates are provided. You just add the copy and the photos from a digital camera. It's truly a cut-and-paste operation.

Consider, for example, building a five-page site that honors your bride as a wife on page one, a mother on page two, a friend on page three, and a volunteer on page four. Use page five as a tribute page where you list the things you appreciate about her. For an added touch, ask several of her friends to send you an e-mail with a few words of praise. Roll those into the back page along with your tribute.

Fill each page with pictures of her in action. Brag about her accomplishments. Praise her beauty. Celebrate her special attributes. Applaud her talents. Find, or better yet, write a poem that communicates your love for her. If you have children, ask them to write a little message for Mommy that you'll include. Use favorite Scriptures. If you have the added skill level and are familiar with QuickTime or Windows Media Player, insert a short personal video greeting.

If that sounds too ambitious, one-page sites can be set up in a matter of minutes. Then once your site is up and running, send her an e-mail. Tell her to check out a link to a very special Web site . . . and then let her bask in the limelight. Whether it's large or small, simple or complex, she's sure to appreciate the creative way you honored her. ⤫

FIRE THE DESIRE 501
Let's Play Detective

One of the most famous television detectives of all time was Lieutenant Columbo. Clad in a crumpled raincoat and chomping on a cigar, he was most well known for his line, "If you don't mind, I have just one more question."

Each episode began with a cleverly planned murder. Using his finely tuned powers of observation, the right penetrating questions, and undying persistence, Columbo always got his man—or woman. By the end of every show, Columbo pieced together enough clues to reconstruct the crime, confront the suspect, and make an arrest.

Using the same skills, you can begin piecing together the clues that will reveal your wife's deepest romantic desires. The "evidence" will be so overwhelming that constructing her perfect romantic weekend and making an "arrest" of your own will be easy.

Begin by asking questions and listening for little hints or comments that she, as the "suspect," makes. She may mention a favorite restaurant or hotel. There could be a certain dress or necklace she'd love to have. She might enjoy watching sunsets or sunrises. These are the easiest clues to pick up on. You could always prompt her with a few questions to draw responses out of her too.

There will also be subtle clues to look for. Notice the things that breathe life into your wife. Is it a small gift that simply communicates you were thinking about her? Is it a compliment? Is it when you take thirty minutes on the sofa together to rub her feet and talk about your day? Begin to notice the times when your wife feels most loved by you. Write them down—every good detective keeps a notebook handy.

You may also want to interview witnesses. They could reveal critical information to your case. Who are your wife's best friends? Ask for their ideas. Of course, swear them to secrecy.

Once you have completed your investigation, which could take weeks or months, and after you feel you have the "evidence" to make your "arrest," carefully plan the confrontation with your suspect. Give this some thought since it's the climax of the show.

If, for example, your investigation has revealed that your wife has her heart set on a little bed-and-breakfast, loves red roses, feels loved when you share your heart, and enjoys taking long walks, then you can begin laying the trap. Make reservations. Write a love letter that you will read to her over dinner. Think through some questions to ask on your walk. Start saving if this will require more than your typical budget allows.

No perfect weekend fits every woman. That's what makes this so much fun and mysterious. Avoid taking shortcuts by copying what a friend might have done. Solve *your* case and make *your* suspect feel extra special. If you haven't been very romantic in your marriage, don't worry. Play that to your advantage. Just as the suspect never imagined Columbo could solve the crime, your wife may not suspect a thing as you plan this encounter and make your romantic arrest. You might even want to dress for the part of Columbo, script out your lines, and make your arrest "in character," as a true detective would. ↷

FOR THOSE THINKING OF GIVING UP

I am the Lord, the God of all mankind.
Is anything too hard for me?
—JEREMIAH 32:27

You may be thinking, *This has been a nice book, Dennis and Barbara, and some of these ideas might have worked for us years ago. However, it's too late for me and my marriage.* If that's what you're feeling, read on.

Several years ago, I was seated in the front row of FamilyLife's *I Still Do* marriage event in Cincinnati, Ohio, surrounded by thirteen thousand men and women who wanted to rekindle their romance. It was late in the day, and as my friend Dr. Crawford Loritts was finishing his remarks, I glanced down at the base of the podium. Seeing four large vases filled with three dozen roses in each, I thought it would be nice to take a dozen roses home to Barbara.

Not wanting all of those roses to go to waste, I considered a few less selfish options. I could give a rose to each member of the volunteer staff, except that there were more than three hundred volunteers working that day. I could give the roses to the pastors, but hundreds of pastors were on hand.

It was then that the thought occurred to me: *There are undoubtedly people in this arena who desperately need a rose.*

Let's see, 144 roses . . . 13,000 people.

As I was giving the closing message for the day, I reached down and tugged a rose out of a vase. Holding up that single rose, I said, "We are going to place these roses on the tables in front of the stage here. I want to invite anyone whose marriage was—for all practical purposes—over to get a rose of reconciliation."

I paused and scanned the faces of the people.

"Let me be clear. This is not an opportunity to score a free rose to take back to your sweetheart. I'm looking for those who came to this event in *serious trouble, heading for a divorce*—I'm not talking about the fact that you might have had an argument this morning about who let the cat or the dog out, you screamed at the kids, or you got upset about being stuck in traffic and arrived late."

It became very quiet in that arena as the ushers placed the roses on the tables.

"I'm talking about men and women who thought their marriages were finished. They came today dragging their heels, leaving skid marks on the marble floor in the lobby all the way out to the parking lot. I'm talking to the person who has decided here today to take steps toward establishing the home upon Jesus Christ. If that is you, come forward, get a rose, return to your spouse, and say, 'I want to ask you to forgive me. I want to be reconciled to you. I want our marriage to go the distance.'"

As the words were leaving my mouth, out of the corner of my eye, I could see a man coming down the stairs to my right. The guy was hitting about every third step. A hush settled on the crowd as every eye in the arena watched him walk up to the front of the stage and tug at a rose. As he did, the audience began to applaud. Moments later, the whole auditorium rose in a standing ovation for him as he made his way back to take that rose to his wife.

She met him halfway between the rows, and I'm told, they literally leaped into each other's arms as he gave her the rose, asking her to forgive him.

Others came. Men, women, old, young.

All 144 roses were gone in 90 seconds.

Those of us on the speaker team were stunned. To think that so many marriages were on the verge of divorce. And yet God was clearly at work. He was breaking down walls in marriages in which the spouses thought they were finished. As you can imagine, we wanted to be prepared to meet the needs the following weekend in Portland. At that event, fourteen thousand people attended, and we did the same thing—we offered the rose of reconciliation.

Four hundred roses were gone in three minutes. We even lost our plant deposit because some took fronds from the palms that were on the stage to their spouses—that's how hungry they were to make the recommitment.

For the next event at the Pond in Anaheim, California, we ordered one thousand roses. Once again, no roses were left—one out of every ten people got a rose. Each time I invited people to come forward, I made it clear that the roses were for couples who felt they couldn't go on in their relationship. To them, it was over. Affirming their love for each other had been the farthest thing from their minds. In fact, seeing the divorce attorney was the next step— or as we later learned, many had already drawn up papers.

My point is that I've seen thousands who thought there was no hope for their marriage and yet, by God's grace and a willingness to stand by their vows, they discovered it is never too late. I've seen reconciliation even in the most difficult of situations.

Earlier I described marriage as a *glorious minefield*. If you are spending more time in the *minefield* rather than embracing the *glorious* delights, if you've lost all hope, it's possible that divorce seems the only way out. If you're hurting that badly, you might be tempted to believe *anything* has to be better than your current circumstances. I want to challenge you to consider the consequences *before you bail out*.

Marci, a single listener to *FamilyLife Today* from Pennsylvania, wrote about divorce from an adult-child's perspective:

I just listened to your broadcast about divorce and felt compelled to write. During your program you mentioned a letter from someone concerned that you're "too hard" on divorce. That broke my heart. I am a twenty-eight-year-old single, professional woman. I grew up in an unstable, non-Christian home. To date, I have had five parents and three sets of siblings. My mother called me just this past Sunday to inform me that she's about to bestow upon me a sixth parent and fourth set of siblings.

In the very depths of my being I understand why God hates divorce and why we should, too. No good thing comes from it. Ever. Divorce has not only stolen from me a family, but also a trust that marriage is a good and desirable thing. The grapes my parents ate with relish have set my teeth on edge.

Divorce answers no question, solves no problem, resolves no conflict, gives no respite, restores no dignity, and grants no peace. Divorce cannot be dealt with too harshly, especially in the church. I bless God that He knows no divorce in this marriage covenant He has established between Himself and His bride!

Thank you for your commitment to teach husbands and wives to honor the covenant they made before God, if for no other reason than the sake of the next generation.

I realize there might be some who, even after reading Marci's letter, are thinking, *Yeah, but, Dennis, my situation is so bad, we're hopeless.* Trust me, I've seen hopeless marriages over the past three decades—by the thousands. But I've also seen the power of God at work and have concluded *there are no lost causes* when spouses are willing to submit to Jesus Christ as the Builder of the marriage.

Take, for example, Todd who attended one of our *Weekend to Remember* marriage conferences:

I wanted to tell you how the Lord and a FamilyLife *Weekend to Remember* marriage conference saved our marriage. On the opening night the speaker said, "If you apply yourselves, by the end of the conference your marriage will change." *Ha!* I thought, *How are you going to take six years of resentment, suspicion, anger, and a ton of damage, and change it in three days?*

Guess what? By the time my wife and I left the conference, something *had* changed. There were faith and hope where there was once hopelessness. We are proof that God can and will fix all marriages if given the chance.

Todd's experience is something we've witnessed in tens of thousands of marriages as more than two million have attended our events. Whether your relationship needs a minor tune-up or a complete overhaul, I'm convinced that "He who has begun a good work in you will complete it until the day of Jesus Christ" (Phil. 1:6 NKJV). The key word in that verse is *He*; God is the One who changes hearts, revives marriages, heals wounds, and breathes life into lifeless relationships.

That is, of course, assuming you don't quit before the payoff. Perhaps the most striking example of quitting prematurely was this fascinating story first told by motivational speaker Napoleon Hill.

Back during America's gold rush, an uncle of R. U. Darby (who many years later built a million-dollar insurance business) was convinced he could strike it rich. Never mind the fact that he knew nothing about mining, that he didn't have a map, or that Williamsburg, Maryland, was a long way from Colorado. Those were minor details compared to the promise of vast riches. He packed pick and shovel and then headed west with Darby toting the bags. Upon arrival, they staked their claim and dug in.

Days of backbreaking labor turned into weeks. At long last, Darby's uncle hit pay dirt. One problem. Convinced this was the

Big One, they needed heavy machinery to excavate their precious treasure. With the mother lode in view, he carefully concealed his find and then hurried back to Maryland to share the news of his good fortune.

Family members pooled their resources and loaned him the funds to purchase the drills and necessary equipment. Darby and his uncle made the several-thousand-mile train ride back to Colorado with dreams of gold dancing in their heads. They were not disappointed. The first car of ore proved to be, according to the smelter, evidence that they had struck it rich. Their vein of gold was estimated to be among the richest in all of Colorado.

Bolstered by their initial success, Darby and his uncle redoubled their efforts. They needed several more loads of gold to clear up their debts. After that, they'd be in fat city. That's when the unthinkable happened. The vein dried up. No gold ore. Just crusty old earth. They drilled on. And on. It couldn't be. They still had debts. Their pot of gold was waiting in those hills; they just knew it. Still nothing.

Weeks and months went by without a fleck of gold. Discouraged and disillusioned, they did the unthinkable. They quit. They packed their bags, sold all of the expensive machinery to a junk dealer for pocket change, tucked their tails between their legs, and headed home to admit their failure.

But the story doesn't end there.

The junk dealer sought advice. He consulted with a mining engineer who had experience in such matters. After further investigation, the engineer explained that the previous owners evidently didn't know about fault lines. He estimated that the gold was probably within three feet of where Darby and his uncle had quit.

The junk man smiled at his good fortune, dug three feet, and struck gold. Big time. Millions of dollars of precious ore were hauled out of what was considered a dead mine. The same principle is true of marriage. Far too often we are tempted to bail on our

efforts before the payoff. We forget that between the investment and the payoff in a marriage is *the waiting*. If we give up too quickly, we miss the rich rewards that await us when we pursue romance and relationship with our spouses God's way.

If you're ready to rekindle the romance God's way, I strongly recommend three steps. First, humble yourself before God, and confess your lack of love for God and the lack of love for His gift of your spouse. Ask His Spirit to ignite a renewed love for your mate. Ask Him to let you see your husband or wife as Christ sees that person—as a precious gift to be treasured and to die for. The Psalmist declares, "Unless the Lord builds the house, they labor in vain who build it" (Psalm 127:1 NASB).

Second, go to the grocery store and buy a single red rose. Splurge a little. Get the long-stem variety. Then leave it on the pillow or hand it to your spouse with a note that says, "Honey, I'd like to try again," "I'd love to love you better," or "I'd marry you all over again." Write whatever is appropriate for your situation.

Third, start investing in growing your marriage. Like any other living thing, marriages need the best nutrients to be able to grow. I'd recommend that you spend a weekend with us at one of our *Weekend to Remember* marriage conferences or a Saturday at one of our *Rekindling the Romance* arena events. You can get more information by calling 1-800-FL-TODAY (358-6329) or going online at FamilyLife.com.

Don't expect amazing results within minutes. Real growth, healthy growth, takes time. But know this: God will add the increase as you plant the seeds of romance in the garden of your mate's heart.

You have His word on that!

ACKNOWLEDGMENTS

We are greatly encouraged by the tremendous people who surrounded us to make this book a reality.

Our thanks goes to those who read the manuscript and gave constructive input along the way: Janet and Tom Logan, Michele English, Todd Nagel, Julie Majors, Phil Krause, Gregg Stutts, Bob Lepine, Anjanette Walchshauser, Tamara Sims, Pam Majors, and Robert and Dora DeMoss. Your honest feedback has made this a better book.

Special kudos go to the fine team at Thomas Nelson: Mike Hyatt and Jonathan Merkh, thanks for the privilege of partnering with you!; Brian Hampton, a great coach who oversaw the entire project with patience and grace; Kyle Olund, an excellent managing editor who kept the project moving and who added many wonderful "touches" to this project—in spite of us; Belinda Bass, whose cover design was THE best ever—you delivered!; and Katherine Lloyd, for the long hours and skill putting together the interior design. Each of you was a HUGE help. Thank you for flexing and for your commitment to excellence.

I must say that Phil Smouse introduced a jolt of humor through his cartoons. Thank you, Phil, for creating these gems for us.

To the 911 Information Service team—thanks go to Bobby Newman, Tim, and Rusty for bailing us out more times than any of us care to recall! You were true servants.

Robert Wolgemuth, you were a great cheerleader and encourager. Thanks for your counsel on this project.

Hats off to Dave "The Slasher" Boehi, whose objective eye and professional opinion were life savers at key points—you are a good friend and great help.

Bob DeMoss, you DID IT! In the midst of incredible opposition, time pressure, and fatigue, you indeed DID IT! Thank you for being on the team, for caring about families, and for making a difference in a bunch of them through this book. We are grateful for you!

And finally, I (Dennis) want to mention a team of people who carried the load of leading and managing a growing ministry while I was out of the office for nearly four months. You juggled everything—e-mails, budgets, personnel issues, emergency calls, scheduling, writing letters, answering calls, making trips in my place, protecting both of us from tons of demands, and staying current on a jillion details that no one will ever know about. THANK YOU goes to Janet Logan, Michele English, Todd Nagel, Merle Engle, and Clark Hollingsworth.

And Clark, one more thing: Thanks goes to you and Julia for carrying the load of the ministry when I couldn't carry much of anything.